THE TWO CULTURES OF ENGLISH

The Two Cultures of English

Literature, Composition, and the Moment of Rhetoric

Jason Maxwell

FORDHAM UNIVERSITY PRESS

New York 2019

Fordham University Press has no responsibility for the persistence or accuracy of URLs for external or third-party Internet websites referred to in this publication and does not guarantee that any content on such websites is, or will remain, accurate or appropriate.

Fordham University Press also publishes its books in a variety of electronic formats. Some content that appears in print may not be available in electronic books.

Visit us online at www.fordhampress.com.

Library of Congress Cataloging-in-Publication Data available online at https://catalog.loc.gov.

Printed in the United States of America
21 20 19   5 4 3 2 1
First edition

CONTENTS

THE TWO CULTURES OF ENGLISH

Introduction

Included in Vincent B. Leitch's 2014 book *Literary Criticism in the 21st Century* is a map that usefully organizes the "unmasterable" sprawl of various fields and subdisciplines in contemporary English studies. As a way of illustrating an emerging "theory renaissance" (8), Leitch's map is structured by a dozen "major topics" with an array of subfields clustered around each one. So, for instance, the major topic "Globalization" is surrounded by six satellites, including "Empire," "Postcolonial Studies," "Diaspora Studies," Multiculturalism," and "New American Studies." Another major topic, "Affect Studies," includes the satellites "Affect Theory," "Testimony," "Sentimentality," "Trauma Studies," "Memory Studies," and "Holocaust Studies." The map offers a more robust, variegated understanding of the discipline than one gets from a strict periodization model (Early Modern, 18th-century British, American Modernism); it also underscores how "Theory" has undergone a significant transformation. Whereas in the final decades of the twentieth-century theory consisted of a range of competing schools and movements (queer theory, Marxism, psychoanalysis, formalism, New Historicism), a model that unfortunately invites comparisons to a buffet, today theory has infiltrated and reshaped the older period groupings, and as a result it exists "everywhere and nowhere" (8). As Leitch explains, theory "now occupies the role of regular practice," serving as "a secondary but indispensable strength" (9) for navigating both long established and emerging fields (some of these fields in fact developed because of crucial critical interventions during the theory era).

Although Leitch clarifies that the ninety-four subdisciplines and fields that constitute the map can "change spheres and fuse into original combinations," his provisional arrangement raises at least one curious point of complication. If one were to use the map as a way of diagnosing the distribution of area groups in English today, one would rightly come away with a sense of the wild diversity of approaches and topics the discipline has to offer. However, the map would provide little in the way of knowing the relative density, in terms of either publications or faculty specializations, of any of these areas. Much as a quick glance at an electoral college map can give a skewed sense of the outcome of an American presidential election, where Montana dwarfs Rhode Island in size even though both states have roughly the same population, Leitch's map doesn't register where certain critical masses may have formed. Of course, Leitch never declared that this was an intention of his schematic, and any attempt to conduct such a project would be complicated by the aforementioned cross-pollination among the fields. Nevertheless, this more than pardonable flaw of the map can be used to emphasize the explosive growth of the area group Rhetoric and Composition, which roughly corresponds to one of Leitch's twelve planets. Looking at recent job trends provided by the MLA, Rhetoric and Composition has notched roughly 30 percent of the positions advertised each year on the Job Information List (JIL). For example, of the 1,621 jobs advertised in the English JIL for 2000–2001, a whopping 30.8 percent were in the area group, matching the entirety of British literature positions (all periods) and outpacing American literature (27 percent). The numbers have remained remarkably consistent over the last decade and a half: in 2012–2013, Rhetoric and Composition counted for 28.9 percent of the advertisements, while British literature received 28.4 percent and American literature received 25 percent.[1]

While examining the MLA's JIL annual report, one might notice that the graph labels the category "Composition and Rhetoric," reversing the order in which I've arranged the two terms. Although "Rhetoric and Composition" has historically served as the preferred nomenclature, the reversed order has recently gained prominence. Elsewhere, the field is simply referred to as "Composition Studies," apparently feeling no obligation to rhetoric whatsoever (I imagine that, if polled, more professors in the area would refer to themselves as "compositionists" rather than "rhetoricians").[2] Complicating matters further, the titles "Rhetoric and Writing" and "Writing and Rhetoric" have also gained currency in the last decade or so, which would suggest some uneasiness surrounding the term composition. "Writing Studies," less common but still in circulation, abandons the two historically significant terms altogether, the generality of its name hinting at previously unexplored territories. The high degree of variation in the name of this field only confirms Leitch's assertion that subdisciplines have a tendency to "change spheres and fuse into original combinations."

But is the volatility surrounding the name a mere trifle or symptomatic of significant underlying tensions? As a way to begin answering that question, we might return to Leitch's map and note that the "major topic" that corresponds to Rhetoric and Composition is labeled "Rhetoric," with "Composition Studies" as one of its satellites (the others being "Literacy Studies," "Discourse Analysis," "History of Rhetoric," "Tropology," "Orality," "Cognitive Poetics," and "Reception Studies"). It would lead us astray to dwell too long on the associations between the eight subfields assembled by Leitch here.[3] Nevertheless, it is worth speculating why Leitch might prioritize "Rhetoric" over "Composition." The former term certainly possesses more gravitas than the latter. The rhetorical tradition dates back to antiquity, its foundational works—texts by Plato, Aristotle, Cicero, Quintilian—predating the entirety of the English literary canon (not to mention the American one). Since antiquity, plenty of intellectual heavyweights who routinely appear in the "Great Books" curriculum have considered rhetoric's significance, including Adam Smith, John Locke, and Friedrich Nietzsche. Put simply, rhetoric has cultural capital to spare. Leitch's decision to prioritize rhetoric might also be motivated by his theoretical orientation—after all, his book reads the current state of the discipline through the fate of theory. Not only did rhetoric serve as a central term in the work of deconstructionist Paul de Man (something we will explore at length in Chapter 1), but the relationship between rhetoric and poetics has a long and complicated history that has been of interest to many within literary studies.[4] "Composition," on the other hand, calls to mind a more practical, perhaps even mechanical, activity, a far cry from the abstractions of intellectual labor; it also carries with it an air of amateurism, or an activity confined to the artificial conditions of a classroom. As Peter Elbow humorously notes, "only children and students (and musical composers) say, 'I'm going in the other room to write a composition' . . . Grown-ups or professionals call their serious writing *writing*" (*English* 138 n. 1). Amateurism is not the first thing one typically associates

with rhetoric, a practice that can be traced back to the agora of ancient
Greece, where dignified statesman implored their fellow citizens on matters of common concern. If rhetoric in antiquity was an elevated form of
discourse reserved for individuals with stature, much of that dignity is preserved in the modern era by treating it as an area of academic inquiry.
To examine rhetoric as an object of serious theoretical interest means
placing it in the realm of professionalized activity, and therefore always a
step or two removed from more mundane, clerical concerns. Just think of
the stereotype of the academic researcher, who is always more interested
in completing the next book or securing the next grant than in teaching
undergraduates or grading their assignments. To privilege rhetoric over
composition, or vice versa, then, is to make a series of judgments concerning the relationship between theory and practice, tradition and innovation,
and professionalism and pedagogy, judgments that are almost guaranteed
to please some and rankle others.

Certainly those judgments have been made, again and again, in various
publications and institutional scenarios, placing more tension between the
two linked terms.[5] Such tension might suggest that Rhetoric and Composition is not a match that can last. The union began in the 1960s, when scholars like Edward P. J. Corbett, W. Ross Winterowd, and Frank D'Angelo
wrote composition textbooks that framed writing instruction in broad
rhetorical terms—that is, analyzing and producing texts with a careful eye
toward issues of audience, purpose, and context—with the purpose of securing greater intellectual status for composition teachers. But as a 2003
article by Sharon Crowley makes clear with its title alone, "Composition
Is Not Rhetoric," the conjunction of these two is far from settled. Perhaps
even more important, the friction between "rhetoric" and "composition"
is indicative of broader antagonisms animating the discipline. Not only are
"rhetoric" and "composition" not linked in any necessary way, but "Rhetoric and Composition" is also not necessarily linked to the broader discipline
of English, either. Indeed, another undeniable trend has been for Rhetoric
and Composition to sever its long-standing ties with English departments,
forming freestanding units within the university and leaving the literary and
cultural critics to their own devices. Institutions like the University of Ken-
tucky, the University of Texas at Austin, the University of Utah, the University of Rhode Island, and Hofstra University have all founded Rhetoric
and Composition programs independent from the English department.[6]

To discern the motivations behind Rhetoric and Composition's increasing separation from the rest of English, we can look to a recent piece of
scholarship that crystallizes some of the tensions in a terse declaration.

In the same year as Leitch's *Literary Criticism in the 21st Century*, *PMLA* published a cluster of articles under its "Theories and Methodologies" section that focused on "Rhetoric, Writing, and Composition Studies." A journal not known for publishing scholarship in this field, the issue was likely the first time many in the discipline encountered firsthand the work of those in Rhetoric and Composition. One of the articles, Patricia Bizzell's "We Want to Know Who Our Students Are," opens with a curious assertion: "Composition Studies concentrates on students, not texts" (442). The opening sentence might be read harmlessly enough as a declaration on the field's focus on undergraduate writing pedagogy rather than literature. But the statement implies that one must make an odd choice between either students or texts; concentrating on one necessarily excludes the other. Posing such a stark choice between students and texts cannot but retroactively attach an aggressive undertone to the article title: other fields have no interest in their students (or, at least, who their students "are"). Opposing students and texts establishes an implicit comparison between the vibrant, often uncontainable, energy of young adults and the motionless silence of dried ink on paper—in short, it invites a comparison between life and death itself. To side with texts rather students, the comparison suggests, is to reject enlivening human connection in favor of more deadening pursuits. "Text" is thus far from an incidental choice, and Bizzell almost certainly intends to invoke Derrida's famous declaration "there is nothing outside the text" to clarify a contrast between lived reality and lifeless abstraction.[7]

But separating students from texts into two distinct categories, particularly in a pedagogical situation, constitutes a rather odd decision. After all, don't composition teachers focus primarily on student texts? Do composition scholars somehow regard these student texts secondary to the students themselves? If so, are students evaluated on their character rather than in their written work? Conversely, could it be possible to concentrate on students *through* texts? In other words, might texts function as a means of illuminating just "who our students are"? Turning to more concrete considerations, if the opposition between students and texts is meant as a subtle condemnation of literary studies, what are we to make of graduate students in literary studies teaching composition? What about composition scholars with lightened teaching loads to accommodate more intensive administrative responsibilities? Indeed, claims about student-teacher proximity according to subject matter begin to unravel when considering that a growing proportion of the adjunct pool, which teaches the majority of the first-year composition and other related composition courses, consists of literature PhDs who have not yet secured (and will likely never secure) tenure-track employment, while a substantial portion of Rhetoric and Composition scholars manage this labor from afar, sometimes teaching few undergraduate courses because of their role as writing program administrators. Bizzell opens her article by establishing a stark opposition that only invites questions about the possible intersections between them.

Before examining the relationship between composition and literature that Bizzell subtly constructs through her students-texts dichotomy, we must first briefly flesh out the history of Rhetoric and Composition itself. While rhetorical education served as the cornerstone of the curriculum for liberal arts colleges during most of the 1800s, composition replaced rhetorical theory as the basis of English-language instruction in the last decades of the nineteenth century; at the same time, rhetoric was rejected in favor of literature. A clear split between composition and literature developed: skilled students (and teachers) involved themselves in literature courses, while less capable individuals enrolled (or taught) composition.[8] And this hierarchy maintained itself in professional scholarship. As Donald C. Stewart's survey of papers from MLA programs at the end of the nineteenth century can attest, composition research was relegated to a decidedly second-class status when compared to literary scholarship. That composition scholarship appeared at all—for most of the twentieth century, it would all but disappear from the MLA convention—was due to the fact that "those who founded the MLA in 1883 were, among other things, professors of rhetoric and oratory, and they were still preoccupied with the problems of teaching writing" (129).

The beginnings of composition's professionalization did not occur until many decades later. Pinpointing a specific origin remains a point of contention, and one could plausibly reference any number of events—the 1949 founding of the Conference on College Composition and Communication (CCCC), the 1963 CCCC meeting that launched a "revival" of interest in rhetoric and thereby initiated an ostensibly more venerable research agenda, or the Dartmouth Conference of 1966.[9] Composition historian Sharon Crowley prefers to see the emergence of the field as an outcome of World War II. From her perspective, the CCCC can find its origin in the demand for "communication" that grew after the global conflict. As Crowley goes on to explain, it was the "communications" course of the 1950s, which combined writing and speech in a single course (under the subtle prompting of the military), which catalyzed the professionalization of composition teachers (*Composition* 158). But even if it lacks a clear start date, the field was clearly beginning to form a critical mass by the beginning of the 1970s, bearing many of the same hallmarks as their literary counterparts. In addition to a professional organization and corresponding conference and journal, Rhetoric and Composition could boast that it had book-length research projects as well. Janet Emig's 1971 *The Composing Processes of Twelfth Graders* and Mina P. Shaughnessy's 1977 *Errors and Expectations: A Guide for the Teacher of Basic Writing* are two of the earliest entries in what would become a booming enterprise by the 1980s, one that began in earnest with the book series "Studies in Writing and Rhetoric" published by Southern Illinois University Press. Additionally, graduate programs in Rhetoric and Composition began to sprout up in English departments at major public research universities across the country, further lending institutional legitimacy to the field.[10]

For a fuller account of these developments, one should consult any number of histories of Rhetoric and Composition, including Crowley's *Composition in the University*, Albert R. Kitzhaber's *Rhetoric in American Colleges, 1850–1900*, John C. Brereton's *The Origins of Composition Studies in the American College, 1875–1925*, and David Gold's *Rhetoric at the Margins: Revising the History of Writing Instruction in American Colleges, 1873–1947*.[11] Although full of insights and surprising anecdotes, many of these histories suffer from isolating Rhetoric and Composition from the rest of the activities occurring within the department at that time, largely because the field is neglected in most other disciplinary histories of English. For instance, in the second page of the landmark *Professing Literature*, Gerald Graff acknowledges that his account deals "only in passing with the teaching of composition" even though "without that enterprise the teaching of literature could never have achieved its central status" (2). More recent entries, like Joseph North's 2017 *Literary Criticism: A Concise Political History*, similarly do not devote any sustained attention to Rhetoric and Composition in recounting the discipline's development in the postwar years. Nevertheless, such understandable critical overcorrections on the part of Rhetoric and Composition historians undersell the interconnections between the two sides that date back many years.[12]

Indeed, the split (and possible reunification) between literature and composition as professional research agendas can be dated as far back as the New Critics. While initially constituting a loose unity of mutually reinforcing values and commitments, New Criticism contained a number of internal tensions that ultimately became untenable, leading to one strand of criticism reminiscent of deconstruction and another strand similar to modern rhetorical studies. The split might best be embodied in the growing distance between John Crowe Ransom on one side and Allen Tate and

Robert Penn Warren on the other. In the later years of his career, Ransom began to abandon the "organic" holistic theories of meaning that had characterized his days during the Agrarian movement. As Mark Jancovich explains, Ransom thought that many New Critics "were concerned with the unity between structure and text, rather than acknowledging their radical difference" (111). Ransom's eventual abandonment of organicism led him to produce proto-deconstructive readings of texts, including a discussion of James Joyce that Jancovich claims "has strong parallels with the positions of Paul de Man in his book, *Allegories of Reading*" (92). Ransom's doubling down on complexity at the expense of organic unity was matched, interestingly enough, by an elevation of the organic over the complex by the very same Agrarians he had instructed and collaborated with during the 1930s.

Indeed, a general humanist spirit informed the latter work of Tate and Warren, who both became less interested in carefully reading literary texts and more preoccupied with defending the democratic tradition and cultivating citizens who could participate effectively within it.[13] This shift to a humanist tradition was rooted in many of the same commitments that motivated the anti-standardization arguments of the early New Critics. For instance, Warren was eager to combat what he called "common manism," a neologism that linked Russian communism with the Fordism of American industrialism ("Knowledge" 240). Warren supported the idea of an individual belonging to a larger collectivity, but he rejected forms of community that sought to eliminate differences between people. Warren believed the complex and sometimes contested interactions between individuals were an asset to the community rather than a liability. Warren worried that industrialism's standardizing logic would further corrupt American politics, which was already suffering from numerous problems. From his perspective, only by cultivating difference could individuals and the collective develop properly. Allen Tate echoed Warren's sentiments, regarding democracy as a political solution to the problems of modern industrialism. Like Warren, Tate links industrialism to political totalitarianism, writing "will it not be born in upon us in the next few years that Hitler and Stalin *are* the Common Man, and that one of the tasks of democracy is to allow as many men as possible to make themselves uncommon?" (*Essays* 24–25). Thus, whereas Ransom ultimately sacrificed the idea of unity in order to pursue complexity for its own sake, Tate and Warren invested their energies in more holistic and organic forms of humanist cultivation, seeing complexity and difference merely as a means to that end.

Kenneth Burke was a critic who embodied this increasing investment in organicism yet retained his attachments to aesthetic complexity for its own sake. While much of his writing in the 1930s rivaled the best New Criticism in terms of its formalist analysis of literary texts (his first book *Counter-Statement* serves as the clearest example), Burke's trajectory following World War II was more like Warren and Tate's than Ransom's. Building on the investigations of political and social phenomena from his works *Permanence and Change* and *Attitudes Toward History*, Burke became invested in the rhetorical dimensions of language and in the process advocated a version of radical democratic practice. In many respects, the 1941 tome *The Philosophy of Literary Form* serves as the most representative of Burke's work, alternating between essays of literary formalist analysis and rhetorical readings of public speech acts. The process of literary interpretation outlined in the long titular essay of the collection provides a useful, albeit simplified, roadmap of Burke's own career: an initial exploration of the internal formal structures of texts that eventually gives way to a study of the external factors conditioning the production of said texts. Indeed, Burke's 1951 essay "Rhetoric—Old and New," which appeared in *The Journal of General Education*, marks a breaking point of sorts in Burke's career where he clearly commits himself to spending more time with these social conditions than with the texts themselves. As he writes in the essay, "by a 'new' rhetoric, we mean one designed to restore structures maimed by the vandalism of the exclusively aesthetic" (203).

Several decades later, the New Critics' split between complexity and organicism was reflected more broadly in the discipline in the warring factions of "literature" and "composition," leaving many figures in the Burkean mold hoping for some kind of truce. Indeed, in his 1982 MLA presidential address, Wayne Booth noted that because the discipline of English couldn't tell a "coherent story" about itself, its members might wonder "whether [they] really belong together at all" (313). The remainder of Booth's speech is an effort to establish some "center" that might create something resembling coherence. Booth articulates the struggle to locate a center emanating from the conflict between professional scholarship and pedagogical commitment. Inspired to pursue a career in academia because of a freshman "Litcomp" course at Brigham Young University in the early 1940s, Booth quickly found himself weary from the rigors of R. S. Crane's graduate seminar at the University of Chicago. Queasy at the prospect of becoming a "dry-as-dust scholar," Booth discovered that he was more interested in teaching first-year composition, the course that initially inspired him, than advanced literature courses. But a legitimate interest in academic research emerged in his early years as a professor at small colleges, and the research-driven University of Chicago hired Booth in 1962. Booth admits that upon accepting the offer, "I still could not, at that time, see any way to reconcile the aims of the learned professors and the aims of the front-line troops, the teachers of freshmen. I decided to return to Chicago because I wanted to join both groups, but I had no conceptual way of uniting the two" (316). After many years of juggling these two competing imperatives, Booth experienced a revelation: They were not as distinct as he had previously imagined. What yoked them together was something he called "critical understanding," a term meant to capture both "thought and passion" (317). More specifically, critical understanding involved replacing "on the one hand, sentimental and uncritical identifications that leave minds undisturbed and, on the other, hypercritical negations that freeze or alienate" (317–318). When in authentic pursuit of "critical understanding," Booth claims that the numerous antagonisms populating the discipline—theory versus practice, the objective versus the subjective, belles-lettres versus "practical" literature, rhetoric versus reality—are all rendered absurd.

Booth believes that only a holistic approach, one that attempts to link the increasingly isolated spheres of the discipline, will have any meaningful and lasting impact. Both sides of the disciplinary divide are guilty of threatening the long-term prospects of English. He chastises the professional scholars for failing to attend to beginning undergraduate students at the expense of graduate seminars. He insists that the real development of critical understanding will happen during the early years of undergraduate education and the discipline makes a grave error in assuming that process will take care of itself. Existing practices have made the undergraduate population at large, as well as the broader public, miserable, all so that a small cohort of professors can derive satisfaction from more advanced pursuits. Booth does not mince words: "The great public fears or despises us because we hire a vast army of underpaid flunkies to teach the so-called service courses, so that we can gladly teach, in our advanced courses, those precious souls who survive the gauntlet" (319). But Booth is equally harsh on composition teachers who lack general intellectual curiosity, those individuals who never explore work outside the confines of "a freshman textbook" and whose pedagogical practices "are parodies of dry pedantry" (320). In Booth's eyes, failing to confront (and perhaps contribute to) more rigorous and demanding intellectual traditions is as equally sinful as shirking the difficult task of effectively ushering young adults into these intimidating but ultimately rewarding traditions. Booth's summary insight—"Only those who fraternize in the no-man's-land between the two camps discover how badly the two sides need each other" (320)—articulated a hope and a challenge for the discipline to pursue in the coming years.[14]

If Booth embodied a split personality, someone unwilling to make a choice between scholarship and teaching, or between composition or literature, many other critics who were forced into making those difficult decisions nevertheless still felt a tug from the other side of the department hallway. The intensification of disciplinary specialization has only widened the gap that Booth lamented in 1982, leaving many within English studies speculating about seemingly impossible unities. Indeed, literary and cultural theorist (and 2004 MLA President) Robert Scholes concludes his 1998 book *The Rise and Fall of English* with a plea for writing and literature to be reconnected in some meaningful way. Scholes asserts that the discipline of English needs to take writing more seriously; he complains that far too many literature professors treat writing as if it were a "mere tool" that students "ought to have picked up along the way" (160). From his perspective, "the ability to write well in a range of expressive modes ought to be a major and explicit goal of any discipline of English" (160). Echoing Scholes's general sentiments, composition scholar Peter Elbow regards his graduate training in literary studies as if it were a phantom limb. Noting that though he has "long been seen as a composition person" even though he didn't consider himself a member of the field until halfway through his career, he feels it necessary to confess, "I miss literature" ("Opinion" 534). The rest of his piece oscillates back and forth between the relative merits of the English divide, reciting a list of traits he wishes the other side might adopt. Both Scholes and Elbow see the entirety of English studies benefitting from a more robust interaction between the two sides; these two figures constitute a "Boothian" strand within English studies, one that holds out hope in the possibility of productive interpenetration of fields that remains in force today.

Attempts to bridge or maintain the divide between literature and composition have remained a staple in the critical diet ever since. Significant works in this scholarly genre include Winifred Bryan Horner's 1983 edited collection *Bridging the Gap: Literature and Composition*, or a 1993 debate in the pages of *College English* between Erika Lindemann and Gary Tate on the possibilities and perils of including literary works in the composition classroom, a debate that solicited numerous critical follow-ups in subsequent years.[15] The very titles of Lindemann and Tate's essays—"Freshman Composition: No Place for Literature" and "A Place for Literature in Freshman Composition"—provide a sense of the general tenor of the proceedings, one that anticipates the stark choice implicitly offered at the beginning of Bizzell's recent *PMLA* article. Reading though much of the material on the literature-composition divide, one would not be incorrect in feeling like they were immersed in a peace treaty negotiation between two warring nation states (a figure like Wayne Booth would amount to a poor soul with dual citizenship).[16]

While *The Two Cultures of English* undoubtedly constitutes another entry within the scholarly genre that considers the relationships among the fields in English studies, my introduction of theory into the long-standing composition-literature divide is not meant to add merely another nation-state to the negotiations.[17] In other words, theory cannot simply be added as another field to the existing area groups that constitute English. In the concluding pages of *Professing Literature*, published just as theory was establishing a firm foothold in the discipline, Gerald Graff wondered how this innovative new discourse would relate to the traditional categories that organized English. He hoped that theory could avoid becoming just another specialized field within the discipline and instead constitute a catalyst for bringing "the different ideologies and methods of the literature department and the university into fruitful relation and opposition" (250). Our analysis of Vincent Leitch's complex diagram of contemporary English studies speaks to the general diffusion of theory throughout the discipline, one that transformed earlier organizational modes. Indeed, theory's incorporation into English forces us to reconceptualize the very terrain on which we understand the divisions and alliances between fields.

To state my case baldly: The introduction of theory invites us to think of the discipline of English less as a collection of discrete camps, a model that resembles a geopolitical landscape consisting of sovereign nation-states, and instead in terms of a globalized network comprising ever-shifting territories and flows. Itself a hybrid product of global flows that transported French intellectuals into the American academy, theory adds to our understanding of English's current configuration by abandoning a model that presumes the stability of older disciplinary divides and treats hybrid formations as secondary. This is not to suggest, however, that existing divides simply vanish, just as globalization has not eliminated the traditional nation-state (despite numerous predictions to the contrary). The decentering of the nation-state does not entail the end of borders, and introducing theory into our accounts of English does not entail thinking of the discipline as a smooth, frictionless space. Far from it. In fact, globalization facilitates the proliferation of borders, an idea I am taking from Sandro Mezzadra and Brett Neilson's 2013 *Border as Method, or, the Multiplication of Labor*. The pair explains that the intensification of globalization accelerates a ceaseless process of breaking down and erecting new, provisional forms of division and connection. As their title "border as method" is supposed to suggest, our ideas concerning borders must be oriented around actions (the act of creating borders) rather than in terms of things (a static border separating two entities). The durability and longevity of any border and accompanying territory is an effect of complex, interconnected, and often unpredictable forces.

The Two Cultures of English argues that the introduction of theory into the discipline simultaneously leveled previous distinctions between old fields and intensified them in new ways. Attempts to place theory on either side of composition or literature, or, alternatively, as some kind of mediator between them, are doomed to fail because theory occupies all and none of these positions at the same time. Put slightly differently, the following analysis introduces theory into the long-standing conflict between literary studies and Rhetoric and Composition, arguing that the rise of theory frustrates all attempts to create clean divisions between the various camps within English. In some instances, theory is often posited as a bridge between literature and composition, serving as a common language that can unite the discipline. As J. Hillis Miller noted in his 1986 MLA Presidential Address, every field requires some form of theorization to ground and legitimize itself. Speaking of the "triumph of theory," he quipped that "in the present context such declarations against theory or such claims to be theoretical end by being obviously theoretical statements. . . . History is not reversible, though it may certainly be reread. Its irreversibility is evident in the way the resistance to theory today is overtly and inescapably theoretical" ("Presidential Address" 286). While Maxine Hairston recommended eliminating all discussions of postmodernism from the pages of *College Composition and Communication*, her canonical 1982 essay "The Winds of Change: Thomas Kuhn and the Revolution in the Teaching of Writing" nevertheless resorted to the theoretical language of "paradigm shifts" to support its claim about the "process movement" within Rhetoric and Composition.[18] But if theory serves as a foundation for the discipline in some instances, elsewhere it is framed as an intensification of literary culture's worst tendencies—elitism, obscurity, abstraction, professionalism—and thereby motivates an alliance between former antagonists who can now unify around a common foe. As Sharon Crowley points out, during the reign of antihumanist theory in the 1970s and 1980s, the composition classroom became a haven for traditional literary critics.[19] Meanwhile, in other instances, theory can be framed as a silent partner with composition in replacing literary studies altogether since neither need the traditional canon to do their work. Despite its jargon-heavy tomes, theory could in fact provide a conceptual arsenal for Rhetoric and Composition to deconstruct the assumptions that authorized literary study's privileged status within the discipline. If Rhetoric and Composition had long seen itself as suffering at the hands of a hierarchy that enshrined literature, it found an ally in theory, a discourse seemingly inseparable from the student and political movements of the 1960s and 1970s.[20] Grappling with the complexities of contemporary English studies means acknowledging that these different dynamics are constantly in flux, sometimes within the same critic or text. It is no longer possible to draw straightforward battle lines. With this in mind, we can now briefly outline some of the important points of contention and compatibility between theory and Rhetoric and Composition, the two terms that will anchor the following analysis and thereby accentuate the volatile nature of the disciplinary relationships under examination.

One area where composition and theory dovetail is their shared emphasis on developing productive capacities. In other words, they both possess a pragmatic orientation rooted in their shared focus on practical activity over static knowledge. As a result, they differ from much of traditional English studies, which, as Bill Readings argues in *The University in Ruins*, was invested in reproducing a national culture through literary study. According to Readings's argument, a nation reproduces its fundamental values through a stable body of privileged texts—that is, the canon—at a privileged site of dissemination—that is, the university. Readings maintains that this model, which he calls "the university of culture," has steadily been losing authority in recent decades. As the centrality of the nation-state wanes in the face of a growing transnational global economy, a "university of excellence" has superseded this "university of culture." The discourses of theory and composition emerge within this new university as the literary text begins to lose the quasi-religious aura that had previously surrounded it.[21] Both theory and composition focus on practices that need to be developed and refined in order for one to navigate within a constantly shifting terrain with few familiar landmarks. Neither theory nor composition is fundamentally oriented around the transmission of stable bodies of knowledge that are consumed in order to reproduce a cultural tradition.

Of course, the split between practice-based arts and bodies of knowledge is anything but firm, since concepts and practices with a pragmatic edge can be transformed into reified bodies of knowledge rather easily. As *The Norton Anthology of Theory and Criticism* and numerous other anthologies demonstrate, many of the figures who interrogated the concepts of authorship and mastery have themselves become consecrated. In composition studies, meanwhile, the process movement, which many have characterized as the origin of the field, can just as easily become another product with its own collection of familiar touchstones and texts (and hence the need for a "postprocess" movement that reorients the field around practices rather than established knowledge).[22] Here comes the new canon, same as the old canon. Conversely, I imagine many would bristle at the notion that literary studies has not departed in substantial ways from the canonical model that long organized the field. As my project discusses, many of the alternatives to the earlier university of culture model that were posited outside of the canon were simultaneously produced *within* it. Rhetoric lies in the intersection between product and process, innovation and tradition, insofar as it constitutes one of the most revered intellectual traditions, but a tradition devoted to detailing modes of practical language use in specific, ever-changing social contexts.

Yoking theory and composition also invites us to examine the ever-renewable tensions between theory and practice. Within the contemporary university, which increasingly envisions its mission as delivering vocational training, "practice" clearly enjoys the upper hand. Accordingly, it is not surprising that composition has assumed a more prominent role in this brave new world insofar as "general" writing skills have, ostensibly, more direct marketability than knowledge of literary and philosophical texts. As Marc Bousquet has explained, "at its most basic, this shift means that members of the educated classes are today far less likely to hail each other at cocktail parties, tennis matches, and job interviews by using such forms of call and response as dropping a book title . . . in order to elicit such appropriate responses as 'Ah, Melville,' 'Call me Ishmael,' or 'Oh, I never finished that!'" ("Figure of Writing" 118). In this environment, theory would appear to be an even graver sin than literature insofar as its head-in-the-clouds abstruse speculation is the farthest thing from hard economic realities. And yet one of the overarching points running through my project is the idea that abstract theorizing may be the most important "practical" skill in the new economy. Indeed, the following analysis urges us to consider the possibility of thinking composition studies and theoretical discourse together as complimentary rather than diametrical opposites.[23] But developing a more robust sense of theoretically informed practice means first untangling the long and complicated antagonisms between certain strains of Rhetoric and Composition and theory. For every James Berlin—who argued in *Rhetorics, Poetics, and Cultures* that a natural affinity existed between scholars working in composition and those working in theory and cultural studies and petitioned the discipline to reorient itself around these two related specializations—there is a Maxine Hairston who regarded theoretical abstraction as an obstacle to the real work of educating students.[24]

Comparing Rhetoric and Composition to theory also raises some pressing questions about the relationship between teaching and research and the role those two practices play in shaping a field's identity. Whereas Rhetoric and Composition leans heavily toward teaching, theory leans heavily toward research. First-year composition is a requirement for just about every college student in America, whereas many students are able to earn an English major without taking a single course in theory. My own work is not so much concerned with the specific practice of teaching first-year writing in the university—that has been going on for quite some time—as it is with the emergence of a research agenda around this teaching practice, particularly one that distinguishes itself from the rest of the department. But if the following analysis will restrict itself to examining the research agendas of these two areas, then it already implicitly favors theory as opposed to Rhetoric and Composition. I would argue that my orientation simply follows the trends that have been reshaping the field of Rhetoric and Composition for some time.[25] Indeed, the emergence of a research agenda is striking considering how teachers of composition have tended to adhere to the "pedagogical imperative" and, à la Joseph Harris, embraced composition as "a teaching subject."[26] Much of Rhetoric and Composition's identity has come from championing, unlike its counterparts in literary studies, teaching over research. At the same time, the publish-or-perish model is more intense than ever before, and today a number of schools that are not research-intensive institutions still expect their faculty to publish. Composition's desire to be taken seriously as a discourse, an equal among its peers in the department, necessitates that it engage in this activity. But, of course, more time spent engaging in research naturally pulls faculty away from the classroom. In an attempt to resolve this dilemma, research in the field is very often about teaching—either improving teaching practices or documenting the history of these teaching practices or making impassioned arguments that other kinds of work not formally recognized as research should be considered as equally valuable. As a result, Rhetoric and Composition has always been something of a schizophrenic discourse, reflected in the difficulty one has separating its research agenda from its teaching practices.

Along similar lines, the discourse's attachment to rhetoric has also always been ambivalent. On one hand, rhetoric provides a more dignified subject matter for the field, one that elevates it above (merely) studying its own pedagogical practices. On the other hand, a field that values pedagogical practices so highly may feel that research into the history and theory of rhetoric is a waste of time if it does not in some way reshape what goes on in the classroom. Regardless, the emergence of Rhetoric and Composition serves as an interesting test case for thinking about the status of disciplinary knowledge in the contemporary university, where the student-centered approach to education confronts a demand for increasingly specialized research.

The role that teaching and research activity play in establishing field identity also points to other material conditions inside and outside the university that shape how Rhetoric and Composition and theory conceptualize themselves. To take just one example, the university's reliance on low-wage instructors is inseparable from the identity of Rhetoric and Composition, which has confronted this problem for decades, long before the recent "crisis in the humanities." Rhetoric and Composition has never completely abandoned its historical identification as members of an exploited class, a group that the late composition scholar Susan Miller once called "the sad women in the basement."[27] And, as Donna Strickland has suggested in her recent *The Managerial Unconscious in the History of Composition Studies*, that self-identity remains in force even when tenure-track positions opened for specialists in Rhetoric and Composition. This book does not study the adjunct labor crisis directly; there are many other impressive ones that do. My analysis is, however, underwritten by the idea that we can read a number of prominent critics within English studies over the last several decades in relation to the material conditions in which they were produced. In what ways do broader social realities inside and outside the university shape the distinct identities between fields within English studies? In what ways might broader social changes increase or decrease the possibility of connections between fields? In what ways do conflicts within the discipline of English, or the university more broadly, inform how critics in these fields understand social dynamics in the larger social world (or vice versa)? English's various camps, while certainly shifting according to internal rifts and alliances, are not immune from outside influence; at the same time, their conceptions of external forces will always be partially filtered through local dynamics.

The following chapters examine a number of critics within English studies that help illuminate the complex process of "bordering" that helps us grasp the dynamic organization of the discipline today. By investigating pivotal figures like Paul de Man, Kenneth Burke, Fredric Jameson, Michel Foucault, Stephen Greenblatt, James Berlin, Susan Miller, John Guillory, and Bruno Latour, we will experience how various fields constantly fluctuate, forming alliances with former foes in one moment and resuming old hostilities in the next. In providing this account, I hope to provide a "cognitive map" of sorts to help navigate the incredibly complex landscape that is contemporary English studies.

Chapter 1, "On the Use and Abuse of Rhetoric in Composition and Theory," examines the varied deployments of the concept of "rhetoric" in these two discourses that have long had antagonistic attitudes toward one another. I analyze the work of Paul de Man and Kenneth Burke as a way of exploring how "rhetoric" has been used as a vehicle for justifying and facilitating the expansion of critical discourse. As my title intimates, Nietzsche serves as the figure that links together two separate versions of rhetoric—one rooted in tropes, the other in persuasion—and, by extension, literary studies with Rhetoric and Composition. De Man adopts Nietzsche's work on rhetorical language as a way of maximizing the ambiguities found in the literary text and thereby ensuring that critical interpretations of canonical texts will remain interminable. Burke, meanwhile, reading against the grain, casts Nietzsche as a thinker of radical democracy, one who underwrites a practice that continually incorporates new voices and perspectives into an "endless conversation." The chapter is a demonstration of the possibilities of *intra*-disciplinary work that rejects the idea that rhetoric (or any other concept, for that matter) is the domain of a single sector of English studies rather than a common good shared by all. The specific articulation of "agonism" that I provide here should not be seen as the property of any existing subdisciplinary specialty but instead a creation that transversally links separate domains.

At another level, this particular notion of rhetoric that I advance—a notion of agonism that prompts the endless expansion of discourse—is also meant to provide an account of the current state of the discipline. The initial boundaries that have long governed the segregation of literary studies from Rhetoric and Composition have slowly broken down. It is precisely because these two discourses are both governed by an impulse to expand their parameters and incorporate new objects so as to spur continued research and criticism that they are approaching a point where no obvious conceptual or methodological principle clearly demarcates them. The field of literary studies is no longer tethered to the principle of "literature" that initially founded the discourse. Similarly, Rhetoric and Composition is quickly finding that the field's initial focus on student writing to be a straightjacket that inhibits future criticism and which must be escaped. Although they began as distinct entities housed within a single department, their expansive tendencies have led them to the shared territory of a generalized "writing studies." In this respect, Chapter 1 not only offers a broad account of how the discipline has arrived at its present condition but also embodies the kind of work that could be done if the existing distinctions (which are becoming increasingly untenable) are ultimately abandoned.

If both a theorized version of literary studies and Rhetoric and Composition have been trending toward the general conceptual category of "writing" or "rhetoric" or, perhaps slightly more broadly, "culture" to contain the ever-expanding nature of their work, this is not to say that the way these terms have been configured are the same. In other words, both fields might now define themselves in terms of broad, open-ended inquiry, but the specific itineraries each has traveled to arrive at the current moment has ensured that they will define their critical enterprise in different and often diametrically opposed ways. As a result, the relationship between contemporary literary studies and Rhetoric and Composition can be both a nearly imperceptible gap and an unbridgeable gulf. Any attempt to facilitate future intradisciplinary work will require taking into account these discrepancies. To that effect, Chapter 2, "Between Standardization and Serialization: Kenneth Burke, Fredric Jameson, and Radical Criticism in the Post-Fordist Era," explores the differences between these discourses through a careful examination of a debate between Burke and Jameson in the journal *Critical Inquiry* in 1978. Burke serves as a pivotal figure for understanding these dynamics insofar as his work has been taken up by both literary studies and Rhetoric and Composition. Surprisingly, however, his fate in these fields could not be more different—while he has mostly been forgotten within literary studies, he has become an enormously important figure in Rhetoric and Composition. As his engagement with Jameson illustrates, the two discourses might be productively split in terms of their understandings of difference and pluralism. While Rhetoric and Composition has largely celebrated these terms as tools to combat a homogenizing hierarchical form of power, literary theory has understood them as simultaneously necessary and dangerous. In more concrete terms, Rhetoric and Composition tends to celebrate difference as an unequivocal good; literary theory, meanwhile, sees the greatest threat to be a lack of cohesion that prevents social collectivities from responding to dispersal and chaos.

Although the schematic outlined in Chapter 2 is a useful way of diagnosing the broad differences between "literary theory" and "rhetorical theory," it would be a mistake to think that these differences have not fluctuated or exceeded the fields I have assigned them (in fact, the model of social change advanced by literary theory anticipates its own appropriation and rearticulation; it also speaks to the concept of "bordering" that I am

borrowing from Mezzadra and Neilson). In other words, although literary theory became an indispensable feature of literary studies, absorbed
into the daily work of the discourse, this absorption transformed much
of "literary theory" into what I earlier characterize as "rhetorical theory."
The work of major figures in the French tradition of continental philosophy was enlisted as theoretical support for multiculturalism and identity
politics during the 1980s and 1990s. Chapter 3, "Mapping the Archival
Turn in English Studies," documents this shift by tracing the reception of
Michel Foucault's work in the American academy. Although his work on
contemporary biopolitics places him firmly within the orbit of "literary
theory," his work was transformed into a version of "rhetorical theory" by
figures within *both* literary studies and Rhetoric and Composition, thereby
complicating the divisions between these two fields (within Chapter 3, "literary theory" is characterized as a "cartographic politics" while "rhetorical theory" is characterized as an "archival politics," for reasons that will
become clear in the chapter).

This chapter also explores how these competing versions of politics—
the cartographic or literary against the archival or rhetorical—circulated
within the contemporary university during this period. I argue that a lack
of attention to the sorts of complications anticipated by a cartographic
politics of literary theory prevent many within Rhetoric and Composition
from properly understanding their position within the university. Because
of its overwhelming commitment to an archival politics, it fails to see that
its low standing has less to do with its relationship to literary studies and
more to do with neoliberal economic imperatives propelling administrative policy. The danger it has long faced but rarely recognizes is the degree to which its embrace of difference does not guarantee its protection
from a central university administration that at least partially subscribes to
these principles of difference. Unexpectedly, difference has become a tool
to create new hierarchies within the university rather than an uncorrupted
principle outside of these hierarchies.

Chapter 4, "Toward an Aesthetics Without Literature," continues to
explore the issues raised in the previous chapter by staging a dialogue between two touchstone texts in English studies: Rhetoric and Composition
scholar Susan Miller's 1991 *Textual Carnivals* and literary critic John Guillory's 1993 *Cultural Capital.* Although both texts constitute full-fledged
attempts to understand the changes occurring within the discipline of English as it approaches the end of the twentieth century, they each understand the relative value or status of literary studies and Rhetoric and
Composition in dramatically different ways. Whereas Miller conceives of

Rhetoric and Composition as little more than a punching bag for literary studies to preserve and strengthen its position within the university, Guillory sees composition as the successor to literary studies, which has long been on a slow but steady path to complete obsolescence. Ultimately, Guillory's understanding of the university as a specific site within society (rather than a small scale replica of that society) prevents him from making the same errors that plague Miller's account.

Beyond navigating the largely incompatible accounts of English studies forwarded in Miller and Guillory's texts, Chapter 4 uses these texts as building blocks for constructing another potential bridge between literary studies and Rhetoric and Composition. Whereas Chapter 1 understood "writing" and "rhetoric" as god terms that could unite the entire discipline, Chapter 4 suggests that "aesthetics" could serve a similar purpose if it is able to shed its long-standing attachment to the problematic concept of "literature" that merely serves as a marker for distinguishing social classes. Indeed, while Miller's *Textual Carnivals* rejects aesthetics entirely, seeing it as inseparable from "literature," Guillory's *Cultural Capital* aims to liberate aesthetic engagement—that is, the experience and analysis of the relationship between form and content that inheres in any cultural phenomenon—from this pernicious relationship. I argue that this reformulation of aesthetics preserves the strengths of contemporary literary studies without being saddled with much of the discipline's historical baggage that has increasingly become a liability in today's university. Similarly, this new approach to aesthetics, which has much in common with a particular version of rhetoric, allows the discipline of English to avoid the pitfalls associated with a form of literalism and immediacy that currently underwrites much of Rhetoric and Composition. Without this version of aesthetics, the discipline is doomed to become a mere service entity on campus once "literature" has finally been marginalized.

In Chapter 5, "New Things, Old Things: Reading the Latourian Turn Symptomatically," I examine the recent uptake of Bruno Latour within both theoretical circles and Rhetoric and Composition. For Latour's followers, his work promises enormous transformations within the critical field. Literary theorists see in him a bold new method of reading that dispenses with one of the most cherished practices in English studies—suspicious, or symptomatic, reading. Meanwhile, scholars in Rhetoric and Composition see Latour providing the field with more intellectual legitimacy than it has ever received before. The chapter demonstrates, however, that such impressions not only overestimate Latour's potential impact but that their overestimation can be attributed to a certain feature within

Latour's work. Over the course of the chapter, I weave together elements from the previous chapters—the examination in Chapter 1 of the critical arena as a system with regular, predictable cycles, the analysis in Chapter 2 of the "serial situation," the treatment in Chapter 3 of the tensions between the singular and the structural, and the exploration in Chapter 4 of criticism's demand to extend beyond academia—as a way of tying together the analysis conducted over the course of the book.

  The Two Cultures of English eschews a straightforwardly linear approach in favor of a constant oscillation between past and present within each chapter. Although a loose chronology exists in these chapters (de Man and the New Rhetoric of the 1960s and early 1970s is followed by Burke and Jameson at the end of the 1970s; Foucault and New Historicism in the 1980s are followed by Miller and Guillory in the early 1990s), all of the chapters include moments or figures from other points on the continuum from 1945 to the present. For instance, Chapter 1 not only discusses Paul de Man and Kenneth Burke but also addresses the New Historicism of the 1980s as well as recent composition scholarship like Sidney I. Dobrin's 2011 *Post-Composition*; Chapter 2 not only examines the Burke-Jameson debate but also gestures toward recent "animal studies" scholarship; Chapter 3 does not limit itself to Foucault's immediate reception in the American academy in the 1980s but also explores recent archival historiography in Rhetoric and Composition. Thus, while I construct a certain narrative in the following chapters, that is an effect of my argument rather than a feature attributable to this period in English studies. Ending in the present day, the work shows how a number of dynamics governing contemporary criticism have a history that stretch back to the origins of theory and Rhetoric and Composition in the American academy.

CHAPTER I

On the Use and Abuse of Rhetoric
in Composition and Theory

In his essay "Roots, Races, and the Return to Philology," Geoffrey Galt Harpham traces the long and contorted history of philology in modern scholarship. Harpham notes that critics as different as Edward Said and Paul de Man each called for a "return to philology" in the final years of their respective careers, and Harpham intimates that this demand "seems to be an urge experienced by those confronting their own mortality" (44). What strikes Harpham as more peculiar, however, is the fact that Said and de Man advanced wildly different conceptions of philology. In fact, both figures envisioned a return to philology as an antidote to what the other critic prescribed. Whereas Said enlisted philology as a means of resuscitating "intimacy, resistance, emancipation, and historical knowledge" (45), de Man defined the term as "a harsh and explicit corrective to precisely such humanistic fantasies" (45). As Harpham explains, "it is as if each had appropriated the term *philology* for his own purposes, without regard to its meaning" (45). Yet as the remainder of Harpham's analysis reveals, the capaciousness of philology, its ability to spearhead disparate and even dramatically antagonistic trends, should not be limited to Said and de Man. For instance, while many hoped that philology would restrain critics from indulging in irresponsible critical explorations that would destabilize disciplinary boundaries (Said and de Man, despite their sharp differences, both belonged to this camp), others championed this disciplinary transcendence as "the defining characteristic and entire point of philology itself" (52). Harpham's analysis would seem to lend credence to the notion that philology was so expansive in its definition that it could mean just about anything to anyone. As he asserts near the conclusion of the piece, "it is difficult to know how to think about philology, because it is difficult to know exactly what philology is" (77).

While Harpham's analysis offers a much needed assessment of how English studies articulates its own history, his use of de Man as a key figure hints at another term that has equal importance in terms of understanding the recent history of the discipline. Indeed, while Harpham cites de Man's "The Resistance to Theory" to document the deconstructionist's commitment to philology, the privileged term in this essay is not "philology" but "rhetoric." In de Man's corpus, rhetoric becomes a pivotal term, one that underwrites his entire critical project (after all, he describes his interpretive practice as "rhetorical reading" and not "philological reading"). As our brief discussion in the introduction illustrated, "rhetoric" has come to occupy an equally nebulous status within English studies, and examining it in more detail should help us better assess the conflicted nature of the discipline over the last fifty years.

While far from the only figure participating in contemporary discourse on rhetoric, de Man serves as an important figure precisely because he highlights the peculiar ends that "rhetoric" has been enlisted to achieve in English studies since the 1960s. De Man's insistence on rhetoric as an indispensable term in his critical toolbox might strike us as odd given the fact that he engages so little with the figures that are typically associated with the rhetorical tradition. Such oddness is emphasized by the fact that a number of literary critics *were* engaging with this rhetorical tradition at roughly the same time. These critics who were invested in the rhetorical tradition—we might, for the sake of convenience, call them "the New Rhetoricians"—saw their work as an antidote to precisely those features that de Man was advancing. In this respect, the split between de Man and these rhetoricians precedes the one between Said and de Man detailed by Harpham. Although serious differences separate de Man from Said, their antagonism remains confined within the discourse of "literary theory." The split between de Man and the New Rhetoricians, however, highlights a more institutionally oriented fault line within the discipline, one that can be best understood by examining publication venues and hiring lines—more specifically, a divide between "literary theory" (which in many respects has come to stand in for the entirety of literary studies) and "Rhetoric and Composition." Given the often tense relationship between these two camps, it is odd that both would turn toward the term rhetoric to underwrite their respective operations.

"Rhetoric" has become a floating signifier of the highest order, so capacious that people working in the same discipline are often unfamiliar with one another's working definitions of the term. Take, for instance, the experience that John Schilb recounts in the beginning of his *Between the Lines: Relating Composition Theory and Literary Theory*. Attending an international summer institute in Chicago in the mid-1980s, Schilb is shocked to learn that the institute's director, famed feminist deconstructionist Barbara Johnson (a former student of de Man's), defines rhetoric as "language that says one thing and means another" (quoted in *Between the Lines* 4). As a composition scholar trained in the rhetorical tradition, Schilb cannot fathom how Johnson's definition could avoid any mention of persuasion: "No one in composition would define *rhetoric* in this way!" Even more alarming is Johnson's complete surprise when Schilb confronts her with the classical definition of rhetoric provided by Aristotle; she seems completely unfamiliar with the notion that rhetoric involves observing the available means of persuasion in a given situation. Schilb is flabbergasted: "How could a theorist of rhetoric be hazy . . . about a definition [that composition specialists] know well?" (5). As the rest of Schilb's *Between the Lines* argues, the fact that practitioners in two different subfields of English studies are completely bewildered by the other's definition of rhetoric is symptomatic of the deep insularity of these two camps.

I would suggest that the line that separating the two fields is not as impermeable as Schilb's analysis suggests. Or, put somewhat differently, the way they grasp the term rhetoric might be understood beyond a simple opposition between "tropes" on the one hand and "persuasion" on the other. While organizing the relationship of English studies to rhetoric along a tropes/persuasion axis is undeniably productive, it fails to offer the entire picture. In Schilb's work, the tropes/persuasion pair produces a number of corresponding binaries, including reading/writing, political quietism/ activism, research/teaching that restrict our understanding of the field. After all, de Man, Johnson's teacher at Yale, was clearly aware of rhetoric in terms of persuasion (see Chapter 6 of *Allegories of Reading*), while plenty of New Rhetoricians, especially Kenneth Burke, focus on figural language's role in persuasion. What if we instead examined literary theory and Rhetoric and Composition's relationship to rhetoric not through their engagement with the tropes or persuasion but instead through another term? Such an approach might help us bypass the deadlock between active and passive that has too long structured discussions of the literature/composition split. Indeed, in this chapter, I will be less concerned with what these respective fields say explicitly about "rhetoric" and more with how ideas from the rhetorical tradition influence the way they understand and organize their practice of scholarly criticism. As Barbara Johnson writes in *A World of Difference* (crediting Schilb in the acknowledgments), "whether one defines rhetoric as 'language that says one thing and means another' (as I do in Chapter 16) . . . or as 'the faculty of observing in any case the available means of persuasion' (as Aristotle and most teachers of composition do) . . . it is clear that the study of rhetoric has everything to do with human politics" (5–6). Modifying Johnson's assertion slightly, I will argue that rhetoric has everything to do with the politics of criticism in the discipline.

The key term for understanding the role of rhetoric in English studies actually comes from within the rhetorical tradition. I argue that the notion of *agon*—strife or competition between two participants—helps us better understand some of the subtle linkages and divergences among various fields within the discipline.[1] Rooted in a conceptualization of the *agon* derived from Nietzsche, the term "rhetoric" has been used to authorize the proliferation of critical discursive acts. For de Man and deconstruction more generally, "rhetoric" serves as a way of signaling the mysterious depths of the literary artifact that inaugurate an endless confrontation between reader and text. For Burke and the New Rhetoricians, "rhetoric" acts as a means of ushering in a more expansive discussion that steadily accumulates new participants and objects. The agonistic principles that have underwritten the continual expansion of scholarship in both literary studies and Rhetoric and Composition have led to a steadily approaching and unavoidable confrontation between these two fields that will likely determine the future of the discipline.

Nietzsche's Agonistic Education

Nietzsche's engagement with rhetoric begins with a series of lectures at the University of Basel during the 1872–73 academic year—lectures only two students attended. Portions of the lectures were translated into French (by Philippe Lacoue-Labarthe and Jean-Luc Nancy) in the 1970s and into English in the 1980s. Consisting of sixteen sections, this work provides a relatively straightforward account of the history of rhetoric and its most important practitioners and theorists. Delivered in a flat, textbook-like manner, Nietzsche's lectures lack his later witty and biting irony. As Sander L. Gilman, Carole Blair, and David J. Parent note in their introduction to the English translation, the "lectures, when they discuss the history and substance of rhetoric, are derivative" (*Rhetoric and Language* xi). Nietzsche merely rehearses arguments from Richard Volkmann's *Die Rhetorik der Griechen und Römer in systematischer Übersicht dargestellt* and parrots historians of rhetoric Gustav Gerber and Friedrich Blass. A recapitulation of common knowledge, Nietzsche's lectures ostensibly offer no unique insights about rhetoric.

A flagrant exception to this assessment can be found in the third section of the lectures entitled "The Relation of the Rhetorical to Language." Nietzsche seizes a marginal feature of rhetorical theory and transforms it into a foundational principle through which language can be grasped in its entirety. After a brief account of how ancient writing strikes modern ears as unnatural, Nietzsche states the case in a way that directly shaped de Man's articulations in *Allegories of Reading*:

> There is obviously no unrhetorical "naturalness" of language to which one could appeal; language itself is the result of purely rhetorical arts. The power to discover and to make operative that which works and impresses, with respect to each thing, a power which Aristotle calls rhetoric, is, at the same time, the essence of language; the latter is based just as rhetoric is upon that which is true, upon the essence of things. Language does not desire to instruct, but to convey to others a subjective impulse and its acceptance. (21)

In fact, as Nietzsche points out, it "makes no sense to speak of a 'proper meaning' which is carried over to something else only in special cases" (25). His assertions not only resonate with the famous essay "On Truth and Lying in an Extra-Moral Sense" (composed the following summer), where he argues that the journey from nerve stimulus to image to sound to concept amounts to a series of metaphorical substitutions that problematize the very notion of a "thing in itself"; they also anticipate the ruminations on perspectivism in all his major philosophical statements of the 1880s.[2]

Nietzsche's confident intervention during the third lecture should initiate a broader revision of the entire course. While much of the material Nietzsche communicated is admittedly derivative, the editors of the English translation point out "the selection, arrangement, and placement of the subject matter are of his choosing" (xvii). Particularly striking is Nietzsche's decision to emphasize Ciceronian stylistics rather than retrace the more predictable path through Plato and Aristotle's work on rhetoric. That

Nietzsche felt comfortable bypassing such familiar landmarks in these lecture sessions challenges the assumption that his only original contribution to the history of rhetoric consisted of an analysis of figural language. Even if his lectures on rhetoric are read as merely a burdensome professional obligation that he fulfilled with little enthusiasm, plenty of other material confirms an investment in rhetoric extending beyond his analysis of tropes. Not only does the lengthy essay "A History of Greek Eloquence" display his nearly encyclopedic grasp of rhetorical practice in ancient Greece, it also gestures toward questions of strife and competition that ultimately became integral to his broader philosophical project. Indeed, many of Nietzsche's primary texts on the Greek culture of competition were contemporaneous with his explorations of tropological language. The interconnections between trope and competition are most clearly pronounced in how Nietzsche reformulates the concept *agonism*.

Nietzsche discusses the *agon* in "Homer's Contest," a brief essay from 1871. Intended as a preface for a book that was never completed (much like his lecture courses in rhetoric the following year failed to culminate in any official or completed text), the essay tracks the startling differences between ancient Greek and nineteenth-century German valuations of contestation and struggle. Lamenting his contemporaries' distaste for competition, Nietzsche asserts that "nothing separates the Greek world more from ours" than differing views on envy (55). The ancient Greeks conceived of envy "not as a blemish" but instead "as the effect of a *beneficent* deity" (55). Rather than a regrettable byproduct of human culture that should be minimized at all costs, competition was actively cultivated through an "agonistic education" (58) that would produce citizens capable of preserving the health and vibrancy of Greek culture.

Although he valorizes envy and competition, Nietzsche warns of the dangers that result when the agonistic sphere becomes unbalanced by unequal competitors. He cites the original meaning of ostracism, which refers to the banishment of figures whose skills far exceed all others. "Why should not someone be the best?" Nietzsche asks rhetorically, offering a firm answer: "Because with that the contest would fail, and the eternal life-basis of the Hellenic State would be endangered" (57). He provides the example of Miltiades, an individual who wielded so much power and skill that he vanquished all rivals who threatened him but whose unchallenged supremacy ultimately ruined both himself and the entire Greek state. To prevent such misfortune, the Greeks advocated perpetual competition that would prevent a single figure from achieving too much glory and thereby dismantling the competitive sphere. Fearing the dangers of autocracy, they desired "a *preventive* against the genius—a second genius" (58). In her recent study of Nietzsche's treatment of agonism, Christa Davis Acampora notes that the philosopher makes a distinction between a positive, productive agonism and a negative, destructive antagonism. The former seeks to perpetuate the competition itself, accords respect to one's opponent, and possesses a desire to maintain the existence of this competitor since their relationship is mutually beneficial. The latter aims to annihilate the opponent and put an end to competition itself.

Reversing typical priorities, Nietzsche privileges competitive action itself over victorious outcomes, introducing a metalepsis between cause and effect that links his arguments about agonism to his ruminations on tropes. No longer can competition be conceived as a mere means to an end, and Nietzsche writes that if one assumes "the Greek was unable to bear glory and fortune, one should say more exactly that he was unable to bear fame without further struggle" ("Homer's Contest" 60). Victory means little on its own without the opportunity to compete again. Rather than a vanishing mediator, the act of struggling within the contest actually constitutes the "glory and fortune" insofar as it develops capacities for individual growth and self-overcoming. The spoils one might gain from the competition should not overshadow the practices that were cultivated in order to secure these rewards. The goal of competition—victory—has now become merely a means through which the goal of a more fully realized competitive spirit—previously just the means for achieving victory—is accomplished. In order to cultivate a competitive spirit, however, one must maintain the desire to defeat one's opponent and secure victory since this objective mobilizes the entire operation. Fighting for victory and fighting for the sake of fighting engage in a sort of duel themselves that must remain unending. Nietzsche adopts the agonistic spirit animating competitive relationships and internalizes it in his later aphoristic writing. Rather than formulating a single position and defending it against potential detractors, Nietzsche's writing instead incorporates opposing positions into its very texture so that a single statement or argument never emerges as anything more than a temporary, provisional victor. Strains of thought emerge and conflict with one another, reconfiguring themselves after these encounters in unanticipated reversals and convergences. Nietzsche's texts might be likened to a competition where a winner is never crowned because the game never ends.

Nietzsche stresses that the productive form of agonism was rooted into the very fabric of Greek culture, such that every Athenian citizen saw it as his duty "to cultivate his Ego in contest, so far that it should be of the highest service to Athens" (58). Crucially, these practices are not limited merely to the most obvious pedagogical settings. Just as "the youths to be educated were brought up struggling against one another, so their educators were in turn in emulation amongst themselves" (59). While Nietzsche mentions jealousies blooming between rival musicians, sophists, and dramatic artists, we might easily see this agonistic spirit animating Nietzsche's own critical project and those inspired by his work in the twentieth century. In fact, Nietzsche's decision to explore rhetoric and offer a decisive reformulation and transformation of its fundamental coordinates may stem from some of these agonistic principles, evident when we consider Nietzsche's historical moment. By the end of the nineteenth century, the field of rhetoric appeared to be completely exhausted, and in his 1936 work *The Philosophy of Rhetoric*, I. A. Richards announced that rhetoric "may perhaps be said to end with Archbishop Whately" (5), whose famous *Elements of Rhetoric* appeared in 1846. Nietzsche's decision to resuscitate rhetoric several decades after Whately may be largely due to its low standing, an effort to return an apparently vanquished foe to the "ring of competition."

De Man and the Ring of Competition

Although the term "rhetoric" features prominently in his corpus, Paul de Man rarely engages with the traditional rhetorical canon. Isocrates, Cicero, and Quintilian fail to generate any commentary, the sophists remain untouched, and Aristotle receives nothing more than a cursory glance. De Man seems content to confine himself to a notion of rhetoric inaugurated during the Romantic period and extended by Nietzsche that focuses solely on tropes and dispenses with questions concerning persuasion and eloquence. Whereas most contemporary rhetoricians have invested their energies in analyzing political discourse, de Man's work exhibits little interest in the public and its problems. Read in this register, de Man's use of the word "rhetoric" to describe his interpretive approach is just a tease, promising a turn toward the politicization of the literary sphere only to double down on the aesthetic object and its precious reflective interiors. The "rhetorical" remains largely indistinguishable from the "literary," signifying the figural or metaphorical dimension of language that frustrates the search for univocal meaning and the frictionless communication of subjective experience. De Man's relentless focus on the nuances of individual literary works has left him vulnerable to charges of a narrow textualism with potentially disastrous political consequences. In *Criticism and Social Change*, Frank Lentricchia chastised de Man for ignoring the important social dimensions of literature, arguing that this omission confirmed a dangerous political quietism. The discovery in 1989 of de Man's anti-Semitic wartime writings only intensified this dismissive reading of de Man, with the fiercest critics asserting that his work cleared a direct path to National Socialism and the Final Solution.

Much evidence exists to counteract this narrative, including de Man's turn to questions of ideology in his late writings.[3] In an interview only months before his death in 1983, de Man asserts that politics and ideology were always "uppermost" in his mind but that they could only be approached through careful linguistic examination (*Recent Imagining* 103). His unfinished manuscript *Aesthetics, Rhetoric, Ideology* (published posthumously in 1996 as *Aesthetic Ideology*) offers a glimpse of an ambitious project that would elucidate the political implications of his earlier textual analyses. But even if these late explorations are discounted, de Man's early work possesses a substantial political undercurrent most evident in his interest in the various allegiances and rivalries that exist within literary criticism. His detailed readings of texts are always accompanied by an erudite awareness of the history of competing critical camps that have long warred over issues of interpretation. The 1971 collection *Blindness and Insight*, which consolidates his explorations of numerous literary critics, suggests that his interest in politics targeted a more immediate and local venue than the broader public sphere or mass democracy. De Man's work likens the discourse of literary criticism to a public forum where pressing matters are assessed and deliberated, thereby making his analyses of the structures and shifts that govern this community an unacknowledged form of rhetorical analysis.

In an interview with Robert Moynihan, de Man acknowledges Nietzsche as the inspiration behind his turn toward rhetoric. Explaining that he had not always had recourse to rhetorical terminology, de Man asserts that

> the main revelation for me was Nietzsche, who I had been trying to read for many years without getting too far, precisely because the moment where Nietzsche reflects on language as a historical structure is a moment which one didn't know or didn't hear about. One was so concerned with problems of good and evil, problems of an ethical nature, or historical attitudes, much of which I couldn't get into. But Nietzsche is highly aware of rhetorical theory, knows those terms and uses them. It gives you a point of entry that is exceedingly fruitful. (147)

In pointing out that Nietzsche possesses an extensive knowledge of the history of rhetoric and uses it to incredible effect, de Man hints at the degree to which he himself is fluent in that history; indeed, as we shall soon see, de Man's own engagement with Nietzsche suggests that his knowledge of rhetoric rivals Nietzsche's. Furthermore, while de Man may appear uninterested in many of the thematic concerns that have troubled commentators of Nietzsche for decades, we should not conclude from his interview comments that his engagement with Nietzsche was limited strictly to those writings meditating on the nature of language—the lectures on rhetoric and "On Truth and Lying in an Extramoral Sense." In fact, de Man engages with Nietzsche's thought in a number of sophisticated ways that inform his practice as a literary critic.

His most obvious engagement with Nietzsche can be seen in the explicitly rhetorical vocabulary he deploys throughout most of his work in the 1970s. An analysis of Nietzsche's writing anchors much of de Man's signature book, *Allegories of Reading*. Three of the six sections in the first part of the book, entitled "Rhetoric," are dedicated to a close reading of the German philosopher's work, with de Man covering a number of texts including *The Birth of Tragedy*, "On Truth and Lying," *The Will to Power*, and *The Gay Science*. In the chapter "Rhetoric of Tropes (Nietzsche)," de Man considers the most significant features of Nietzsche's thoughts on language that first appeared in the third rhetoric lecture. De Man claims that Nietzsche regards the figural dimension of language not as a peripheral feature but instead an essential one. As de Man emphasizes, Nietzsche's comments constitute a profound intervention into the theory of language, one that "marks a full reversal of established priorities" (106). In fact, Nietzsche's critique of language is merely a proxy for his broader project of undermining metaphysics more generally. De Man assures his reader that "we can legitimately assert therefore that the key to Nietzsche's critique of metaphysics . . . lies in the rhetorical model of the trope or . . . the language most explicitly grounded in rhetoric" (109). As de Man's analysis unfolds, determining his differences from Nietzsche becomes increasingly difficult; he becomes so tightly sutured to Nietzsche's metalanguage that separating the two seems impossible, much like the impossibility of separating the dancer from the dance that de Man explores in the opening chapter of *Allegories of Reading*.

In his famous 1982 essay "The Resistance to Theory," de Man even mobilizes Nietzsche's formulation of rhetoric as a synecdoche for theory in its entirety. Responding to a request from the Committee on Research Activities of the Modern Language Association for a succinct overview of recent trends in the field of "literary theory," de Man defines the term as "the introduction of linguistic terminology in the metalanguage about literature" (8) that "upsets rooted ideologies by revealing the mechanics of their workings" (11). He conceptualizes theory in terms of the classic trivium that includes grammar, rhetoric, and logic. A symbiotic relationship between grammar and logic, de Man explains, underwrites any belief in a transparent and self-assured knowledge of the world. However, by focusing on the rhetorical dimension of language, a residue of indetermination emerges that grammar cannot solve. Language always defies the easy assurances promised by a grammatical definition. "Rhetoric," de Man writes, "by its actively negative relationship to grammar and to logic, certainly undoes the claims of the *trivium* (and by extension, of language) to be an epistemologically stable construct" (17). The "resistance" to theory that de Man addresses is a resistance to the rhetorical dimension of language.

But Nietzsche does more for de Man than simply help him deconstruct metaphysics. De Man continually returns to Nietzsche's writing because it forces him to think more deeply about the consequences of the deconstructive operation. Put slightly differently, de Man's analyses of Nietzsche can be understood as meditations on his own work, the closest that de Man would come to deconstructing one of his own texts. De Man learns from Nietzsche that the deconstructive operation is one that is not completely antagonistic with metaphysics. A rather shortsighted reading of de Man's work would conclude that language's referential, metaphysical properties and its deconstructive, rhetorical ones are diametrically opposed: deconstruction eliminates the phantasmagoric metaphysical ideals that illusorily allow the text to cohere in a transcendent unity. De Man's work actually proposes a more nuanced dynamic where the confrontation between these two forces does not end in the elimination of one but instead engenders an endless restaging of the conflict. Instead of a goal or value to be cultivated through deliberate action, the agonistic forces that reside in language always already exist and only become more apparent in those moments when resisted.

Consider, for example, how in "Semiology and Rhetoric," de Man's fairly straightforward deconstruction of a literary text does not complete his analysis but merely produces a provisional conclusion that is then subjected to its own fierce interrogation, instigating a process that will continue ad infinitum. De Man begins his analysis with the recognizable move of deconstructing an ostensibly stable and coherent set of statements in a passage from Marcel Proust. He shows how a series of tropes, including metaphor and metonymy, preclude the unified meaning the text initially promises. De Man calls this procedure the "grammatization of rhetoric" since he has provided a fixed group of rhetorical concepts—a grammar—that complete this subversive function. However, an important tension emerges: if rhetoric is supposed to undermine the universal claims of grammar, de Man's analysis repeats such universalizing gestures by privileging the rhetorical tropes as a conclusive explanation. Metaphysics reemerges with renewed strength in the moment that it has apparently been vanquished. The negative knowledge that de Man's analysis produces nevertheless constitutes a form of knowledge that was earlier deemed problematic. Continuing the interpretive process, de Man's analysis reveals the agonistic relationship between metaphysics and its deconstruction, suggesting that these competing tendencies within language cannot be suspended.

The agonistic relationship between metaphysics and deconstruction reemerges in the final moments of "The Resistance to Theory." Although the early portions of the piece demonstrate how rhetoric undermines the stabilities promised by logic and grammar, de Man ends by emphasizing how a logical impulse reemerges within rhetorical reading. Deconstructive criticism, while claiming to foreground the "rhetorical" dimension of any text—its endless interpretability, its profound depths that prompt infinite speculation and analysis—simultaneously contains conceptual safeguards that neutralize the threat posed by this rhetorical dimension. De Man asserts that rhetorical readings are "irrefutable" and "totalizing" since they are "the most elastic theoretical and dialectical model to end all models" (*Resistance* 19). Even though his rhetorical readings come to a dramatically different position than "naïve" thematic readings—namely, they provide a kind of negative knowledge—these conclusions nevertheless embody the totalizing tendencies that the deconstructive reading initially set out to eliminate. He writes that this approach is simultaneously "theory and not theory" since their capacity to be "teachable, generalizable and highly responsive to systematization" necessitates that they "still avoid and resist the reading they advocate. Nothing can overcome the resistance to theory since theory *is* itself resistance" (19). In a startling twist, de Man implies that his own work constitutes the purest instantiation of the resistance named in the essay's title. He ends with an uncertainty: "literary theory is not in danger of going under; it cannot help but flourish, and the more it is resisted, the more it flourishes, since the language it speaks is the language of self-resistance. What remains impossible to decide is whether this flourishing is a triumph or a fall" (19–20). Given the agonistic impulses undergirding his analysis, we might wonder whether this language of triumphs and falls, of victory and defeat, properly foregrounds de Man's interest in the site of the struggle that produces such winners and losers.

The ultimate triumph is precisely the undecidability of whether theory's flourishing amounts to a triumph or a fall.

At this point, it might be appropriate to respond to a potential criticism of my analysis: the concept of agonism never appears as a significant term anywhere in de Man's work. Beyond the more straightforward concern of whether de Man actually read Nietzsche's essay "Homer's Contest"— considering de Man's level of erudition, it would be surprising if he hadn't read it—there exists the crucial question of whether we might reasonably impose a foreign concept on de Man's corpus to understand his writing. Doing so enacts violence upon his texts and produces the very kind of reading that de Man rejected. "Deconstruction is not something we can decide to do or not do at will" he insists, arguing that it is instead "co-extensive with any use of language" (*Allegories* 125). However, the modifications de Man made between preliminary drafts and the final version of *Allegories of Reading* reveal explicitly agonistic language later eliminated from the published texts.

The editorial changes occur in "Rhetoric of Persuasion (Nietzsche)," the sixth chapter of *Allegories of Reading*, one of the few moments in his writing where de Man talks about rhetoric in terms of persuasion. He mentions Aristotle in the opening moments of the chapter, but instead of gesturing toward the *Rhetoric* as one might expect based on the chapter title, he cites the philosopher's principle of noncontradiction. This principle is discussed as a way of approaching the central concern of the chapter: the relationship between constative and performative language and each form's relationship to truth and reality. The first portion of the essay covers familiar ground, problematizing the idea that language is constative, able to describe a state of affairs and thereby secure clear knowledge of the world. De Man outlines how Nietzsche troubles these claims to arrive at the conclusion that all language must be understood as performative. But de Man then questions the ostensible supremacy of the performative over the constative, since other writings of Nietzsche undermine the concept of "action" that underwrites performative language. The difference between the constative and the performative proves to be "undecidable" (130) and de Man maintains that this "aporia between performative and constative language is merely a version of the aporia between trope and persuasion" (131) that constitutes rhetoric.

Undecidability, however, is only one way to characterize the relationship between rhetoric as persuasion and rhetoric as trope. Couldn't it just as easily be represented as agonistic rather than undecidable? Although there is a great deal of overlap between agonism and undecidability, agonism highlights the process that makes a final decision impossible rather than the impossibility itself. According to this alternate formulation, rhetoric as persuasion and rhetoric as trope enter a duel for supremacy that never concludes decisively; their confrontation multiplies the ways we understand the connections and divergences between these two terms. In *Textual Allegories*, a recently published draft of what would eventually become *Allegories of Reading*, constative and performative language are treated as agonists. In an appendix to the draft entitled "Nietzsche I: Rhetoric + Metaphysics," certain phrases in the final pages (which later became the conclusion to the sixth chapter of *Allegories of Reading*) are highly suggestive of an athletic competition or physical confrontation. The version from "Nietzsche I: Rhetoric + Metaphysics" reads:

> What seemed to lead to an established priority of doxa, opinion and persuasion, over truth never quite reaches its target: it under- or, in this case, over-shoots it and reveals, by mis-hitting it, another target which one assumed to have been long since eliminated. The *episteme* is hardly restored intact in its former glory; it has been badly battered, but one has not entirely managed to eliminate it either. (189)

The published version in *Allegories of Reading* reads:

> What seems to lead to an established priority of "setzen" over "erkennen," of language as action over language as truth, never quite reaches its mark. It under- or overshoots it and, in so doing, it reveals that the target which one long since assumed to have been eliminated has merely been displaced. The *episteme* has hardly been restored intact to its former glory, but it has not been definitively eliminated either. (130)

Beyond some of the more straightforward cosmetic adjustments (the change in tense, for instance), the finalized text removes some telling features. The substitution of "action" for "doxa, opinion and persuasion" shifts the emphasis from a realm of force and contestation toward one of mere movement. This shift causes the word "target" to lose its more violent connotations and become simply a synonym for goal or objective. The deletion of "mis-hitting" in the final version only compounds the feeling that de Man has forcibly removed elements from the text that suggest a combative relationship between trope and persuasion. The elimination of the description of constative language as having "been badly battered" in its encounter with the performative confirms a decisive pattern within the passage. These discrepancies suggest that de Man couldn't decide—

or, perhaps more appropriately, was at war with himself over—whether to characterize the tension between constantive and performative language in terms of undecidability or agonism. While the agonistic language was ultimately badly battered itself, removed for the published version *Allegories of Reading*, the recent release of the archival material reveals that it was not definitely eliminated either.

As de Man's editorial changes here suggest, agonism not only served as a thematic element in his work but also operated at the stylistic level. I would like to suggest that Nietzsche offers a more important contribution to de Man's work than simply lending terms from the rhetorical tradition. Whereas the language of tropes and figures is unavoidable in de Man's prose, the agonistic principles cultivated and explored by Nietzsche find themselves filtered into de Man's writing in more subtle yet no less important ways. Agonism, as opposed to tropism, plays just as an important role in de Man's method or style as it does in the specific principles that inform his treatment of language. Specifically, the concept of agonism plays a central role in how de Man positions himself with respect to other critics and how he envisions deconstruction's place within the history of literary and rhetorical criticism.

Agonistic vocabulary certainly captures the combative nature of literary criticism at the time de Man composed *Allegories of Reading* in the 1970s. He noted that a "quarrelsome tone" (21) had begun to permeate literary criticism in his essay "Return to Philology," and he had either contributed to this atmosphere or parodied its aggressive pretensions several years earlier when he boldly declared that rhetorical reading should be "the task of literary criticism in the coming years" (*Allegories* 17). Josué Harari's *Textual Strategies*, a well-known anthology of literary theory published in the same year as *Allegories of Reading* that included de Man's "Semiology and Rhetoric," intensifies this agonistic language even further. Comparing the collection to "a ring of criticism" where contemporary theorists engage in "various critical struggles," Harari admits that he has yet to "determine how the rounds are to be scored" for this competition but nevertheless feels confident that "in this game, everyone is eventually a loser" (68–69). Harari's belief that a decisive victory can never be achieved hints at the complicated rules governing the game of criticism.

As an integral part of this game, de Man recognizes that criticism is an agonistic structure that his own writing cannot help but perpetuate. Winners cannot be determined insofar as the teams in the contest continually bleed into one another, a fact that de Man alludes to in his discussions of the discipline. De Man simultaneously embraces and disavows a range of discourses—philology, rhetoric, New Criticism—through which he configures his own deconstructive project. If his work seeks to correct the fundamental errors of these other forms of criticism, he nevertheless readily describes his work as an extension of these movements. Against those critics who regard his work as a threat to humanist literary criticism, he repeatedly characterizes deconstruction in terms of traditional schools of thought. For all the fury surrounding the New Critics and the deconstructionists, de Man confesses that he can "live . . . very easily" with his work being classified as "just more New Criticism" (*Resistance* 117). When responding to charges by Walter Jackson Bate that he has contributed to undermining the humanities, he attaches himself to New Criticism, specifically the work of Reuben Brower, when pinpointing crucial influences on his methodology. De Man's endorsement of Brower appears in an essay entitled "The Return to Philology"—not, as the essay's content might suggest, "The Return to New Criticism"—a point that further complicates the connections among various movements in the history of literary criticism. De Man not only characterizes his scholarship as philological in nature but also suggests a certain degree of contiguity between New Criticism and philology, which should surprise anyone who recalls Gerald Graff's account in *Professing Literature* of how New Criticism competed with and ultimately replaced the philological enterprise that dominated the American academy during the late nineteenth and early twentieth centuries. And philology itself, inseparable from the beginnings of the American research university based on the German model, can be said to have marginalized the rhetorical education that was the norm in American colleges in the early and middle portions of the nineteenth century. If de Man is unwilling to draw clear demarcations between critical friend and foe, illustrating how a range of discourses implicitly support one another in spite of themselves, what might this ambivalence reveal about de Man's understanding of literary history more generally?

To answer this question, we must once again return to Nietzsche since de Man uses him as a vehicle for articulating his own ideas about the historical evolution of critical discourse. Nietzsche certainly possessed an agonistic relationship with philology, a discipline he often ridiculed but remained unwilling to abandon altogether. As a young scholar at the University of Basel, he frequently combatted stifling scholarly protocols. Securing tenure at the astonishingly early age of twenty-four, Nietzsche was knocked off this lofty perch when the conservative community of philologists rejected the speculative quality that marked his first major work, 1872's *The Birth of Tragedy*. In response, he penned the blistering "We Philologists" in

1874, condemning philologists as a haughty and superficial specimen with a barrage of not so subtle insults. "Ah, it is a sad story, the story of philology!" Nietzsche mockingly announces before he derides "the disgusting erudition, the lazy, inactive passivity, the timid submission" that plagues these scholars (140). Regarding philological investigation as directionless "ant-like work" that is "simply nonsense, and quite superfluous" (115), Nietzsche characterizes its practitioners as "intellectually crippled" individuals who have "found a suitable hobby in all this hairsplitting" (140). He proclaims that "ninety-nine philologists out of a hundred *should* not be philologists at all" (110). Nietzsche tellingly does not condemn all one hundred, however, and the first-person plural found in the title suggests that he counts himself among those select few who might steer philology in a worthwhile direction (in 1881's *Daybreak*, Nietzsche would be more explicit about philology's potential, conceptualizing it as a "venerable art" of "slow reading" that is "more necessary than ever today" [5]). At the same time, Nietzsche refuses to immunize himself completely from the criticisms he launches at the philologists. Throughout the piece, Nietzsche targets the majority of philologists for pursuing their work out of either sheer inertia or simple careerism. After reiterating this claim in the seventieth aphorism in the essay, Nietzsche concludes by grouping himself within these timid scholars: "I know them—I myself am one of them" (146).

A similar ambivalence marks Nietzsche's engagement with rhetoric as well. At first glance, Nietzsche appears to dismiss the rhetorical tradition and his largely derivative lectures on the subject would be symptomatic of such disregard. As de Man points out, any philologist of the time would have possessed the requisite knowledge to teach an introductory course on rhetoric, so Nietzsche's 1872 lectures should not be seen as "zwingend proof of an overriding interest" ("Nietzsche" 191 n. 13). When de Man's colleague J. Hillis Miller commented on Nietzsche's rhetoric lectures in a 1993 article, he suggested that their dry, straightforward tenor could be read as an ironic treatment of the humanist underpinnings of the rhetorical tradition. The third lecture in the series, where Nietzsche advances his iconoclastic notion of rhetoric as constitutive of language as such, serves as the point where such irony comes into sharp focus. For Miller, the lectures are "the ironically solemn repetition of a colossal, centuries-long mistake, a mistake based on a false idea of language and epistemology that dominated both Greek and Roman ideas about rhetoric" ("Nietzsche" 324). Only during the third lecture "does Nietzsche allow his own opinions to break through the ironic deadpan miming of what Aristotle, Quintilian, and the rest had to say" (324). The entire metaphysical edifice of the rhetorical tradition crumbles when Professor Nietzsche briefly intervenes with his own commentary on the textbook material.

While Miller offers a compelling reading of the lectures, de Man suggests that Nietzsche had a more complicated relationship to the rhetorical tradition than outright dismissiveness.[4] If Nietzsche disparages this tradition in explicit statements, he does not hesitate to employ every rhetorical technique available for his highly stylized compositions. The ostensible contradiction only underscores the agonistic tension between Nietzsche's philosophy and this competing canon. In the very moment when he seeks to dismantle traditional rhetoric and its focus on persuasion, Nietzsche cannot help but reinvigorate it through his very denunciation of it, thereby returning it to the "ring of competition" among academic discourses. From de Man's perspective, Nietzsche's interest in rhetoric stems in part from its relegation to a dead past, since he is suspicious that the past can ever remain dead. Whatever animosity he initially possesses toward the rhetorical tradition, Nietzsche also acknowledges his inescapable indebtedness to this work.

De Man explores these issues in the 1970 essay "Literary History and Literary Modernity," tackling the question of critical practice and its relationship to past tradition through a careful reading of Nietzsche's "On the Use and Abuse of History for Life." The analysis begins by outlining how Nietzsche establishes a clear antagonism between "history" and "modernity." "History" refers to the lamentable condition of humanity that prevents it from forgetting the past. Adopting a crucial distinction between nature and culture that he inherits from Rousseau, Nietzsche argues that humans differ from animals insofar as they remain shackled to memories that inhibit action in the present. The historical man hopelessly relies on the past to understand his immediate surroundings, and in doing so, ensures that he suffocates from the dead weight of his ancestry. To characterize "modernity," Nietzsche uses the word "life," which he conceives of as an active faculty of forgetting that casts off historical deadwood in order to create a better future. De Man stresses that Nietzsche aligns himself clearly with the life-giving spirit of modernism against the stultifying demands of the historical record; Nietzsche regards an active mode of forgetting as an essential ingredient for any action in the present, noting that "modernity exists in the form of a desire to wipe out whatever came earlier" so as to reach "a true present, a point of origin that marks a new departure" (*Blindness* 148). "Moments of genuine humanity" are achieved only when "all interiority vanishes" (147). Only by cultivating this capacity to discount the past and grasp the present without the debilitating perspectives of previous generations can true "life" be achieved.

De Man insists, however, that Nietzsche subtly undermines his breathless affiliation with modernity within the essay by proposing a dynamic between modernity and history that cannot be reduced to a simple "antithesis or opposition" (151). The moderns of the present cannot dispense with the past because it is inseparable from them. Modernity privileges the present over the past but ultimately learns that "in severing itself from the past, it has at the same time severed itself from the present" (149). The present is so inexorably tied to the past that it always risks destroying itself when it attacks the past. In an effort to clean house and start anew, the present pulls the carpet out from under itself: "the more radical the rejection of anything that came before, the greater the dependence on the past" (161). Although this relationship between modernity and history is described as a "self-destroying union that threatens the survival of both" (151), his examination suggests that these destructive tendencies also possess a regenerative quality. History and modernity may continually threaten the stability of one another, but they also remain crucial to one another's survival; like any agonistic relationship, history and modernity simultaneously rejuvenate and destroy one another. History, threatened by the innovation that modernism promises, nevertheless needs these forces for its own perpetuation. Modernity, refusing the traditions erected by literature and history, simultaneously contributes to these traditions simply by adding to the heap of written material that it sought to overcome. Nietzsche, de Man explains, realizes that even his own essay on modernity will ultimately become "nothing but another historical document" (151).

De Man's analysis of "On the Use and Abuse of History for Life" not only provides an alternate way of interpreting Nietzsche's relationship with the rhetorical tradition but also offers a key for understanding de Man's use of the term "rhetoric" in the years following "Literary History and Literary Modernity." Within de Man's later writing, "rhetoric" functions as a way of highlighting deconstruction's indebtedness to past tradition even in the moment when it seems to have departed from it completely. As de Man periodically alludes to throughout his essay but never addresses directly, the dynamics between modernity and history have a particular significance to contemporary "theoretical speculations about literature" (143). De Man seems to have read Nietzsche's essay allegorically, replacing the general modern man who attempts to overcome the detritus of history with the more specific formulation of the deconstructive critic dispelling the erroneous readings of the critical commentary that he has inherited. "Literary History and Literary Modernity" was composed during the transitional phase of de Man's career when his early interest in phenomenological and psychological concerns was giving way to the rhetorical terminology with which he is now indelibly linked.[5] The use of "rhetoric" thus constitutes a decisive break from his past work. On a much broader scale, de Man connected "rhetoric" to a bold new interpretive paradigm that promised to expose the shortsightedness of previous critical movements. The term would have a particularly strong charge during this time, when the reigning critical orthodoxy, New Criticism, was allergic to thinking about literature as anything but an isolated object existing outside everyday social discourse—that is, as rhetoric. Within these texts, "rhetoric" is thus marked as decidedly modernist, as if de Man were severing ties with his own past work as well as the larger critical community in order to embark on a daring new adventure in criticism. Yet at the same time, the unfashionable and antiquated connotations surrounding the word "rhetoric" simultaneously dashes these modernist aspirations, underscoring how the specter of the past haunts de Man's discourse despite his best efforts to overcome it.

Close inspection reveals that de Man's turn to rhetoric weaves together a number of discourses and figures that the present had all but forgotten. Not only was rhetoric a fairly marginal discourse when de Man published his work, but the specific version of rhetoric that he advanced—one centered on tropes rather than persuasion—was neglected even by those few scholars who were arguing for a "revival of rhetoric."[6] Furthermore, Nietzsche was a marginal figure within philosophical discourse during this time. As has been well documented, Nietzsche had long been dismissed by the philosophical establishment in France before he was resurrected during the 1960s (de Man approvingly cites some of this work, including that by Gilles Deleuze, Phillippe Lacoue-Labarthe, and Sarah Kofman). His reemergence offered a fresh perspective for a young generation of French thinkers weaned on Hegel, Heidegger, and Husserl.[7] But even most of these scholars did not see Nietzsche's minor lecture course on rhetoric as a pivotal point for his entire corpus. De Man seizes upon this seemingly "eccentric and minor part of Nietzsche's enterprise" (*Allegories* 103) as a way to examine a number of central questions concerning the relationship between philosophy and literature. De Man was not only resuscitating a marginalized figure or a marginalized discourse that had been relegated to the dustbin of history, but a doubly displaced entity—a marginalized figure's engagement with a marginalized discourse.

Ultimately, de Man's use of "rhetoric" helps emphasize the inexhaustible nature of the critical enterprise. Texts will not be conquered by perceptive readers; instead they prompt endless speculation about them. Perhaps this is why de Man advances the bizarre claim that every reading is always a misreading—a position he clarifies, unsurprisingly, when discussing Nietzsche. In a conference on the philosopher, whose proceedings were published in *Symposium* in 1974, de Man asserts that "perhaps we have not yet begun to read him properly" ("Nietzsche's Theory" 49). He chastises those who cling to a "false literalism" when reading the philosopher, arguing that "we risk to produce the wrong kind of misreading" if we seek to apply Nietzsche's work practically too quickly. But how can there be such a thing as a "right" kind of misreading? De Man clearly believes such a thing exists, complimenting the participants in the conference for generating "very productive misreadings" (50). After engaging with Walter Kaufmann about whether a plurality of complementary interpretations is possible, de Man rejects the idea, saying that the production of any interpretation necessarily must rule out all others in its attempt to be "unique" (51). The conversation ends with de Man clarifying the distinction: "by a good misreading, *I mean a text that produces another text* which can itself be shown to be an interesting misreading, a text which engenders additional texts. *If you have a poor text, you cannot make up a very rewarding construction.* But with Nietzsche, the possibilities are endless" (51, my emphasis). For de Man, the best criticism is that which solicits the most additional commentary on the literary work.

"Rhetoric" functions, then, in two distinct yet interrelated ways in de Man's work. First, it refers to the specific dimension of language found in literary texts that defies any final, decisive interpretation. The figural status of language ensures that the agonism between critic and text will never be exhausted but instead perpetually renewed with each successive interpretation. Second, it refers to the way in which the present always remains indebted to the past. This alternative use of rhetoric helps reinforce the first—the ceaseless dynamic between critic and text—by broadening the scope in which we see criticism functioning. Any attempt to grasp the text's essence, to cast off previous misinterpretations, will ultimately become part of this failed tradition. By aligning himself with marginalized discourses and figures, including Nietzsche, rhetoric, and philology, de Man foreshadows the inevitable failure of his own project. But this failure is simultaneously a triumph insofar as it perpetuates critical discourse as a whole.

Burke and the Unending Conversation

While de Man offers a rich interpretation of Nietzsche's meditations on agonism, incorporating it into his account of the relationship between metaphysics and deconstruction, he is not the only prominent figure in English studies to draw upon this thinker. Although his engagement with Nietzsche is much more subdued in terms of explicit references, Kenneth Burke drew a great deal from the German philosopher and this influence had a significant impact on the discipline in the late twentieth century and beyond. There is no evidence to suggest that Burke ever read Nietzsche's lectures on rhetoric. However, his engagement with other work by Nietzsche suggests that he took insights about the fundamental nature of language and adapted them to many of his own concerns about rhetoric and social practice. As Burke says in *A Rhetoric of Motives*, rhetorical acts work not only on direct acts but more general beliefs. Thus, while the references to Nietzsche are few and far between in Burke's efforts to sketch his own understanding of rhetoric—Burke mentions him, briefly, only four times in all of *A Rhetoric of Motives*—we should regard this relative absence as a greater presence. Burke had already absorbed Nietzsche into his bloodstream, so to speak, and the influence could be felt through his entire disposition. But this transfer from Nietzsche to Burke, much like the one from Nietzsche to de Man, must be understood not as a frictionless translation but itself a metaphor—that is, as a "leap from one sphere to another" that should not be understood as a simple reference to "the original." Burke's working through Nietzsche produced what Gilles Deleuze might call "a monstrous offspring"—a philosophical formulation that Nietzsche might be horrified to see but could nevertheless not completely disavow as his own.[8] Like de Man, Burke uses Nietzsche to theorize a critical practice rooted in the agon, but he links it to a radical democratic practice that Nietzsche would hesitate to endorse. Or, perhaps more appropriately, Burke conducts his own form of agonism with Nietzsche himself.

Although numerous commentators have ignored or downplayed Nietzsche's influence on Burke, doing so only underscores their limited understanding of both figures. There are indeed many different "Burkes," but the Nietzschean Burke must certainly rank as one of the most central.[9] Burke's apprenticeship with Nietzsche began as early as the late 1920s. Like de Man, Burke found fertile ground in Nietzsche's meditations on language and its fundamentally metaphorical qualities. Burke also emphasizes the unavoidable metaphorical properties of language, particularly in scientific language that flatly rejects such characterizations. Interrogating the truth claims of the scientific community in *Permanence and Change*, Burke asks the following question: "as the documents of science pile up, are we not coming to see that whole works of scientific research, even entire *schools*, are hardly more than the patient repetition, in all its ramifications, of a fertile metaphor?" (95). Burke is thus connected to de Man in advancing the Nietzschean position that there is no "natural language" upon which metaphor could be understood as a derivative or decorative element. The irreducible metaphorical quality of language eliminates the possibility of an absolute, transcendent position that could see the world as it actually exists and grasp an object "in itself."

For Burke, this inescapably limited and partial nature of language demands that we revise our understanding and evaluation of rhetoric. Indeed, when he offers his most straightforward definition of the term, it bears an uncanny resemblance to the one initially given by Nietzsche in his lecture course in 1872–73. In *A Rhetoric of Motives*, which he considers nothing less than a "philosophy of rhetoric" (xv), Burke argues against the belief in language as a transparent medium between a subject and the world, instead asserting that the persuasive dimension of language is incompatible with a scientific, descriptive one. This persuasive feature of language is not "sheer decadent decoration" (66) but instead "of the essence of language" (252). Italicizing his claim for emphasis, Burke maintains that rhetoric "*is rooted in an essential function of language itself . . . as a symbolic means of inducing cooperation in beings that by nature respond to symbols*" (43). Like his philosophical forefather, Burke seizes an ostensibly marginal dimension of language and transforms it into the groundwork through which to understand language more generally. And like de Man, who would follow several decades later, Burke uses this rhetoric-centric vision to challenge the principles of scientific rationalism that typically guide our understanding of language and the world more broadly.

Like de Man, Burke also forges subtle connections between these insights and Nietzsche's work on agonism. Much of *A Rhetoric of Motives* finds Burke framing rhetoric in agonistic terms, part of a broader effort to rescue it from its usual associations with antagonism. The book begins with a lengthy treatment of rhetoric's relationship to violence, with Burke declaring in the opening moments of the introduction that an "imagery of killing is but one of many terminologies by which writers can represent the process of change" (xiii). Burke insists that conceptualizing rhetoric solely in terms of violence must be rejected, asserting "we can treat 'war' as a 'special case of peace'—not as a primary motive in itself, not as essentially real, but purely a derivative condition, a perversion" (20). At the same time, however, Burke maintains that "invective, eristic, polemic, and logomachy" (20) are undeniable elements in rhetoric. But how can Burke downgrade war to a perversion of peace while at the same time maintaining the combative elements of rhetoric as essential? Rather than read these twin statements as evidence of sheer contradiction, we should recognize their fundamentally agonistic tenor. Positing a clear distinction between mere strife and outright violence, Burke reverts to the distinction between productive and destructive agonism outlined in Nietzsche's "Homer's Contest." While strife and conflict remain unavoidable, we should be careful not to conflate them with outright bloodshed and death. Violence is strife that has been improperly channeled, a corruption of an initially productive impulse. Burke maintains that war should be understood "not simply as strife come to a head" but instead "a disease, or perversion of communion" (22). This "communion" does not avoid conflict in pursuit of a final stasis but instead regards conflict as necessary and generative so long as it does not descend into pointless antagonism.

Extending this agonistic impulse, Burke emphasizes that his primary term for understanding rhetoric, "identification," treats unity and division as complementary rather than fiercely antagonistic. After explaining that *A Rhetoric of Motives* deals primarily with "the ways in which individuals are at odds with one another, or become identified with groups more or less at odds with one another," Burke pauses to explain this emphasis given that his primary term is "identification," which would ostensibly minimize or altogether eliminate division. From his perspective, identification forces one "to confront the implications of *division*" because "identification is compensatory to division" (22). To suggest that a pure unity without division could be achieved amounts to sheer utopianism; unity and division require one another for their respective coherence. Only because a fundamental division among people exists can a rhetorical act seek unification. For Burke, rhetoric occupies this always indistinct region between identification and division, serving as "a mediatory ground" between opponents "that makes communication possible, thus providing the first condition necessary for their interchange of blows" (25). Burke's conception of rhetoric as a unity through division (or a division through unity) clearly draws on the paradoxical relationship between agonistic opponents, where strife holds the participants together in a productive tension that avoids conclusive victory. During his analysis, Burke writes that the line between cooperation and exploitation remains forever vague since it is difficult to determine "just where 'cooperation' ends and one partner's 'exploitation' of the other begins" (25). It would seem that Burke also affirms the converse, emphasizing that exploitation (or competition) involves an equally unclear degree of cooperation. In this respect, agonism is inseparable from how Burke conceives of rhetoric as both a feature of language and as a social practice.

Once identified, this agonistic spirit proves impossible to escape in *A Rhetoric of Motives*. For instance, Burke argues that competition, rather than bitterly dividing the community, actually unifies its members by cultivating habits of imitation and conformity. Competition encourages men to either "crudely imitate one another's actions as revealed on the surface, or subtly imitate the *underlying principles* of such actions" (131). Competition does not break down the social bonds but actually preserves and even strengthens them by reproducing valuable social beliefs through subtle mechanisms. Elsewhere in *A Rhetoric of Motives*, Burke revises the long-standing opposition between image and idea, maintaining "the antithetical relation" between the two should be "replaced by a partial stress upon the bond of kinship between them" (90). Furthermore, Burke rejects a "flat antithesis" between body and spirit in favor of a more dynamic relationship where spiritual awakening "is made *through* body, nature, image" (189).

Throughout *A Rhetoric of Motives*, Burke does not simply describe agonistic principles and argue for their centrality to a proper understanding of rhetorical theory and practice. He simultaneously embodies this agonistic spirit through a carefully measured treatment of his critical predecessors. Although boldly pursuing a thorough reconceptualization of rhetoric, he does not reject earlier work on the subject so much as preserve these original contributions as recurring points of contrast or complication to his own work. In doing so, he acknowledges his debt to a critical tradition that cannot be surpassed and which remains essential to any innovations Burke might achieve. The most prominent example can be found in his treatment of Aristotle, an undeniable touchstone in the rhetorical tradition who first yoked rhetoric to persuasion. While *A Rhetoric of Motives* aims to replace "persuasion" with "identification" as the skeleton key to rhetoric, he emphasizes in the book's introduction that "our treatment, in terms of identification, is decidedly not meant as a substitute for the sound traditional approach. Rather, as we try to show, it is but an accessory to the standard lore" (xiv). Burke's deference to Aristotle, even as he attempts to land a decisive blow to the philosopher's key term, only reinforces his keen awareness of the agonistic dynamic underwriting critical practice. Accordingly, in the closing moments of the book's first section, Burke defies readers who expect "identification" to replace "persuasion." For Burke, such a clear-cut victory is impossible, since an inexorable connection exists between the two concepts. In what initially seems like a radical departure, the analysis ultimately returns to familiar ground, with Burke noting "we have thus, *deviously*, come to the point at which Aristotle begins his treatise on rhetoric" (46, my emphasis). As his use of the word "deviously" should suggest, Burke recognizes that any attempt to completely reject past origins will only find itself returning to them through unexpected, circuitous routes. In showing that attempts to flee the tradition are futile and that change requires the preservation of this historical combatant, Burke possesses a keen awareness of the dynamics that de Man would later explore in Nietzsche's musings on history.

However, unlike de Man, who would invest little time considering the explicit political consequences of Nietzsche's meditations on language, Burke explored how these insights could be sutured to democracy, an unusual decision given Nietzsche's allergy to this form of government. Throughout Nietzsche's corpus, we can see a general distaste for democracy and its emphasis on equality and the masses. For instance, in Section 203 of *Beyond Good and Evil*, Nietzsche writes that the democratic movement should be understood "not only as a degenerating form of political organization, but as equivalent to a degenerating, a waning type of man, as involving his mediocrising and depreciation" (307). From Nietzsche's perspective, the urge for democracy originates in Christianity insofar as it mobilizes life-denying forces and subtly inflicts the herd's resentment on innovative individuals. While the unambiguous tone of Nietzsche's declarations might discourage efforts, a number of recent critics have attempted to reread the philosopher's work in a way that unearths a democratic undercurrent (or could in some way be amenable to democratic processes). In *Politics Out of History*, Wendy Brown suggests that apologists of liberal democracy should take Nietzsche's critiques seriously insofar as they prevent democracy's creative and rejuvenating impulses from degenerating into a confining institutional proceduralism that overrides the ever-changing demands of life: "democracy requires antidemocratic critique in order to remain democratic . . . the democratic state may require democratic resistance rather than fealty if it is not to become the death of democracy" (137). Meanwhile, Lawrence J. Hatab has argued that "Nietzsche indeed is anti-egalitarian but . . . egalitarianism may not be the *sine qua non* of democratic politics, and . . . many elements of democratic practice and performance are more Nietzschean than he suspected" ("Prospects" 133).[10] The efforts to illustrate Nietzsche's compatibility with democratic practice date back much earlier, however, if we recognize Burke's efforts beginning in the 1930s.

Of course, Burke was not the first person to link agonism with democratic practice, largely because these connections have always existed. As Jeffrey Walker has demonstrated in *Rhetoric and Poetics in Antiquity*, agonistic practices were regarded as essential to the health of the body politic. For citizens of Ancient Greece, it was beneficial "to go downtown to the marketplace, or to some banquet or festivity, and hear some interesting disputation, or to have some poet's psychagogic eloquence carry one's mind into unusual positions and provoke one into thought" (163). However, Burke explored agonism at the level of language itself, incorporating Nietzsche's concept "perspective by incongruity" for this purpose. As the concept suggests, Burke finds Nietzsche's emphasis on one's perspective in creating knowledge to be critical—our perspectives are always already interpretations of phenomenon geared toward specific goals. More important, these various perspectives used to interpret the world undoubtedly conflict with one another as they are deployed in shifting contexts. When vocabulary from one domain is introduced into another, a certain degree of conceptual dissonance emerges. While his engagement with Nietzsche would, at first glance, appear relegated to his early years, culminating in the 1935 text *Permanence and Change*, Burke clearly carried over many of these insights when developing his thoughts on a "New Rhetoric" and its relationship to democratic politics.

Against Nietzsche, Burke illustrates how the cognitive dissonance produced through "perspective by incongruity" translates into democratic practice. He argues that one should "bring several *rhetoricians* together, let their speeches contribute to the maturing of one another by the give and take of question and answer" to produce "the *dialectic* of a Platonic dialogue" (*Rhetoric* 53). For Burke, "the dialogue seeks to attain a higher order of truth, as the speakers, in competing with one another, cooperate towards an end transcending their individual positions" (53). Rather than see this dissonance as a problem that must be resolved by clearly determining "winning" and "losing" perspectives, Burke instead regards the conflict as a productive one. In highlighting their respective strengths and weaknesses, disparate perspectives play a crucial role in a more fully realized understanding of the world. He elaborates on this point later in the text, offering a picture of how competing conceptual schemas interact: "Any such 'unmasking' of an ideology's limitations is itself made from a limited point of view. But each such limited perspective can throw light upon the relation between the universal principles of an ideology and the special interests which they are consciously or unconsciously made to serve" (198).

For Burke, this deliberative process does not have a final correct answer. At one level, this is obvious since rhetoric concerns practices where truth and falsity are not central. Burke explains that rhetoric "is essentially a realism of the *act*: moral, persuasive—and acts are not 'true' and 'false' in the sense that the propositions of 'scientific realism' are" (44). There can be no final synthesis to the debate precisely because of the practical dimension of their language, which responds to a range of ever-shifting political problems. One reason that this final synthesis proves impossible is that practical solutions to political problems themselves produce new political problems, the least of which includes an inability to adapt to new contexts and their corresponding problems. Ironically, the effectiveness of a certain conceptual strategy reinforces blindnesses that create more problems than they initially solved; success produces a form of inflexibility that guarantees future failure. In *A Rhetoric of Motives*, Burke characterizes these successful strategies as forms of "occupational psychosis," where certain perceptions or concepts harden and prevent a full appreciation of the highly complex texture of reality. For Burke, language is structured hierarchically such that these kinds of blindnesses are inevitable. Such tensions are present in Marxism, which Burke argues operates according to a process of ideological mystification. While Marxism aims to reveal the blind spots of competing conceptual systems, it claims that it itself has no blind spots and has a final representation of reality. Burke clearly rejects these claims, emphasizing that other perspectives must be put into dialogue with Marxism so as to reveal its conceptual weaknesses.

Accordingly, the democratic practice Burke envisions is one without end, devoid of any final utopian goals, precisely because the deliberative, agonistic process produces new values, new goals, and new positions. It is a self-generating, self-reproducing system that rewrites its fundamental coordinates with each successive move. Rather than a final synthesis and a termination of the dialogue amongst competitors, the trajectory is reversed: conclusions are always provisional, stopping points along a journey that never concludes. Recalling the Roman Saturnalia festival "where master and servant changed places," Burke argues that democracy serves "as a kind of permanent but minute Saturnalia, with constant reversal in the relation between up and down" (224). The only way to avoid the dangers of occupational psychosis and the hardening of provisional schemas into reified objects is through the proliferation of conversation, incorporating newer voices into the fold. Indeed, the result of these clashing perspectives is simply the creation of even more perspectives: "we invent new terms, or apply our old vocabulary in new ways" (36).

In *The Philosophy of Literary Form*, Burke offers a vivid metaphor for understanding the democratic process. Here, he speaks of the "'unending conversation' that is going on at the point in history when we are born" (110). For Burke, the democratic process can be likened to the rambunctious chatter of a social event, where the participants simultaneously shape and are shaped by the material, material that slowly drifts from one topic to another ad infinitum:

> Imagine that you enter a parlor. You come late. When you arrive, others have long preceded you, and they are engaged in a heated discussion, a discussion too heated for them to pause and tell you exactly what it is about. In fact, the discussion had already begun long before any of them got there, so that no one present is qualified to retrace for you all the steps that had gone before. You listen for a while, until you decide that you have caught the tenor of the argument; then you put in your oar. Someone answers; you answer him; another comes to your defense; another aligns himself against you, to either the embarrassment or gratification of your opponent, depending upon the quality of your ally's assistance. However, the discussion is interminable. The hour grows late, you must depart. And you do depart, with the discussion still vigorously in progress. (110–111)

Crucial to this metaphor is how the conversation transcends any of the individual speakers. No one precedes the conversation and no one manages to see it to any fitting conclusion. Nevertheless, each person contributes to the overall tenor of the conversation (once they've determined its basic parameters) and steer it in a direction that it had not been previously chartered.

Burke regarded this form as a compelling model for critical practice, evident in his remarkable ability to incorporate democratic agonism into the stylistic elements of his writing. Reading *The Rhetoric of Motives* can often prove to be incredibly laborious, since it is a text that does not clearly signal any forward momentum or logical progression. Burke introduces ostensibly disconnected themes and texts, interrupts himself with lengthy digressions, and refuses to offer any final word of wisdom. While it would be easy to account for these stylistic attributes and organizational decisions as symptoms of an unsystematic intellect that darts haphazardly from one topic to the other, we might also interpret them as a sophisticated enactment of the book's content. The cacophony of voices presented in *The Rhetoric of Motives*, which often has a bewildering effect on the reader, should be seen as intentional. Burke's motives can also be seen in a number of small stylistic choices in the work. For instance, the use of "we" throughout, even if nothing more than an often-used convention of critical writing, contributes to the feeling of a collective engagement. More important, Burke's use of "friends" to supply anecdotes also lends this collaborative tone. In several spots in *The Rhetoric of Motives*, Burke introduces an anecdote with "A friend said" (259, 261) or "A teacher once told us" (287). Whether these anonymous characters are fictional or not is largely irrelevant—as rhetorical devices, they add other voices into the conversation, momentarily forcing Burke to the side of the stage while foregrounding that his work is indebted to others. The culmination of this collaborative style occurs in the book's final pages. Here, detailing William James's *The Varieties of Religious Experiences*, Burke elects to create a collage of voices consisting of short quotes from different people describing religious fervor. At nearly two pages in length, the individual statements prove largely inconsequential to the effect created by stacking quotation upon quotation, as if Burke wanted his reader to skim the surface of the page so as to hear something else altogether: the wondrous effects produced by a collection of voices in an endless conversation (329). This is ultimately the dream he has for criticism.

Criticism's Expanding Borders

For both de Man and Burke, the turn to "rhetoric" becomes part of an effort to broaden the scope of criticism, and in their desire to expand the borders of the critical conversation, we see an impulse that characterizes discursive formations more generally. In *The Archaeology of Knowledge*, Michel Foucault analyzes the nature of discursive formations, attending to the way that they function by not fully grasping their object but by maintaining a gap that allows the work of criticism to remain in motion. For someone like Foucault, the prospect of conclusive definitions ever being secured is impossible based on the very terms that structure the process. In the introduction to *The Birth of the Clinic*, Foucault notes that "the possibility of commentary . . . dooms us to an endless task that nothing can limit: there is always a certain amount of signified remaining that must be allowed to speak, while the signifier is always offered to us in an abundance that questions us, in spite of ourselves, as to what it 'means'" (xviii). A more familiar assessment can be found in his essay "What Is an Author?" where he characterizes an "authored" text as one that facilitates endless discourse about it. Against a figure like Barthes, Foucault asserts that the "death" of the author isn't the birth of the reader; instead, both author and reader are birthed in the same moment, since they are two sides of the same coin.

I would like to supplement Foucault's account by outlining another tendency within discursive formations. If he rightly contends that discourse is structured in a way that commentary on its chosen object can perpetuate itself indefinitely, it should be pointed out that the value of this commentary tends to erode over time unless it modified in some way. Critics are still talking about Shakespeare's plays and Wordsworth's poetry today, but they're talking about them in ways that differ from previous eras since old approaches became, for lack of a better word, "exhausted." I propose that we understand this dynamic within the discourse of literary criticism according to a crucial concept found in Marx's political economy: the tendency of the rate of profit to fall over time, a tendency which accounts for capitalism's inevitable expansion. Because capital's capacity to extract surplus labor value within a circumscribed area diminishes over time, it must seek out new territories and create new markets in order to maintain stable profit rates. I argue that a similar process is governing criticism in English studies—that is, the "surplus value" of work on a particular text or topic tends to diminish over time, prompting criticism to seek out new objects of study and modes of inquiry. In order to perpetuate itself as a discourse, English studies must revitalize exhausted texts by connecting them to other discourses or by seeking out new texts altogether.

Before I provide a few concrete examples to clarify, allow me to explain how "surplus value" functions in criticism (acknowledging that critical discourse both is and is not an economy in the traditional sense). It seems to me that the supposed goal of literary criticism is to innovate or produce difference. While this can be achieved in a number of ways, ideally, every critical intervention will be judged by how it makes the object, and by extension, the entire field, appear in a slightly different light. Such a valuation system certainly pans out in terms of rewards in the field—the critics that help us think completely differently about Romanticism in general are generally regarded as more "valuable" than the ones who merely bring to light a neglected poet working during that time (of course, if that neglected poet helps critics reconsider the entire field of Romanticism in an interesting way, then you have a whole different story). To put it in terms familiar to our undergraduate students, value is based on the "so what?" question. What I'm arguing is that achieving a satisfying answer to the "so what?" question becomes an increasingly difficult prospect within certain demarcated fields of study, and this difficulty underwrites the desire to transcend the boundaries of these fields by establishing new areas of study and modes of investigation. From now on, I'll refer to the value that this work produces its "innovative differential."

Let's take New Criticism as our prime example largely because it constitutes the starting point of criticism as we understand it today. The New Critics began by looking carefully at the literary text, something previous historical scholarship had largely ignored. What could we learn, the New Critics asked, by examining the literary text directly? At first, such a move was enormously productive, generating all sorts of insights about the literary work—the "innovative differential" was fairly substantial during the early stages of the process, since each new reading highlighted elements of the text that had been previously overlooked. As commentary on a given text begins to saturate, however, these overlooked sections of the text begin to disappear, and each subsequent reading finds itself in the precarious position of having to account for all the previous scholarship. Not only is it difficult to do innovative work in this context, but the innovations themselves will also become less meaningful with each iteration. I imagine most of us have had the experience of diligently reading through an extensive bibliography of secondary material on a text only to suffocate under the weight of this scholarship, wondering what we might say about the work that had not already been addressed (or the equally depressing experience of producing a new reading of a text, only to discover that this intervention was published by someone else seven years ago). Undoubtedly, whatever intervention we make into this conversation, it undoubtedly feels deflating in the grand scheme of things.

Literary theory, specifically deconstruction, played a fundamental role in redefining the boundaries of the discipline by introducing an entirely new way of reading texts. Deploying a version of language that guarantees endless commentary—rather than haggle over the correct interpretation of *The Scarlet Letter*, it shows in innumerable ways how a correct, totalizing interpretation of the novel is impossible—deconstruction made an entirely different mode of commentary on literary objects possible. The entire canon could be approached from a fresh perspective, making a whole new set of readings possible. But this innovative approach, which initially produced a number of analyses with a high "innovative differential," would eventually succumb to the same fate of the previous era. As our earlier analysis of "The Resistance to Theory" shows, de Man himself recognizes the limitations of the interpretive practices he has initiated, seeing that they ossify into the mechanical processes they originally sought to overcome.

While both de Man and Burke seek to mobilize a criticism that can perpetuate itself indefinitely, Burke advances a form with more flexibility than de Man's insofar as it is not anchored to the concept of literature. When Burke begins to broaden the scope of literary criticism, he realizes that this operation will cease unless the "literariness" that defines it is called into question. In *The Philosophy of Literary Form*, he outlines a mode of analysis that broadens the scope of the investigation at each stage, incorporating more texts and perspectives with every move. As *A Rhetoric of Motives* makes explicit, it is precisely the notion of "literary" that proved to be the fundamental problem with continued expansion. Burke claims that disciplinary specialization ultimately inhibits the growth of a vibrant criticism. Attempts to sequester oneself in a single disciplinary location prove exceptionally detrimental when one studies rhetoric, which Burke stresses "has no systematic location" (41). Indeed, he believes that rhetoric has fallen into disrepute precisely because of disciplinary boundaries, which have configured rhetoric as an idiosyncratic mode of discourse (public political speech) rather than language as such. From his perspective, disciplinary specialization has prevented insights from related fields from having a substantial impact. Burke regards rhetoric as a sort of clearinghouse for the disciplines, where the work in one field can modify and be modified by the work in related areas. In this respect, rhetoric as a concept helps facilitate agonistic relationships among practitioners in a number of disciplines insofar as it offers them a common ground on which to exchange critical blows.

It is this moving across disciplines that ultimately points toward the fundamental difference between de Man and Burke—a process of connection rather than interpretation. The entire discipline becomes a free-floating operation without a canon to anchor it. We might think about this in terms of a "gold standard." Of course, the most obvious way to read this term would be through Matthew Arnold, who conceives of literature in terms of the most valuable items produced by a culture. But we might also think about it in economic terms, where the gold standard helps stabilize economic transactions and minimize financial speculation. If criticism has discarded the "gold standard" of the canon it has done so in order to facilitate the critical work that the canon initially made possible (just like the foundationless, ever-fluctuating market that replaces a "gold standard" economy merely intensifies the logic that made the "gold standard" possible in the first place). Criticism has developed in a similar manner, using the notion of the canon as a "gold standard" to underwrite a flurry of critical interpretive activity that was guaranteed as legitimate (recall Foucault's conceptualization of the author as a function that operates within a discourse). Unfortunately, if the canon mobilizes this activity, it also prevents its long-term growth prospects. The canon allows for the proliferation of discourse at the same time that it guarantees this process will slowly grind to a halt, with the "innovative differential" trending closer to zero. Only by departing from a privileged set of texts and the specific interpretive practices attached to these texts can criticism maintain its forward momentum.

Put in a slightly different way, much like financial capitalism produces additional money through money itself (in Marx's terminology, M—M' rather than C—M), criticism has gradually weaned itself off of the literary object to perpetuate itself. Rather than sacred objects around which critics circulate endlessly, texts become tokens passed among critics who are invested in exploring more nebulous conceptual questions (hence, the rise of various studies concerning concepts like race, gender, media, animals, affect, the body—recall Leitch's diagram of "planets" and "satellites" that opened our general introduction). When fidelity to the text dissipates, the relations among critics become that much more important, with texts becoming instruments by which critics position themselves in alliance or opposition to other critics. Such a shift is indicative of another change in the disposition of criticism: the difference between a hermeneutic criticism and a creative or constructive criticism. Granting that these two categories can never be cleanly distinguished, we can see that an emphasis on the latter has much more promising prospects than the previous one, insofar as the text can be *used* in any number of ways rather than *interpreted* endlessly without a final interpretation emerging. The innovative differential is always much higher insofar as the ways in which the text can be taken up is not determined in advance by a predisposition to the object. Interpretive questions of "rigor" are replaced by pragmatic questions of "interest" largely because the latter formulation eliminates many of the limits imposed upon criticism.

De Man's work nevertheless serves as an important reminder that even though criticism may no longer be oriented around the single foundation of the canon, it nevertheless erects new foundations. These new foundations serve as internal limits that criticism approaches and ultimately destroys, repeating the process anew. In other words, Burke and de Man alert us to two important moments in criticism's growth and development. While Burke's work suggests that a foundationless model will guarantee the long-term expansion of the critical enterprise, de Man's work supplements his formulation by pointing out that this expansion always involves the creation of localized, provisional limits. Indeed, if Burke offers a model of rhetoric that isn't tethered to a canon of texts (despite its heavy indebtedness to Aristotle), the field of Rhetoric and Composition that has been inspired by his work nevertheless deployed new canons through which to produce criticism, the most obvious being the "rhetorical canon." This rhetorical canon does little to distinguish itself formally from the literary canon, since it authorizes the same sorts of critical practices that will succumb to the same fate as their counterparts in literary criticism.

But these provisional foundations do not necessarily have to be located in concrete texts; they can also assume more abstract forms. While the "rhetorical studies" wing of Rhetoric and Composition most closely resembles literary criticism's attachment to a set of texts, the vast majority of the rest of the field is still governed by an internal limit which simultaneously makes criticism possible and inhibits its long-term growth. As has been clear to an increasing number of Rhetoric and Composition specialists in recent years, this nearly unconscious internal limit has been the "pedagogical imperative." That the pedagogical imperative has ultimately inhibited the discourse can be seen in Sidney I. Dobrin's 2011 *Postcomposition*, where he asserts that Rhetoric and Composition must redefine itself as "writing studies" if it wants to remain vibrant. From his perspective, composition studies has been hobbled by its myopic focus on college writing, particularly the first-year course. Dobrin is particularly worried about the focus on "student improvement" that preoccupies the vast majority of scholarship in the field. He asserts that "the work of theorizing writing is—and must be—bigger than the idea of students" (15). For composition studies to remain a compelling area of inquiry in the coming years, it must shed its previous attachments to these issues and begin to study "writing" in general in all the various guises it has assumed throughout history and contemporary life. Dobrin's text registers an exhaustion with the current territory that composition studies has staked out for itself, and only an outward expansion to uncharted ground will prevent the field from collapsing under its own weight.[11]

Interestingly enough, the inevitable expansion of literary studies has also pushed it in the direction of becoming a wide-ranging "writing studies." The rise of the New Historicism in the 1980s and 1990s marks the beginning of this movement. New Historicism can be seen as a response to deconstruction's exhaustion as a critical method, which, while departing with the New Criticism that preceded it, nevertheless maintained a strict attention to closely reading isolated texts. New Historicism sought to reinsert the isolated literary work back into the broader network of texts in which it was originally produced. Obviously, this maneuver initiated a further expansion of critical work. As Catherine Gallagher and Stephen Greenblatt explain in *Practicing New Historicism*, their turn toward noncanonical literature and nonliterary texts was initially just a way of revitalizing canonical authors. Their use of historical anecdotes was intended to better illuminate the great texts of the tradition: "in the earliest essays of new historicism . . . the anecdote worked if it illuminated a major literary work" (47). But this strategy produced an emerging countercurrent. In some cases, anecdotes and other minor historical documents could steal the show and become the primary focus of analysis, relegating the canonical work to a mere supporting actor. Rather than being evaluated according to how well it illuminated a canonical text, the critical work could instead be "measured by its success in captivating readers. If the attention—one's own and that demanded of one's readers—seemed justified, then it was a successful intervention" (46–47). New Historicism is thus pulled in opposite directions. On one hand, the literary text remains the primary object of interest—that is, other texts (both noncanonical and nonliterary) are sought out and colonized simply to further illuminate this literary work. On the other hand, the literary text loses its primacy and merely becomes a launching point from which one departs to ask questions about culture and written material more generally.

If the internal shifts within a discourse like New Historicism hint that contemporary literary studies is heading toward what we might call the "postliterary," then its differences with the discourse of "writing studies" proposed by Dobrin becomes a central question. Indeed, if composition studies is eager to shift away from only studying student writers and toward writing more generally, than the most obvious boundaries separating theory, literature, and composition cease to exist. It could be said, then, that the various fields that constitute the discipline of English are loosely united around the concepts of "writing" and "rhetoric." Indeed, what exactly separates a mode of critical inquiry like Dobrin's "post-composition," which studies writing and the various contexts in which it is produced and consumed, from the version of New Historicism that has little attachment to the concept of "literature"? Wouldn't the ecological and networked models that Dobrin advances in *Postcomposition* have much to say to New Historicism's notion that texts circulate within a general economy of written material? Thanks to the expansive impulse of any critical discourse, attempts to produce new decisive distinctions between literary and composition studies would only temporarily halt their inevitable convergence.

Today, literature and composition studies might be likened to two neighboring cities that have gradually expanded to the point that the border separating one from the other has become increasingly difficult to pinpoint. If composition studies began as a small outpost far outside the center of the city of literary studies, it has expanded quickly enough that it may eventually dwarf the original settlement. Complicating matters, both are seeking to claim the fertile territory of "writing" that exists between them and that may be necessary for long-term survival. Of course, each municipality has cultivated its own set of customs and practices over the course of several decades, and additional growth will require negotiating the sometimes sharp differences between these two cultures. Will one side manage to wrest control of this territory, leaving the other side vulnerable? Will a symbiotic or parasitic relationship emerge? What hybrid cultural formations might be produced from such negotiations? In order to predict how this uncertain future might (or should) unfold, we must first retrace the previous interactions between the two cities, beginning with a contentious foreigner who has spent considerable time in both locales—French theory.

CHAPTER 2

Between Standardization and Serialization: Kenneth Burke, Fredric Jameson, and Radical Criticism in the Post-Fordist Era

By the early 1980s, the stage was set for Kenneth Burke to assume a prominent role within the canon of literary theory. During this period, many critics eagerly called for more socially oriented forms of inquiry to replace (or at least supplement) the formalistic approaches that had long dominated literary study. In his influential 1983 work *Criticism and Social Change*, Frank Lentricchia argued that Burke's examination of a literary work's practical effects served as a useful antidote to the narrow focus found in New Criticism and deconstruction. Positioning Kenneth Burke against Paul de Man, Lentricchia's book embodied an emerging demand for literary criticism to engage more directly with broader social questions while remaining theoretically savvy. "Not all social power is literary power," Lentricchia explains, "but all literary power is social power. . . . The literary act is a social act" (19). For Lentricchia, Kenneth Burke offered a compelling model for critics wanting to pursue this mode of inquiry.

Although literary theory did in fact begin to explore literature's relationship with its social context, Kenneth Burke's work did not become a touchstone within this movement. The 1980s witnessed the emergence of many new approaches, all of which criticized the strict formalisms of the preceding era. However, rather than look to Burke for crucial insights, theoretical discourse largely dismissed him in favor of thinkers like Michel Foucault and Fredric Jameson. Despite periodic calls by Lentricchia and others to give Burke the attention he deserves, his marginalization within literary theory has persisted, most evidently with the complete elimination of his entry from the revised edition of *The Norton Anthology of Theory and Criticism* published in 2010.[1]

Whatever readers Burke failed to gain within literary theory, he more than won within rhetorical scholarship, particularly in Rhetoric and Composition, a subfield of English studies that has been steadily developing its own research agenda and publishing venues for the last several decades. Even the most cursory glance at some of the most prominent journals of rhetorical scholarship—*Quarterly Journal of Speech, Rhetoric Society Quarterly, Rhetoric Review, JAC, Philosophy and Rhetoric*—quickly confirms Burke's unparalleled prominence in this field. Additionally, the number of book-length publications analyzing Burke's work outright (Debra Hawhee's *Moving Bodies: Kenneth Burke at the Edges of Language*), deploying his insights to explore other topics (Gregory Clark's *Rhetorical Landscapes in America: Variations on a Theme from Kenneth Burke*), or combining these two approaches (Bryan Crable's *Ralph Ellison and Kenneth Burke: At the Roots of the Racial Divide*) has increased dramatically in recent years, featured prominently by university presses like Southern Illinois and South Carolina. How can we account for this startling dissymmetry? How is it that Burke could experience two wildly different fates within the same discipline?

Indeed, Kenneth Burke serves as an important figure for understanding the complicated relationships that have developed over the last four decades among the various subdisciplines comprising English studies. Typically housed within a single academic unit—"the English Department at X University"—these various subdisciplines maintain irreconcilable and sometimes hostile differences even as they share a number of texts, approaches, and concepts.[2] Certainly, the relationship between literary theory and rhetorical theory has been one of the most complicated, with Burke serving as the figure that simultaneously unites and separates the two camps. On the one hand, rhetorical criticism and theory has often sought to link Burke to the other big names in theoretical discourse (Derrida, Foucault, de Man), demonstrating how he poses the same methodological questions and belongs to the same philosophical heritage (Nietzsche, Freud, Marx, Hegel).[3] On the other hand, rhetorical criticism has also aimed to distance itself from literary theory, suggesting that Burke's protean yet digestible prose constitutes a dramatic improvement over the obfuscating provocations of Parisian intellectuals, as if Burke shielded American rhetorical scholarship from a dependence on foreign theory, a homegrown alternative to continental imports. In one swift stroke, Burke both belongs to the discourse of literary theory and transcends its most obvious limitations. While this ambivalent deployment of Burke certainly alerts us to the undeniable tensions that exist between rhetorical and literary theory, it can often obscure the precise contours of these tensions, reducing them to unhelpful stereotypes. What exactly distinguishes rhetorical theory and criticism, which champions the work of Kenneth Burke, from literary theory, which has relegated him to an easily deleted footnote in the theory canon? More important, what might this tell us about the status of English studies today?

I propose that these questions can be usefully explored by examining a well-known debate between Burke and Marxist literary critic Fredric Jameson in the journal *Critical Inquiry* in 1978.[4] While ostensibly focused on the merits of Burke's work, their exchange actually illuminates important differences between literary theory on one hand and rhetorical theory on the other. The Burke-Jameson debate illustrates how the emergence of various subdisciplines can be traced back to differing responses to liberal pluralism. While I would argue that pluralism constitutes the starting point for the entirety of English studies today, the discipline fractures when it comes to assessing the effects or political efficacy of this pluralism. In fact, the Burke-Jameson debate shows that literary and rhetorical theory diverge most decisively on this issue, and it is on precisely this issue that the discipline is now divided.

Throughout his lengthy career, Burke remained the consummate pluralist, assembling a range of concepts that both illustrate and enact the principles of difference, flexibility, and innovation that underwrite this doctrine. For Burke, pluralism is an indispensable political tool, the only thing that can adequately address the numerous challenges posed by modernity. While literary theory has its own pluralist tendencies—Derridean *différance*, Foucauldian history, Deleuzian multiplicity—it has also stressed, perhaps with less fanfare, that pluralism alone will not save us: Far from a simple blueprint for a better world, it actually contributes to the troubles of the contemporary social landscape. And, as Jameson's analysis of Burke implies, liberal pluralism has become increasingly indistinguishable from the imperatives of late postindustrial capitalism. In other words, rhetorical theory's attachment to pluralism might be better understood as an unacknowledged promotion of the very neoliberal principles it claims to be defying. As the Burke-Jameson debate will reveal, much of English studies, particularly rhetorical theory and criticism, remains tethered to a set of historical conditions that is no longer dominant.

A Missed Encounter?

To fully appreciate the differences between Burke and Jameson, one must understand the venue that hosted the exchange. Long before sponsoring Burke's debate with Jameson, *Critical Inquiry* had already assembled many of the major practitioners of both literary and rhetorical theory. While the role of *Critical Inquiry* in incorporating French theory into the American academy is widely acknowledged, the fact that the journal was the brain-child of the Chicago School of literary criticism, which advocated for a pluralistic approach to interpretation, remains less well known. During the first decade of the publication's existence, the editors of *Critical Inquiry* clearly counted Kenneth Burke among their most prominent philosophical proponents. Not only did Burke serve as a member of the editorial board, but he also contributed a number of articles to the journal during this time. Furthermore, *Critical Inquiry* highlighted Burke's underappreciated contributions to American criticism; for the first article of the debut issue, co-editor Wayne Booth—who would soon become one of the most important figures in rhetorical theory—offered a thinly veiled encomium celebrating Burke's career achievements and placing him firmly within the tradition of pluralism. In his response to Booth (which appeared in the same issue), Burke never objects to being characterized as a pluralist.[5] Indeed, early in his essay, Burke fondly recalls that his ideas concerning the relationship between language and poetry "were largely sharpened by the vigorous and friendly hagglings I had with 'that Chicago crowd'" ("Dancing" 24). Moreover, both Burke and the editors at *Critical Inquiry* often spoke of "literary theory" in harsh terms and differentiated their own pluralistic approach from it. For instance, in a 1979 letter, Booth commended Burke for managing "to say just about everything worth saying that the Frenchies are now saying, long since. You run circles around [Roland] Barthes" (quoted in Rood, "'Understanding' Again: Listening with Kenneth Burke and Wayne Booth," 461).[6] Jameson's engagement with Burke, then, amounted to a direct confrontation between literary theory and pluralism that had been germinating since the inception of *Critical Inquiry*.

The exchange between Burke and Jameson actually began under circumstances more fitting of a memorial service than a title fight. In September 1977, Harvard's English Institute organized to discuss Burke's

legacy, naming the event "The Achievement of Kenneth Burke." Given
that Burke's major critical statements had been composed decades earlier, the participants' comments couldn't avoid a retrospective tenor and
Burke's attendance could have easily lent the proceedings the atmosphere
of a retirement party full of glowing remembrances of towering intellectual feats (or, at the very worst, a good-natured roast full of humorous
quibbles). Burke, who had turned eighty a few months earlier but still possessed a spritely and pugnacious demeanor in his old age, had completely
different expectations for the event and took Jameson's keynote address,
"The Symbolic Inference; or Kenneth Burke and Ideological Analysis," as
a personal affront. When Jameson's paper was published in *Critical Inquiry*
in the spring of 1978, Burke penned a lengthy response, "Methodological
Repression and/or Strategies of Containment," for the journal's Winter
1978 issue that not only defended his work but also condemned Jameson's
entire methodological approach. Jameson provided a further rejoinder to
Burke in this same issue, a brief piece entitled "Ideology and Symbolic
Action."

Defying any attempt at straightforward summarization, their exchange
could nevertheless easily be understood as an academic comedy of errors,
with both sides struggling to marshal a range of ambiguous philosophical
terms that evaded their complete command. To worsen matters, the mischaracterizations that resulted from this slippery terminology only intensified the undeniable antagonism between the participants. In other words,
the heated nature of their exchange obscures both the surprising affinities
and more inconspicuous differences between Burke and Jameson. Only by
bracketing its more theatrical qualities can we appreciate the important
stakes of this encounter.[7]

Jameson's initial analysis of Burke might best be conceived of as an an-
ticipation and refutation of Frank Lentricchia's book several years later.
Jameson opens the piece by contrasting philosophical criticism from the
first half of the twentieth century with more recent "literary theory," noting that the latter emphasizes "the primacy of language" (507). Jameson
quickly points out that Kenneth Burke's work in the 1930s and 1940s constitutes a notable exception to this schematic, since his "pioneering work
on the tropes mark him as the precursor of literary theory in this new,
linguistics-oriented sense" (507). Praising Burke for anticipating many of
the limitations of overly formalistic theoretical methods, Jameson suggests
that Burke's conception of "the symbolic as act or *praxis* may equally be
said to constitute a critique of the more mindless forms of the fetishism
of language" (508). Although Burke may share important similarities with

more recent theoretical models, his sustained emphasis on language as a social practice prevents him from making the same mistakes that characterize much literary theory. As Jameson asserts, Burke's writing has the ostensible goal of "restoring to the literary text its value as activity and its meaning as a gesture and a response to a determinate situation" (509). Generally speaking, then, Jameson agrees with Lentricchia about Burke's potential as a great theorist of literature as a form of social action (a position Jameson also endorses). The remainder of the essay assesses whether Burke's work fulfills these expectations.

In his typically circuitous fashion, Jameson announces that Burke does not successfully document how literature constitutes symbolic action. Although his work seems to promise an escape from formalism, Burke ultimately succumbs to these very same limitations, repeating them in a much more subtle form. More specifically, Burke tends to reduce a literary work's social activity to its engagement with other literary works; he sees authors participating in an unending conversation with other authors about the vagaries of the human condition. Jameson asserts that Burke, by limiting literature's engagement with the social to "literary history" broadly construed, has excluded considerations of a "vaster social or historical or political horizon" (515). As a result, "his conception of literature as symbolic act, which began as a powerful incitement to the study of a text's mode of activity in the general cultural and social world beyond it" actually supports "those who want to limit our work to texts whose autonomy has been carefully secured in advance" (518). Focusing solely on philosophical and aesthetic debates within the literary world, Burke is condemned to overlook the social and political forces that shape the production and circulation of these works.

Instead of refuting Jameson's central argument, Burke's essay responds to a number of seemingly tangential issues in the original piece. Burke criticizes Jameson for failing to read his work closely and spends a large portion of his response simply listing the various ways in which he has used the word "ideology" over the course of several decades (Jameson had mentioned Burke's "strange reluctance" to use this word [521]). As Burke sees it, Jameson's critique lacks credibility because it remains ignorant of a large portion of his writing, most evident in Jameson's failure to even attempt a recapitulation of Burke's arguments: "since he is differentiating his position from mine . . . the proper expository procedure would require that he explicitly 'report' my statement of my position . . . and then proceed to demolish it as he sees fit. Surely Jameson is not asking his readers to take the sheer Quietus as a 'model' for his way of 'rereading' or 'rewriting' a text" (403). Throughout the essay, Burke reiterates this reservation about Jameson's methodology.

Jameson spends the bulk of his subsequent response to Burke clarifying that his use of the word "ideology" differs substantially from Burke's. Jameson explains that Burke conceives of ideology in terms of "our old friend 'false consciousness,' so unavoidable a part of the baggage of thirties Marxism" (418). When Burke labels an object or practice "ideological," it constitutes "a purely negative judgment" that "leave[s] nothing of its object intact" (419). But Jameson rejects this formulation, asserting that matters of truth or falsehood are irrelevant to understanding ideology. Given that all ideas and concepts possess a practical function, helping to organize society in one way rather than another, they are all equally "true." In other words, as forms of activity, ideological concepts produce real effects in the world that cannot simply be dismissed as delusional. Jameson puts the matter bluntly: "Are 'courtly morality' or the bourgeois concept of 'nature' true or false?" (420). For Jameson, ideology is synonymous with praxis, bypassing the epistemological concerns that seem to preoccupy Burke. In claiming that Burke has a "strange reluctance" to think in terms of "ideology," Jameson is merely reiterating Burke's failure to address the true social function of a literary work—in other words, the main thesis advanced in his original essay.

Interestingly enough, despite his passionate resistance to Jameson's characterization of him in "The Symbolic Inference," Burke seems to admit the validity of Jameson's central critique. In an offhand comment in his response to Jameson, he writes that "my method of analysis is designed to strike a balance between the New Critics' stress upon the particular work in itself and Jameson's 'ideological' stress upon 'the ultimate horizon of every cultural artifact'" (411). Here, Burke fully admits to not being "ideological" in Jameson's sense due to his desire to preserve many of the formalist tendencies found in the work of the New Critics.[8] In this respect, the entire debate can be understood as a colossal misunderstanding, a severe complication of terms that has two figures agreeing about the differences in their methodology but failing to recognize this fact because of the terminology that their respective methodologies deploy.

However, the heatedness of their debate suggests that there were important tensions between the two figures that their scuffle over the word "ideology" only served to obscure. Jameson's critique implies that Burke's work, in failing to be a form of proper ideological analysis, could not have a positive social impact—instead of being wrong it was ineffective, perhaps even detrimental. Burke obviously took offense to this implied accusation and suggested that Jameson's work was equally irrelevant as a tool for engaging with the social world. Put otherwise, this debate implicitly explored each thinker's work to the social world in which it functioned. If Burke and Jameson's respective writings are symbolic actions (Burke's term) or ideological (Jameson's term), then how exactly are they functioning within society and history more broadly? What role might criticism play in advanced capitalist society? Naturally, this question cannot be answered without a relatively clear idea about the nature of advanced capitalist society itself, and much of Burke and Jameson's disagreement pivoted on the current state of capitalism. Accordingly, to better understand the debate between Burke and Jameson in *Critical Inquiry*, we must not only examine each thinker's broader body of work but also the seemingly trivial moments in their exchange that intimate how each understands the specific historical moment in which their work operates.

Marxism as Terministic Screen

Throughout his response to Jameson, Burke sounds a familiar refrain: Jameson's critique lacks credibility because it ignores a large portion of his writing. In addition to the example offered in the previous section, Burke reiterates the same reservations: "If . . . his model encourages him simply to *ignore* my way of developing the term 'ideology' and to 'dispose of' the issue by regretting my 'strange reluctance' to use the *term* as often as he would, does that speak well for his model?" (409). On the following page, he underscores the point once more: "if Jameson decides that I'm quite off the track, he might show in detail why, rather than simply grading my paper without further ado" (410).

Burke regards Jameson's failure to follow the basic decorum of critical exchange—namely, the proper citation of an interlocutor's work before criticizing it—as the result of a much larger problem: the inability to see his own position as one among many. In other words, Jameson's failure to cite Burke's words within his essay stems from a troubling attachment to his own terminology and perspective. The title of Burke's response—"Methodological Repression and/or Strategies of Containment"—encapsulates the general thrust of his response. As he explains in the opening moments of the essay, "methodological repression" (his assessment of Jameson) and "strategies of containment" (Jameson's assessment of him) become difficult to distinguish. In other words, Burke suggests that both parties involved are making the same fundamental criticism. If Jameson has criticized him for focusing on certain aspects in the texts he analyzes (namely the text's inner workings rather than its broader social effects), Burke in turn thinks that Jameson is too focused on the social effects rather than these inner workings.

Although Burke finds no problem with Jameson's emphasis in itself, he does flinch at the prospect that Jameson does not seem to recognize this perspective *as* a perspective. Indeed, Burke asserts that "any expression of something implies a repression of something else, and any statement that goes only so far is analyzable as serving to forestall a statement that goes farther" (401). He repeats this same point near the end of the piece, explaining, "I would call any 'historicist' ideology like Jameson's an implicit 'strategy of containment' to the extent that it deflects attention" away from other considerations (412). Anyone familiar with Burke's larger philosophical project should find this statement unsurprising. For instance, in his essay "Terministic Screens," Burke asserts that language does not accurately reflect the world but instead constitutes a deliberate selection and arrangement of details for a specific end or purpose: "any nomenclature necessarily directs the attention into some channels rather than others" (*Language as Symbolic Action* 45). A neutral perspective is fundamentally impossible since emphasizing some features of a phenomenon will require neglecting others. Burke's notion of "terministic screen"—or what he calls "methodological repression" in the debate—underscores that any given concept or strategy does not transcend the world but instead offers a limited perspective on it.

Wanting to avoid the trap of committing too deeply to a single, limited perspective, Burke develops a technique he calls "perspective by incongruity." Inspired by the writings of Nietzsche and Bergson, this procedure scrambles the vocabularies of competing conceptual systems, thereby calling into question any claims of comprehensive knowledge. As Burke explains in *Permanence and Change*, the combination of contradictory concepts will not offer "the whole of reality" but will at least "give us something more indicative than is obtainable by the assumption that our conceptualizations of events in nature are real" (94). In other words, Burke's "perspective by incongruity" calls attention to the fact that concepts are pragmatic and constructed devices rather than natural entities in the world merely waiting to be discovered by mankind. By placing words or metaphors from one interpretive schema into a completely different framework, Burke thinks that many of the dangers embodied in modern scientific attitudes can be avoided.

Given that he sees Jameson failing to acknowledge the constructed nature of his own discourse, Burke appropriately mentions this concept "perspective by incongruity" during his *Critical Inquiry* response essay, defining it here as a process that "puts together terms usually thought of as mutually exclusive" which can often "startle by giving new insights" (409). Before proceeding to elaborate on the concept and its significance, Burke includes a single provocative sentence, one intended as a jab at Jameson: "the device can become trivial, mere irresponsible smartness slapped out by city-slickers" (409). Why characterize Jameson as a "city slicker"? Lacking the proper context or explanation, we must briefly turn to an important dimension of Burke's writing in order to understand this off-hand barb.

Burke's biting remark should be read as an instance of his deep-seated suspicion of industrialization and the bureaucracies that facilitated its growth. Committed to the idea that any given perspective must be recognized as a perspective, Burke was dismayed at the industrial world's strident unwillingness to consider its own hidden biases or question its underlying values. His work underscores how bureaucracies, rather than grappling with the messy and ever-shifting details of the world, devise complex vocabularies to shield themselves from this conceptual turbulence and perpetuate their existence. Burke's antagonism toward institutions stems from these organizations actively working against enacting a process like "perspective by incongruity." In a section of *Attitudes Toward History* entitled "Bureaucratization of the Imaginative," he explains that actualizing one possibility necessarily restricts actualizing other possibilities. Characterizing the foreclosure of alternative forms of thought in terms of a bureaucracy, Burke suggests that we "call the possibilities 'imaginative.' And call the carrying-out of *one* possibility the *bureaucratization* of the imaginative" (225). In order to maintain internal consistency and order, any large-scale organization must standardize its vocabulary, effectively limiting the evolution of ideas and perspectives. Institutions, which rely on fixed quantities and qualities for their continued existence, are diametrically opposed to the strategy of "perspective by incongruity." The problem resides not so much with the specific principles advanced by a given institution but with the structural limitations of institutions themselves. Overemphasizing any one set of principles will prove damaging in the long-term. For instance, big business's stubborn attachment to "efficiency" effectively "violates 'ecological balance,' stressing some one ingredient rather than maintaining all ingredients by the subtler requirements of 'symbiosis'" (250). In calling him a "city slicker," Burke suggests that Jameson is guilty of a similar error, a point reinforced when he criticizes Jameson's "*over investment* in the term 'ideology'" (401, my emphasis).

Although Jameson's Marxist disposition ostensibly casts him as an antagonist to big business and its imperatives, Burke stresses an unsettling commonality that unites these otherwise diametrically opposed foes. Burke's suspicion of institutions extends beyond the usual suspects of government and business agencies to include philosophical systems as well, most notably Freudian and Marxist frameworks. By clinging to a rigid set of concepts and vocabulary, these grand interpretive schemes produce the same effects as traditional bureaucracies, rendering themselves incapable of dealing with the complexities that escape their limited perspectives. Burke finds Marxism particularly guilty of this bureaucratizing tendency, since it not only claims to possess a broad and totalizing knowledge of society but also seeks to employ this knowledge in order to mobilize a disciplined and potentially dogmatic political party. Indeed, one moment during his *Critical Inquiry* essay confirms that Burke's response to Jameson was shaped by this broader skepticism of Marxism as a form of bureaucratic routinization. Near the end of the piece, he states that the tendency toward ritual and routine that characterize "contemporary bureaucratizations" is not "likely to be 'abolished' as is *routinely or ritualistically promised* of the classless society in the Marxist dialectic" (413, my emphasis). Despite affirming many of Marx's insights into the nature of capitalist exploitation, Burke had refrained from joining the Communist Party during the 1930s out of fear that this organization would probably repeat many of the same errors it sought to correct (George and Selzer, *Kenneth Burke in the 1930s*, 2–3), and the same anxiety concerning Marxism influenced Burke in his response to Jameson.

Naturally, then, Burke regarded Jameson's unqualified confidence in Marxism as incredibly dangerous. Only bolstering Burke's suspicions, Jameson peppers his writing with declarations of Marxism's theoretical supremacy. In perhaps his definitive work, *The Political Unconscious* (1981), he boldly announces in the opening pages that "only Marxism offers a philosophically coherent and ideologically compelling resolution to the dilemma" of interpreting history and that "only Marxism can give us an adequate account of the essential *mystery* of the cultural past" (19). Self-assured claims like these explain why Burke decided in his *Critical Inquiry* essay to paint Jameson as a dogmatic figure. From his perspective, Jameson's insistence on the correctness of his Marxist interpretive scheme actualizes all of the bureaucratizing and totalitarian tendencies seen in the businessman and scientist. Indeed, Burke charges Jameson with failing to acknowledge the constructed nature of his own discourse, evident when Burke asserts in his response essay that his own methodology freely grants the charge [of being anthropomorphic]. But when one man-made nomenclature accuses another man-made nomenclature of being anthropomorphic, if the accusation is intended to imply that the accusant nomenclature is *not* anthropomorphic, at that point my brand of Logology likens such ideological behavior to the verbal tactics of the politician who would imply his purity by accusing another politician of playing politics. (413)

From Burke's perspective, Jameson's bold declarations are implicitly totalitarian, illustrating how Marxist discourse ignores other interpretive possibilities by claiming itself as absolute truth.

In this respect, we should understand this retort as Burke's demonstration of Jameson's overly simplified philosophical positioning, one lacking literary theory's awareness of language's subtle vicissitudes. Trapped behind one terministic screen, Jameson brushes aside all evidence that does not conform to his static, lifeless system. Burke clearly found humor in Jameson's desire to have a positive political effect since his work contributed to political problems rather than solving them. In fact, from Burke's perspective, Jameson's bureaucratizing and standardizing tendencies constitute *the* fundamental problem of modern society. In revealing how poorly Jameson read his work, Burke sought to expose the dangerous, antipluralist effects of this Marxist orientation.

Marxism as Perspective by Incongruity

Throughout his rebuttal to Jameson, Burke emphasizes that his opponent commits egregious acts of misreading. As he sees it, Jameson conveniently overlooks any evidence that defies the assumptions he possesses about Burke's thought. Interestingly enough, however, a similar charge could be leveled at Burke. While Jameson's insistence on the superiority of Marxism certainly seems to confirm anxieties about totalitarian undertones in his work, Burke's accusations miss much in Jameson's writing. A close reading of Jameson's engagement with Marxism illustrates that he actually shares a similar investment with producing a flexible and adaptable methodology.

Like Burke, Jameson maintains a suspicious attitude toward any positivistic account of the world. In his 1971 *Marxism and Form*, he dedicates a substantial amount of time to outlining the differences between his Marxist approach and these other perspectives. In the book's concluding chapter, he writes that the dialectic is designed "to project us in spite of ourselves out of our concepts into the world of genuine realities to which those concepts were supposed to apply"; he continues by explaining that "every time [our concepts] begin to freeze over," the task of "genuine dialectical thinking" is to "spring us outside of our own hardened ideas into a new and more vivid apprehension of reality itself" (372). And when discussing Lacan in another essay from that period, Jameson echoes Burke by re-iterating that "in terms of language, we must distinguish between our own narrative of history—whether psychoanalytic or political—and the Real itself, which our narratives can only approximate in asymptotic fashion and which 'resists symbolization absolutely'" (*Ideologies* 110). But if both Burke and Jameson reject the simplistic positivism that ensnares so much con-temporary thinking, why does the latter nevertheless retain the Marxist label?

For Jameson, Marxism is simply the name for antisystematic thinking. In his 1979 essay "Marxism and Historicism," he argues that "a Marxist hermeneutic can be radically distinguished from all the other types . . . since its 'master code,' or transcendental *signified*, is precisely not given as a representation but rather as an *absent cause*, as that which can never know full representation" (*Ideologies* 452). Distancing himself from the many limitations of vulgar Marxism, Jameson insists that his own frame-work does not operate according to straightforward concepts like econom-ics or production but functions instead according to the nebulous concept of "history." For Jameson, history can never be examined directly but can only be observed in its different manifestations over time. His version of Marxism does not seek to offer a stable, unchanging vocabulary for accu-rately describing society's operations but instead illustrates the very impos-sibility of ever achieving such a feat due to continuous historical transfor-mation. As the opening declaration of *The Political Unconscious*—"Always historicize!"—indicates, the only constant in Jameson's approach is the perpetual need to modify his analytical tools for each concrete situation.

Jameson departs from Burke, however, by insisting that one can be flexi-ble and change over time while remaining within a single institution. While Burke posits that institutions present a continual threat to the possibility of true change—their bureaucratic apparatuses necessarily disrupting the natural flow of ideas and the ability to adapt to new demands—Jameson suggests that one enacts change through an institution. For him, institu-tions constitute spaces of collectivity where concepts are reflexively modi-fied over time. Even a rather abstract institution like Marxism facilitates such a process. In self-identifying as a Marxist, Jameson does not dogmati-cally uphold every point advanced in Marx's writing. For him, Marxism consists of a body of general problems and broad guidelines with a flexible vocabulary that can (and must) be adapted over time to suit ever-changing contexts. Even though they belong to the same lineage, Jameson's Marxism differs noticeably from Lukács's Marxism, or Adorno's Marxism, or Marx's Marxism. In adapting and refiguring the work of previous thinkers, Jameson actually enacts the process of reflexive modification that his work so highly values.

This tension between Burke and Jameson manifests itself clearly in the pair's divergent understanding of Marx's concept of ideology. Writing to his lifelong friend Malcolm Cowley about Jameson's initial essay about him, Burke complains that Jameson

> had managed to tangle Marx's notion of "ideology" (as per the *German Ideology*, which he presumably never understood, if he ever read it) in ways that only the Hermeneutics is capable of. I was furious that, although I had brought all sorts of baggage with me, I didn't have p. 104 of *A Rhetoric of Motives*, and thus couldn't dispatch the guy as quickly as I could of. Marx's meaning is as clear as a flash, yet the guy was in a fog . . . which would have led Marx to damn him as an ideologue [*sic*]. (Burke and Cowley, *The Selected Correspondence, 1915–1981*, 409)

For Burke, the concept of ideology has a clear and definite meaning that can be attributed to a particular author in a specific text. One either grasps the meaning of "ideology" as described by Marx in *The German Ideology* or one does not. Accordingly, Burke believes that Jameson's reconfiguration of the term can only signify that he never even bothered to read Marx's work in the first place. With a meaning "as clear as a flash," how else could one explain Jameson's wild misinterpretation?

Burke's assessment of Jameson underscores these two thinkers' differing approaches to texts and philosophical traditions. Although both find Marx's work in *The German Ideology* to be compelling yet incomplete, their competing strategies for addressing these inadequacies reveal important assumptions underwriting their respective methodologies. For Burke, the Marxist perspective is just another terministic screen, offering some useful insights into the world while simultaneously ignoring others. Aware of the inherent limitations of the Marxist system, Burke employs its insights sparingly as he darts from one interpretive method to the next in an effort to avoid dwelling too long in one fixed perspective. Unlike Burke, Jameson elects to transform Marxism from the inside. The Marxist framework should not be regarded as the static monument of a singular thinker but rather a dynamic body of concepts that naturally evolves over time. In a 1982 interview with the journal *Diacritics*, Jameson asserts that dialectical terminology is "never stable in some older analytical or Cartesian sense: it builds on its own uses in the process of development of the dialectical text, using its initial provisory formulations as a ladder which can either be kicked away or drawn up behind you in later 'moments' of the text" (*Jameson on Jameson* 23–24).

Jameson's commitment to modifying a discourse from the inside extends beyond traditional Marxist texts to include other thinkers and methodologies. Indeed, he regards other interpretive strategies as "incomplete" rather than "incorrect," explaining that they are merely "provisory formulations" that further exploration will transform into a properly Marxist analysis. As Jameson argues, any given methodology that rigorously applies its own procedures to their logical conclusion will inevitably arrive at Jameson's Marxist perspective. In his 1976 essay "Criticism in History," he addresses the proliferation of interpretive frameworks that were then flooding the academy, arguing that "the Marxist point of view is secretly present in all those methods—if only as the reality that is repressed, or covertly opposed" (*Ideologies of Theory* 125). Rather than an alternative to so many formalisms and sociological approaches, Marxism should "be seen as their completion, and as the only method that can really finish what it is they all in their various ways set out to do" (126). For Jameson, other interpretive regimes only appear adequate because they place arbitrary limits on their own unique reading procedures. As Jameson later points out, "I would like to show that if you prolong any one of these methods even on its own terms, you always reemerge into the historical dimension itself" (126). Most methodologies stop short at precisely the moment when they must reflexively consider their own historical conditions of possibility; in taking that crucial last step, they would effectively become Marxist.

During his debate with Burke in *Critical Inquiry*, Jameson scrutinizes Burke's method in exactly this way. Jameson sees Burke's pentad as subtly reinforcing many of the capitalist principles that Burke seeks to undermine, noting that he "has anticipated many of the fundamental objections to such a rhetoric of self and identity at the same time that he may be counted among its founding fathers" (521). Burke's dramatism is "not so much the archetype of praxis as it is the very source of the ideology of representation and, with it, of the optical illusion of the subject" (522). In spite of these reservations about Burke's methodology, Jameson insists that if the underlying structure of the pentad is pushed to its limit, it will become a more rigorous form of analysis. Ironically enough, the pentad can be deployed to demonstrate Burke's own failure to use this paradigm adequately:

it is a measure of the ambiguous power of Burke's dramatism that we can use it to study its own strategies of containment, and to flush out those concepts external to his own system to which he tends to have recourse when it is necessary to arrest the evolution of his concept of symbolic action in the direction of a full-fledged analysis of the ideological function of literary and cultural texts. ("Symbolic Inference" 518)

Taken to its logical conclusion, the pentad will necessarily lead to the ideological analysis that Jameson believes essential for criticism. Burke simply has not used his philosophical concepts to their fullest potential.[9] Thus, Burke's worry that Jameson is not a dynamic, mobile thinker proves unfounded. Although his approach differs from Burke, Jameson manages to produce a flexible, ever-changing methodology that avoids the standardizing impulses that had doomed earlier forms of Marxism.

An Omitted Third Term

If Burke advances a largely unspoken criticism of Jameson's work as potentially totalitarian, Jameson launches an equally oblique suggestion concerning the obsolescence of Burke's work in the late twentieth century. While Jameson makes clear that Burke fails to offer a compelling account of symbolic action, much remains left unsaid regarding the reasons for this failure. We should understand Jameson's assessment of Burke as a critique of the very idealization of difference and flexibility that underwrites all of Burke's thought, including everything from a specific conceptual practice like "perspective by incongruity" to his larger "logological" philosophy and pluralist disposition. While the previous section outlined the similarities between Burke and Jameson on this matter, it remains crucial to recognize that Jameson regards these techniques of difference and innovation as necessary but not sufficient to respond effectively to contemporary capitalism. Jameson's critique unearths the dark underside of Burke's ostensibly liberating vision of language and creativity by showing how late twentieth-century capitalism actually thrives on the continual process of differentiation that Burke champions. Occurring roughly midway through the twentieth century, this shift from standardization to differentiation as the primary motor of capitalism strips Burke's philosophical pluralism of its politically radical edge.

Burke's "Methodological Repression and/or Strategies of Containment," beyond offering extensive documentation of his use of the word "ideology," stressed the creative potential buried within language, a potential that Burke regards as central to human flourishing. Burke's ideas about language here rest upon a distinction between "nonsymbolic motion" and "symbolic action"; Burke had initially elaborated upon this distinction in an article published in *Critical Inquiry* in its Summer 1978 issue and subsequently returned to it when responding to Jameson. In a move that underwrites Burke's entire "logological" perspective, the article "(Nonsymbolic) Motion/(Symbolic) Action" establishes a "critical distinction" between "human animals and other animals," one that makes possible "the realm of technological counter-nature" (414) where humankind can "guide its own evolution rather than being subject to the instincts and laws of natural selection" (415). For Burke, humankind should be defined by its capacity for inventiveness through "symbolic action" that allows it to transcend the law-bound structures of a natural world consisting of "nonsymbolic motion." Human beings transcend the limitations of their physical bodies through the creative powers of language. He criticizes Darwinism for privileging the natural realm of nonsymbolic motion over the social realm of symbolic action; Darwinism problematically endorses a unidirectional notion of causality that ultimately posits human civilization as a mere effect of inflexible natural processes. In doing so, Darwinism treats humans as just another kind of animal, reducing them to their "sheer physiology" (414).

Burke condemns Marxism for committing the same sin as Darwinism. He argues that Marxist discourse prioritizes the material world and thereby downplays the enormous creative potential that accompanies the human's status as "the typically symbol-using animal" (415). For Burke, doing so constitutes a "kind of 'genetic fallacy'" where "overstress upon the *origins* of some manifestation can deflect attention from what it *is*, regardless of what it came from" (415). Even if humankind and symbolic action originated in nonsymbolic nature, that does "not imply that such a realm of symbolicity cannot be an originating force in its own right" (414).

We can now begin to see how all of Burke's numerous criticisms of Marxism—its positivistic pretensions, its attachment to the primacy of material origins, its unsettling tendency toward institutional routinization—fit with his own logological philosophy. If Burke targets Marxism for failing to recognize its perspective as a perspective, he clearly sees this failure stemming from its belief that the material conditions of the world completely determine human thought. Marxism can claim to be a completely accurate account of the world because it believes that it is merely representing the world's natural laws; Marxism sees itself as merely a "reflection" of the fundamentals of the "economic base" (which Marxism regards as an extension of unchanging processes of the natural world). Marxism's strident self-assurance inevitably leads to an increasing standardization in its thinking, which prevents it from considering alternative perspectives and encourages it to become just another inflexible and uncritical institution that plagues the modern era. Despite this grim situation, Burke believes that hope lies in the human's often unrecognized but nevertheless essential capacity to creatively remake the world. Its status as a "symbol-using animal" offers the liberating potential to overcome the stifling procedures of standardizing institutions, which deny these human capacities by taking certain creative human acts—that is, particular concepts used to describe the world—as accepted, unchangeable facts. For Burke, recognizing and subsequently cultivating humankind's linguistically based creative powers will help modern society overcome its dangerous inclination toward standardization.

Jameson's critique centers on Burke's entire schematic being outmoded. Although he fails to elaborate much on this point during his assessment, elsewhere in his writing Jameson describes a significant historical shift in the mid-twentieth century that complicates Burke's politics. He maintains that "the fundamental difference between our situation and that of the 1930s is the emergence in full-blown and definitive form of that ultimate transformation of late monopoly capitalism variously known as the *société de consommation* or as postindustrial society" (*Ideologies* 444). After the Second World War, postindustrialism—or what is often called "post-Fordism"—began to emerge as the dominant social formation in advanced nations, eclipsing the industrial practices that previously supported these societies. Within the context of a post-Fordist society, Burke's work provides few tools for political resistance because it remains so firmly entrenched in the dilemmas of the preceding industrial era.

In "The Symbolic Inference," Jameson illustrates Burke's inability to grasp this significant historical shift through an analysis of the latter's notion of "ritual." Here, Jameson writes that Burke's "idea of ritual indeed entails as one of its basic preconditions the essential stability of a given social formation, its functional capacity to reproduce itself over time" (519). For Jameson, however, this precondition of "essential stability" does not accurately describe the world of the late twentieth century. As Jameson explains, "it would seem to me misguided, not to say historically naïve, to attribute a Parsonian stability and functionality of the former primitive or tribal type to a social formation whose inner logic is the restless and corrosive dissolution of traditional social relations into the atomized and quantified aggregates of the market system" (519).

Although he confidently dismisses Jameson's objections, Burke actually reconfirms this critique by continuing to overlook this shift to post-
Fordism. After admitting that Jameson has "a good point" about the differences between tribal and modern societies, he qualifies his original
assertion by saying that he is "mostly concerned with ritualization *aris-
ing perennially anew, largely out of contemporary bureaucratizations*, since I
am specifically concerned with the indeterminate *shifts between ritual and
routine*. History can show different transformations of ritual in the modes
of symbolic action. But . . . the tendency is not a mere 'survival' nor is it
likely to be 'abolished'" (413, emphasis in original). In other words, Burke
admits that contemporary practices are not synonymous with the rituals of
past societies. Nevertheless, important underlying similarities exist among
disparate historical moments. As a way of rebuffing Jameson, he points to
his *Attitudes Toward History*, which contains a fifty-page outline of historical development, culminating in the contemporary moment. Within this
schematic, he labels the twentieth-century as "Collectivism," describing it
as one dominated by "the conditions of modern technology and accoun-
tancy, encompassing such a variety of polities as Fascism, 'Police States,'
socialism, communism, the 'Welfare State,' and the giant industrial corporations which are typical of our own nation at the present time" (410).
Burke claims that various political and economic agendas can be grouped
together under a single category; a structural homology exists between
repressive totalitarian governments and capitalist corporations since both
seek to organize society according to a standardizing logic. He even ap-
proves of the term "business governments" (410) to describe contemporary corporations precisely because he believes their organizational structure accomplishes similar goals—rigid standardization and the elimination
of flexibility and difference.

As this analysis illustrates, Burke's work treats "totalization" as the defining social dilemma of his day, and his emphasis on openness, difference,
and flexibility are clearly responses to this dilemma. For him, economics
and politics follow a similar logic: Both aim to standardize a diverse range
of perspectives and practices. For Burke, this truth was evident in the twin
evils of fascism and industrial capitalism. Without question, when Burke
wrote the majority of his critical work, this compulsory standardization
was nearly identical in both politics and economics. Burke could not be
faulted for seeing parallels in German fascism and American capitalism
since both operated according to this logic. In Burke's view, acts of difference, innovation, and flexibility are necessarily resistant because of these
broader social structures. Jameson believes that Burke's conceptual out-

look aptly diagnoses the problems of a "standardizing society" and prescribes a useful solution to said problems. Unfortunately, this standardizing society no longer exists—or, at least, it no longer constitutes the dominant cultural formation as it did when Burke composed his most celebrated works.

Burke's ideals of innovation, fragmentation, and flexibility place him squarely within what Jameson would call a "modernist aesthetic." For Jameson, modernism as an aesthetic movement can only be adequately understood in relation to Fordism and industrialism more generally; that is, modernism ("make it new") was directly responding to the stifling imperatives of the economic realm, which aimed to standardize all industrial production ("make it the same"). But this relationship between the economic and the aesthetic, with the modernists and their innovative ideals seeking a small space of freedom in an otherwise conformist society, was a temporary moment in history, one that no longer holds in the contemporary first world. Today, the modernist aesthetic and general economic production coincide. In his essay "The Ideology of the Text," Jameson asserts that modernism "has integrated itself into an economy functionally dependent on it for its indispensable fashion changes and for the perpetual resupplying of a media culture" (*Ideologies* 74–75). This historical transformation became the centerpiece of his definition of "postmodernism"—largely interchangeable with postindustrialism and post-Fordism—a historical era where the aesthetic values of innovation and speculation coincide with the dominant mode of economic production. Fragmentation, difference, and flexibility are not antagonistic toward late capitalism but have actually become its central axioms.

The complete refashioning of the relationship between the aesthetic and the economic has stripped Burke's work of its politically radical core. If the Fordist production model once threatened fragmentation, innovation, and difference with extinction—therefore necessitating the impassioned defense of Burke and other modernists—this threat itself no longer exists, having been replaced by a host of new problems corresponding to this post-Fordist era. If innovation and openness were once the solution, they are now part of the problem. Burke's medicine for the ills of modern capitalism is precisely the poison that plagues the postmodern era. As Jameson explains, a previously "oppositional and antisocial phenomenon" has become "the dominant style of commodity production and an indispensable component in the machinery of the latter's ever more rapid and demanding reproduction of itself" (*Ideologies* 445). The rebellious qualities of Burke's work have now become the cultural dominant.

Jameson foregrounds Burke's problematic modernist impulses when he interrogates the "motion-action" binary that Burke advances in the final pages of "Methodological Repression and/or Strategies of Containment." In the conclusion of "Ideology and Symbolic Action," Jameson criticizes Burke's "binary opposition" between "'nature' vs. human transcendence" for having "omitted an essential third term" which must be recognized as "distinct from either of these" (422). Jameson announces "the realm of history" as this "third term," which he defines as "the alienated forces of human institutions which return on people as external forces with a dynamism of their own." He continues to explain that "this is the realm of what Marx called 'prehistory,' the space in which class dynamics" function as if they were "a natural law" (422). From Jameson's perspective, "Burke's too immediate celebration of the free creativity of human language (in its broadest symbol-making sense) overleaps the whole dimension of our (nonnatural) determination by transindividual historical forces" (422).

Coming in the closing moments of his response essay, Jameson does not elaborate on how these "transindividual historical forces" might emerge. In *Marxism and Form*, however, Jameson outlines the undesirable consequences that a completely free collection of individuals can produce. This analysis speaks directly to his critique of Burke's valorization of difference and flexibility. Here, using Jean-Paul Sartre's notion of "seriality," he illustrates how a "host of collective actions and wills" working independently of one another ultimately produces an "uncontrollable result" (246). This assemblage of "individually positive actions . . . add up to a negative sum" (247). Unexpected social formations erupt from the haphazard combinations of individual actions, creating a context that was willed by no one yet nevertheless constrains all. If the immediate effects of an individual's actions can be clearly observed and understood, the longer-term consequences of such actions remain harder to anticipate and often return on the original actor as an alien and unalterable force. Like the sorcerer's apprentice, humans discover that their actions produce consequences that take on a life of their own, well beyond the original intention of their creators. As Jameson explains, even when individuals agree and have positive, well-intentioned desires, the combination of their identical demands can produce the completely opposite effect: "a million freedoms seemed to cancel each other out in total helplessness" (247). Therefore, as Jameson's analysis reveals, Burke's proposed space of innovation, fragmentation, and flexibility overlooks the fact that the combination of multiple acts of individual freedom can paradoxically create a set of conditions that inhibit further action.

The Unconscious of the Political

If the slipperiness of the term "ideology" has long constituted the focal point for critics interested in the Burke-Jameson exchange, another form of terminological confusion during the debate also needs to be considered, one that obscures our understanding of a concept that is already difficult to grasp—namely, the "political unconscious." At several points in his critique of Burke, Jameson targets his interlocutor for what he sees as a problematic attachment to the "individual." In "The Symbolic Inference," he writes that even though Burke "has anticipated many of the fundamental objections to . . . a rhetoric of self and identity," he also "may be counted among its founding fathers" (521). When assessing this facet of Burke's work, Jameson's terminology shifts rapidly, as if he is unwilling to settle for a single word to signify the issue. Indeed, the language of "self" and "identity," which is first used in a transitional paragraph where Jameson forecasts the material he will discuss for the remainder of his essay, gets reformulated when he finally turns his attention to this topic several pages later. Here, he reintroduces the issue as "the concept of the self or the subject in Burke's criticism" (520). In the very next sentence, Jameson seems to recognize the wide range of options at his disposal, adding yet another term: "this whole issue of the subject, or the ego, or the self" (520). During his analysis over the following several pages, he extends this list, adding "individualism" (520) and "anthropomorphism" (522). At one level, these various terms become interchangeable, all meant to signify the same essential concern (underscored by use of the word "or"); Jameson intends no substantial difference between "self" or "ego" or "subject." At another level, however, Jameson's critique of the "self" (or "identity" or "subject") in Burke possesses several interrelated but distinct features that the sprawling array of signifiers only risks muddying. Untangling this lexical confusion creates a pathway for outlining how Jameson's critique of the "self" is intimately connected to his critique of Burke's inability to grasp the "political unconscious."

At first glance, it would be easy to assume that Jameson's critique of Burke's attachment to the "individual" or "self" simply refers to a difference between the two figures concerning individual versus collective action. After all, Jameson does write that the uncontrollable historical forces produced in the late twentieth century far exceed the "possibility of the individual subject" (422). When Jameson dismisses Burke's attachment to "the individual subject" in this moment, he does so to assert that serial situations (or "the realm of history") can only be countered through a "collective project" (422). As our analysis has already shown, promoting decentralized, uncoordinated individual action will do nothing to resolve the dilemmas presented by serial situations. Beyond alluding to it in his initial assessment of Burke, Jameson also articulates this idea elsewhere in his writing. In *Marxism and Form*, he writes that "given the impotence of individuals in the serial situation, the motivation behind the formation of genuine groups is easily understood as a way of regaining autonomy, of reacting against dispersal through a new type of unity and solidarity" (249). And in "The Symbolic Inference," he reiterates these goals, announcing his aim to achieve "a transcendence of the older individualism" and to produce "new and post-individualistic categories" (521) that will facilitate "new collective structures" (520).

Jameson's sustained insistence on totality should be understood in precisely these terms. Rather than a Stalinist project of domination, his call for totality constitutes a sincere attempt to overcome the dilemmas of the serial situation. For Jameson, the realm of Necessity's grasp over the realm of Freedom will never be undone simply by allowing the individual to flourish in his own unique space of difference and flexibility. As the serial situation demonstrates, the helplessness that most people feel is partially a product of these very strategies. Only through collective action can the serial situation be addressed.[10] Burke and Jameson therefore appear to be split on the prospects of collective action. Where Burke sees only totalitarian outcomes emerging from collectivity, Jameson sees collective action as the only realistic response to the serial situation.

Of course, Jameson's assessment of Burke's notion of the "individual" is much more ambivalent—after all, if he may be counted among the "founding fathers" of individualistic rhetoric, he must also be understood as anticipating "many of the fundamental objections" to this rhetoric. Closer inspection of Burke's work suggests its compatibility with the sort of social democracy that Jameson envisions. In fact, Burke makes a number of positive assessments of democracy, linking its procedures to his own philosophical principles. In his early work *Counter-Statement*, he writes that democracy is a system of "organized distrust" and "a babble of discordant voices, a colossal getting in one's own way" (114). He then responds to those who criticize democracy for being inefficient by saying "inefficiency is the one thing it has in its favor" (114). The democratic deliberative process enacts many of the principles that his work advances—most notably, perspective by incongruity—as a way of organizing society. Regardless of its limitations, democracy at least prevents the totalizing impulse that characterizes the efficiency-obsessed capitalist from assuming the reigns too firmly and leading society to fascism. It would seem, then, that Jameson has misread Burke in a manner similar to how Burke misreads Jameson. Just as Burke erroneously accuses Jameson of harboring fascist tendencies, Jameson erroneously charges Burke with being a neoliberal avant la lettre. In both instances, such condemnations obscure that both critics' projects are underwritten by many of the same presuppositions and goals.

Yet a different valence of the words "individual" and "self" in Jameson's work remains to be explored, one that illuminates the real distinction between Burke and Jameson. Rather than simply juxtaposing the "self" or "identity" with some kind of collective entity, Jameson simultaneously uses these words as shorthand for a problematic belief in human control over its own actions and creations. In critiquing Burke's attachment to the "self," Jameson is actually highlighting what he sees as a faulty understanding of capitalism. In yoking Marxism to certain dimensions of poststructuralist thought, Jameson advances a vision of capitalism as a system that, although it emerged out of human activity, has become powerful and decentered enough to resist attempts to undermine its primary coordinates.

To better explain Jameson's approach, we should begin with an unusual tension within his work: He advocates for a collective response to the serial situation at the same time that he demonstrates that all collective movements are destined to fail. Jameson's hopeful orientation toward the future is tempered by his mournful reflections on the past. While the Marxist tenor of his work suggests a full-blooded notion of revolutionary agency, Jameson's emphasis on the failure of all social movements throughout history calls into question these assumptions. Addressing the dialectic between Freedom and Necessity in *The Political Unconscious*, he writes that "Necessity is here represented in the form of the *inexorable logic* involved in the *determinate failure* of *all* the revolutions that have taken place in human history" (102, my emphasis). For him, "the failure or the blockage, the contradictory reversal or functional inversion, of this or that local revolutionary process" should always be "grasped as '*inevitable*'" and the effect of "objective limits" (102, my emphasis). His Marxist perspective argues that "history is what hurts, it is what refuses desire and sets inexorable limits to individual as well as collective praxis, which its 'ruses' turn into grisly and ironic reversals of their overt intention" (102).[11]

Briefly turning to a concrete example that Jameson takes from Marx should clarify these assertions. In his recent reading of *Capital*, Jameson seizes on a particularly distressing insight concerning the introduction of new technology within capitalism. Rather than stemming from "the ingenuity of the inventors" as one might expect, it instead arises out of intensified "labor unrest." As Jameson explains, "the new machine is the capitalist's answer to the strike, the demand for higher wages, the increasingly effective organization—or 'combination'—of the workers" (*Representing Capital* 58). He underscores Marx's "somber conclusion": "if the progress of capital produces the ever greater misery of the workers . . . then it must also be said that class struggle—the increasingly articulate and self-conscious resistance of the workers themselves—is itself responsible for the ever greater productivity of capitalism" (58). In one of history's "grisly and ironic reversals," organized labor's resistance to capital actually accelerates its own immiseration.

Jameson explains this paradoxical example and other inexorable failures to what he refers to as the "political unconscious," which he uses as the title of his major 1981 work. While it might be tempting to read this phrase simply in terms of political ideologies that have escaped detection from conscious thought, Jameson intends an additional meaning: For him, the "political unconscious" must also be understood as "the unconscious" *of* the political or social sphere. Our analysis has already characterized this "political unconscious" in terms of the serial situation and what Marx calls "prehistory": "the alienated forces of human institutions which return on people as external forces with a dynamism of their own" (422). Indeed, in the last sentence of "Ideology and Symbolic Action," he argues that the relationship between human society and this "realm of alienation" corresponds to the relationship between "individual experience" and "the unconscious" (422). Within the system Jameson has fashioned, the failure to reflect perfectly the objective world through language (which connects him with Burke) must be paired with an equally necessary failure for concrete actions to produce the consequences intended by the actors involved (or, more precisely, for those intended consequences to be preserved over time). A failure in epistemology must be accompanied by a failure in political practice.

Jameson's declaration that "Burke's system has no place for an unconscious" (521) should therefore be understood as a critique of Burke's failure to account for these alienated forces. Jameson undoubtedly counts liberal pluralist democracies among the casualties of the political unconscious and his reservations about Burke stem from his unabashed attachment to these ideals. Jameson criticizes Burke for being fully invested in the "Deweyan rhetoric of liberal democracy and pluralism, federalism, the 'Human Barnyard,' the 'competitive use of the cooperative,' and the celebration of political conflict in terms of what the motto to *A Grammar of Motives* calls the 'purification of war'" (520). The decades since the New Deal have revealed that liberal democratic practice has not lived up to the expectations that Burke and others have ascribed to it: "from the nostalgic perspective of the present day . . . what tends to strike us today about the *Grammar* and *Rhetoric of Motives* is less their critical force than Burke's implicit faith in the harmonizing claims of liberal democracy and in the capacity of the system to reform itself from within" (520). In this respect, Jameson's problem with Burke's notion of "self" or "identity" involves its all too-comforting investment in the idea that human society can reliably contain the effects of its own creative potential—and here we should think of "self" and "identity" in terms of self-possession and control at a collective level. Indeed, Jameson criticizes Burke's dramatistic approach for appealing too heavily on "categories of consciousness": "the Burkean symbolic act is thus always serenely transparent to itself, in lucid blindness to the dark underside of language, to the ruses of history or of desire" (522).

While Jameson never directly illustrates how democracy might endanger its own functioning, his discussion of small group practice in *Marxism and Form* offers the best hint of the shape that analysis would assume. Here, Jameson offers an account of a collective organization that would respond to the serial situation while avoiding rigid organization. He notes that this decentered group makes decisions according to a process of "rotating or revolving thirds" (253), where a "third" designates a leadership position within the group. As the name "rotating thirds" suggests, leadership positions are never fixed in this highly egalitarian structure.

Almost immediately after praising this group for its democratic principles, he suggests that its longevity is doomed from the start. The laudable process of revolving thirds can disintegrate in one of two ways. The first: Because decentered organization will prove to be ineffective in dealing with the enormous complexity of the serial situation, the group will inevitably attempt to protect itself by establishing some guise of stability, typically in the form of rules or principles. Unfortunately, this produces a hierarchy that slows down and eventually halts the shared responsibility that initially defined the group. The group prolongs its life by becoming better organized, yet "the demarcation of separate responsibilities, the assignment of tasks of different orders, the division of labor, are ultimately inconsistent with the total democracy and equality of the revolving thirds" (269). The second: If the group somehow manages to address the serial situation effectively, it will nevertheless attempt to maintain its existence so as to prevent or address future serial incidents. But without an imminent threat, the group will only be able to preserve itself through an oath of allegiance, thereby opening up the possibility of political terror.

As Jameson writes, "born of an attempt to prevent the return of seriality and dispersal, [the group] engages instead in the liquidation of individual freedoms" (255). Regardless of its ability to successfully address the serial situation, the group itself fails to preserve the dynamics of equality and "rotating thirds" that marked its origin.

Jameson's analysis highlights how democratic practice cannot be posited as a solution to the problems of standardization and bureaucratization precisely because these problems were outcomes implicit at the very beginning of the group's formation. Upholding democratic practice as an unproblematic ideal is untenable because it fails to recognize the relationship between democracy and a centralized form of power. Democracy does not replace a sovereign mode of power; instead, a centralized sovereignty necessarily emerges out of any form of democratic practice, since "it is part of the natural history of the group that as the rotation of thirds slows down, as institution and organization begin to come into being," that "a single third finds himself in the dominant position in the now petrified group structure" (271). According to Jameson's analysis, Stalin's takeover of the Soviet apparatus is not an unfortunate accident. While effectively dispelling the forces of seriality that surrounded the Soviet Union, Stalin subjected the members of this organization to an equally distressing system of political oppression.

The fundamental misgiving of democratic utopianism stems from its failure to recognize the broader flows of historical development. Jameson explains that "history can be seen alternatively as either a perpetual oscillation between moments of genuine group existence and long periods of serial dispersal, or, at any given moment, as a complicated coexistence of groups at various stages of their development and masses of serial individuals surrounding them" (249). Any social formation—chaotic seriality, equal democratic practice, rigid hierarchical organization—will inevitably succumb to internal contradictions, leading to the emergence of one of the other forms. While it might be tempting to see all social formations trending inevitably toward totalitarianism—this seems to be Burke's conclusion, with human history ending in a wide-ranging "Collectivism"—Jameson insists that totalitarian regimes will fail when their oppressive structures lead to a revolution producing serial dispersal or a new small-group formation. We therefore have a cyclical process that moves from the helplessness of individuals in isolation crushed by the serial situation to the formation of democratic groups combatting this serial situation to the inevitable transformation of these groups into standardized hierarchies that will eventually dissolve and return individuals to a starting point of freedom, which will soon enough create another serial situation. Democratic practice can only be understood as an ideal when it ignores the broader historical currents from which it has emerged and that ensure its eventual dissolution.

Jameson's analysis of the "rotating thirds" anticipates Derrida's late work *Rogues*, where he offers a dramatic illustration of democracy's autoimmune structure. Here, Derrida points to a recent political incident to illustrate what he sees as an aporia inherent to any democratic process. In the weeks leading up to a 1991 election in Algeria, a group of Islamic fundamentalists had generated enough popular support to gain control of the government. Once in power, these fundamentalists would dismantle the existing democratic practices like free elections and install a dictatorship. The current holders of power, moderate secularists, sought to stop this outcome by suspending the elections. For Derrida, this situation illustrates two ways in which democracy's autoimmunity manifests itself. On the one hand, nondemocratic governments can always be elected through the democratic process. One can always vote to have one's right to vote eliminated. As Derrida explains, "the *alternative to* democracy can always be *represented* as a democratic *alternation*" (31). On the other hand, those who recognized the threat posed by the Islamic fundamentalists and attempted to stall or alter the outcome of the election also killed the democratic process from within. From their perspective, the normal democratic practices had to be temporarily suspended in order to preserve these practices in the long term, but in stopping the fundamentalists, they had already dismantled these democratic principles. Regardless of the outcome in this particular situation—the election of the Islamic fundamentalists or their failure at the hands of the more moderate secularists—the democratic process fell victim to a nondemocratic force. For Derrida, this force is inextricable from the democratic practice itself, since "democracy has always been suicidal" (33).

Central to Derrida's analysis of democracy is the concept of ipseity. As he explains, "ipseity names a principle of . . . accredited or recognized supremacy of a power or a force" (*Rogues* 12). In spite of democracy's opposition to a sovereign monarch, it shares with this alternative political form a belief in ipseity. Indeed, Derrida argues that democracy is "a force (*kratos*), a force in the form of a sovereign authority (sovereign, that is, *kurios* or *kuros*, having the power to decide . . .), and thus the power and ipseity of the people (*demos*)" (13). In other words, it is a capacity "to do as one pleases, to decide, to choose to determine *oneself*, to have self-determination, to be master, and first of all master of oneself" (22). Democracy might be understood as a sort of distributed or dispersed sovereignty.

Derrida's analysis illustrates how this sovereign self-possession, regardless of whether it assumes a concentrated form like a monarch or a distributed form like democracy, is structurally exposed to an outside that will disrupt its constitution. In the case of democracy, the only political form that actively welcomes this exposure to the outside, its willingness to change itself is paradoxically what makes it possible to become rigid and hierarchical. As Derrida's concrete examples demonstrate, its very openness makes it vulnerable to closure, and therefore, it fails to preserve its capacity to determine itself as a self-creating, transformative phenomenon. Derrida's analysis of the inherent autoimmunity of democracy does not suggest this failure can be attributed to some internal weaknesses of the governing or the governed; instead, it points to the unnerving prospect that the very desire to preserve these democratic structures indirectly participates in their unraveling.

In this respect, Jameson's critique of Burke's "anthropomorphism" is less an indictment of his attachment to the individual than his investment in the ipseity of any entity, whether individual or collective. In spite of this dire analysis, however, Jameson firmly maintains hope in the prospect of a better future where Freedom could overcome the limitations of Necessity. He understands Marxism as a commitment to this hope, arguing that "no Marxism is possible without a vision of a radically different future" (*Jameson on Jameson* 26). In the conclusion to *The Political Unconscious*, he writes that "one of the most urgent tasks for Marxist theory today" involves the creation of "a whole new logic of collective dynamics, with categories that escape the taint of some mere application of terms drawn from individual experience" (294). Thus, Jameson's Marxism consists of equal parts pessimism (the failure of all social movements through history) and optimism (the possibility that some future social movement might transcend these past failures), attempting to hold these incompatible notions in dialectical tension. The ease with which both Burke and Jameson become almost indistinguishable from their opponent, often in their most polemical and antagonistic moments, remains one of the most fascinating hallmarks of their debate.

By introducing Derrida into Burke and Jameson's exchange, a diverse array of anti-essentialist positions comes into focus. While a traditionalist would likely dismiss them all as so many lost causes, the differences among Burke, Jameson, and Derrida warrant careful consideration. Anti-essentialism may constitute the starting point for these thinkers (and most left-leaning political theorists today), but they depart from this shared ground in unexpected directions. As a way to organize the differences among them, we might chart their respective treatments of ipseity, producing a spectrum from least to most critical assessment of the concept (with an awareness that these thinkers shift on the spectrum depending on what we emphasize or marginalize in their writing). On one end of the spectrum lies Burke, who, while only occasionally indulging in the problematic fantasy of individual world making, consistently regards collective organizations as powerful agents who largely determine their destiny. His broad historical vision traces society's increasing ipseity that culminates in the nightmarish totalitarian extremes of the twentieth century. On the other end of the spectrum lies Derrida, who outlines a set of ontological conditions that call into question the capacity of any individual or collective formation to remain in control and self-possessed for any significant duration. Finally, in the middle of the spectrum rests Jameson, the puzzling figure who combines features of both Burke and Derrida.[12] Despite sharing many similarities with Burke's vision of political action, Jameson diverges most sharply with him concerning the ultimate effectiveness of these movements, engaging in a critique of ipseity that resembles Derrida's. At the same time, his commitment to utopian hope, which he sees as inseparable from Marxism, prompts him to regard ipseity as a promise that may be achieved by collectivities at some point in the future that would overcome, or at least minimize, the dilemmas posed by Derrida's analysis.[13] Based on this analysis, it is Jameson, rather than Burke, who constitutes the pivotal figure joining literary theory with Rhetoric and Composition. Within theoretical discourse, Jameson's Marxist utopian impulses place him in an odd position, yet his emphasis on the complete and utter failure of all human revolutions in history clearly justifies his inclusion in this group. Indeed, for these thinkers, the historical record is a symptom of a fundamental condition that no amount of Utopian desire on Jameson's part could ever hope to counteract.

Indeed, while the tensions between Derrida and his outright detractors have received the most critical attention, the subtle differences that separate him from his more sympathetic interlocutors—in other words, Jameson and others positioned along the anti-essentialist spectrum— speak more directly to the vicissitudes of leftist political theorizing today.[14] Take, for instance, the work of Ernesto Laclau and Chantal Mouffe, which is in the same spirit as Burke's (their notion of radical democracy resonates nicely with Burke's "parlor metaphor" found in *The Philosophy of Literary Form*). The pair enlists Derrida both as a means of challenging the notion of consensus-oriented democracies and of advancing the robust, "agonistic" model of democracy that they champion.[15] What their analysis tends to underemphasize is the degree to which the concept of democracy, even their highly amorphous version that escapes the trap of being tied to concrete forms or procedures, remains forever vulnerable to its own internal impulses. Deconstruction not only problematizes the notion that rigid, hierarchical societies can remain stable but also suggests that democracies, which cultivate perpetual contestation and transformation, will suffer a similar fate. Despite their best efforts to internalize a constitutive outside, democracies cannot fully protect the flexible mechanisms that promise perpetual transformation from foreclosure. Attending to the nearly negligible interval between figures like Laclau and Mouffe on the one hand and Derrida on the other remains crucial in assessing the prospects of democracy in the contemporary world.

Ultimately, then, it is precisely Burke's enthusiasm for the human's creative potential (which rests at the heart of the motion-action distinction) as well as his faith in the liberating nature of difference (which underwrites logology and his pluralistic outlook more generally) that rendered him a problematic figure when literary theory began to direct its attention to social questions in the 1980s. The big figures of literary theory would, each in their own way, examine the dangers associated with flexibility and fluidity—Derrida and his treatment of democracy's suicidal autoimmunity mechanisms, Foucault and his examination of the capillary and distributed nature of biopolitical power in neoliberalism, Deleuze and his diagnosis of capitalism's schizophrenic character.

Although it never garnered as much attention as other high-profile debates in *Critical Inquiry*, the confrontation between Kenneth Burke and Fredric Jameson constitutes a critical moment in English studies, one that anticipates important fault lines that would soon structure much of the discipline. While pluralism quickly became an assumed starting point for both literary and rhetorical theory, replacing the essentialisms of the preceding era, the nature of this pluralism and its effects remained much more contentious. Broadly speaking, then, two versions of pluralism have circulated in English studies over the last few decades. Following Burke and other figures of the Chicago school like Wayne Booth, rhetorical theory and criticism have tended to endorse liberal pluralism wholeheartedly, seeing in it a utopian ideal.[16] When engaging with figures from continental philosophy, rhetorical theory has tended to emphasize those features in their work that align most closely with Burke's pluralist position. Literary theory, meanwhile, has remained more skeptical about pluralism's prospects, with Jameson's analysis of Burke characterizing the broad strokes of that skepticism. At every turn, the canonical figures of literary theory have sought to distance themselves from the "anthropomorphic" tendencies evident in the Chicago pluralists, instead emphasizing that the plurality of which they speak is an impersonal, structural one that continually makes (and unmakes) individual subjects (and not the other way around).

If these two versions of pluralism have circulated in the discipline over the last few decades, English studies has often embraced rhetorical theory's version of pluralism without fully acknowledging it. While the widespread incorporation of "theory" into the discipline has become a generally acknowledged fact, close inspection should reveal that much of what passes for literary theory is actually some version of rhetorical theory. Take, for instance, the discipline's recent investment in "animal studies," a turn at least partially motivated by Jacques Derrida's late work *The Animal That Therefore I Am*. While the vast majority of the work on animals has assumed a liberal pluralist register, demanding that rights be extended to nonhuman subjects, Derrida's text gestures in precisely the opposite direction, questioning whether humans even possess those qualities that make them subjects capable of bearing rights in the first place.[17] In other words, much of the effort to trouble the boundaries between the human and the animal is aligned more closely with Burke's pluralism than Derrida's. If the discipline is split between two competing pluralisms, rhetorical theory's version appears to hold the clear advantage. The next chapter will further explore this tendency and its implications in the contemporary university.

CHAPTER 3

Mapping the Archival Turn
in English Studies

More than thirty years after Kenneth Burke's heated exchange with Fredric Jameson, another significant but understated debate occurred in *Critical Inquiry*. In 2012, Jeffrey J. Williams responded to Evan Kindley's article "Big Criticism." While the particulars of their argument concern the funding apparatuses involved in the rise of literary criticism following World War II, a significant methodological point emerges in the final moments of Williams's critique. Here he admits that his investment in criticizing Kindley's piece, beyond a shared commitment to generating a more cultural materialist version of modern literary criticism, stems from the article embodying problematic assumptions that are endemic to contemporary critical work. Williams argues,

> If the master word defining the theory era was *text*, the master word
> of our era is *archive*, and there is a tendency to present intriguing and
> very local archival material from which one makes a grand speculation.
> The speculation gains credibility from the accumulation of archival
> material. It's impressive when you read notes that reveal their sources
> as box 6, folder 15, and they seem inarguable. Similar to what Roland

Barthes called the reality effect, they perform I believe a history effect. Such procedure broadcasts a realistic account, but it is in fact primarily rhetorical; because the scholar has access to such arcane material, we assume that other statements are based on this bedrock of fact. (411)

Here, Williams criticizes Kindley for conflating the universal and the particular. Unearthing material from a specific historical site, Kindley draws broad conclusions about postwar literary criticism that his work cannot reasonably support. The specificity of his research materials does not adequately represent the more complicated realities of the period under investigation. Williams's critique of Kindley only begins to address the complex issues that surround what we might refer to as the "archive era." To understand the implications of the shift from "text" to "archive" that Williams insightfully posits, we must first detach these two terms from their concrete referents. After all, archival work existed long before the rise of Big Theory and texts continue to be read and analyzed today even though, as Williams claims, the "era of the text" has ended.

A useful starting point for outlining some of the underlying tensions between text and archive can be found in Kurt Spellmeyer's 1996 piece "After Theory: From Textuality to Attunement with the World." Like Williams, Spellmeyer equates the era of literary theory with the concept "textuality." And while the word "archive" does not figure prominently in his discussion, Spellmeyer complements Williams's text/archive dichotomy by supplying a broad organizing principle for the latter term. In his opening paragraph, he maintains "theory's successor's all share among themselves at least one identifying feature—a commitment to descending from textuality into the particulars of everyday life" (893). As the rest of Spellmeyer's argument unfolds, the transition from the text to the archive becomes clearer: Against an ahistorical, institutionally sanctioned form of criticism that implicitly supports the status quo, a socially conscious criticism emerges to advance a broadly progressive democratic agenda. For Spellmeyer, the practice of writing criticism has unfortunately become a conservative act insofar as it only further separates academics from the society they are meant to serve, pulling them out of the undergraduate classroom at startling rates. Whatever the merits of Spellmeyer's position, his piece points to a "social turn" in literary scholarship following the demise of Big Theory in the discipline.

But the shift from text to archive was far from a decisive split. If critics' turn toward social and political questions, best seen in (but not limited to) a deep investment in archival research, can be seen in many ways as a reaction against literary theory and "the text," this new paradigm also drew much of its energy (or at least some cultural capital) from these theoretical texts. Much of the discipline's recourse to these theoretical works is puzzling, however, since these texts do not directly speak in the name of the progressive political movement into which they were assimilated. As François Cusset explains in his history of French theory's American legacy, "if Derrida or Foucault deconstructed the concept of *objectivity*, the Americans would draw on those theories not for a reflection on the figural power of language or on discursive constructions, but for a more concrete political conclusion: *objectivity* is synonymous with 'subjectivity of the white male.' What they developed was an entirely unexpected link between literary theory and the political Left" (131). Those who had been skeptical or simply bewildered by the "black box" of French theory could be reassured that it "had a focus after all, and it was none other than unearthing minority identities, and the lot of subjugated groups" (131–132). In other words, the shift from text to archive could be seen as both a birth and death of theory in the American academy. If theory was simultaneously expelled from the academy and embraced all the more tightly, the love it received was through rose-tinted glasses.

If French theory found itself being used as a support for a broad democratic coalition, the writings of many of its key practitioners predicted such an outcome. Indeed, what links diverse figures like Derrida, Deleuze, and Foucault together is a shared understanding of social or political organization rooted in contingent dispersal and appropriation (what, in the previous chapter, Jameson referred to as "history"). This is not to say that the truth of French theory was corrupted and made to be something it was not, but that French theory provides an account of how historical phenomena are seized and deployed for different ends—and, more important, how these phenomena cannot be separated from the forces that capture and deploy them. Because French theory advances a notion of the socius that functions according to the principle of difference, it can be fairly easily assimilated into a democratic identity politics. While not diametrically opposed, the two systems do possess substantial differences that warrant exploration.

The previous chapter outlined the differences between these two versions of politics using the debate between Kenneth Burke and Fredric Jameson as an example. This chapter extends that analysis by showing these two models at work within the discipline of English over the last several decades. Indeed, the relationship between these two competing models can be productively examined in contemporary English studies where literary

theory, identity politics, democratic practices, and a decentered social organization all collide. First, I trace how many of the insights of French
theory were confirmed by the way they were incorporated into English
studies during the "social turn" in criticism. Then I outline how the democratic identity politics movement that redeployed French theory for its
own ends ultimately became subject to these same forces of appropriation
and redeployment. More specifically, I examine how the concept of the political in the discourse of Rhetoric and Composition, in many ways shaped
by local disciplinary matters (including its relationship to literary studies), had unintended consequences that has worked against its progressive
goals. The model of identity politics that the field advances shares much
in common with an emerging discourse within the university's central administration that is invested in making the university more hierarchical.

The Archival and the Cartographic

The shift from "text" to "archive" has been quite decisive throughout literary criticism, so decisive, in fact, that even those paradigmatic figures
of textuality have experienced a flurry of archival research around their
own work. The ambitious project of translating and publishing thirty-five
years' worth of Derrida's lecture courses can be seen as a symptom of this
shift. The same can be said for many of Paul de Man's unpublished works
and unofficial writings that have recently been unearthed. In 2012's *Theory
and the Disappearing Future*, Tom Cohen, Claire Colebrook, and J. Hillis
Miller take a series of notes by de Man on Walter Benjamin as a starting point for a reevaluation of the Yale critic (the book also includes a
transcription of these notes). The same year also saw the publication of
The Post-Romantic Predicament, a collection of essays that were part of the
critic's papers that are housed at the library at the University of California
at Irvine. Other material from this collection, including the rough draft
of *Allegories of Reading*, spurred Martin McQuillan's recent collection of
essays *The Political Archive of Paul de Man*. And the recently published *The
Paul de Man Notebooks* emphasize the extent to which this archival impulse
has taken a decisive hold of many of the fundamental protocols structuring
criticism today.

While the shift from "text" to "archive" can be understood as a reaction to French theory, its abstruse ruminations rejected in favor of more
certain historical realities, it might also be said that the shift occurred
within the discourse of theory as well as outside of it. If the "era of the
text" was underwritten by Jacques Derrida's infamous statement from *Of*

Grammatology that *"there is nothing outside the text"* (158), critics targeted this approach for dismissing the social and historical factors determining the literary work. Although Derrida's assertion is certainly one of the most misunderstood phrases in the theory canon (here, "text" does not refer to specific written materials but a certain type of ontological structure), these critiques nevertheless adequately capture how his work was deployed within much American literary criticism throughout the late 1970s and 1980s. Those looking for a fully formed challenge to Derrida didn't need to look beyond the confines of recent French writing, since Michel Foucault both detailed the limitations of Derrida's approach and promised a more socially committed model for literary criticism. In *The World, the Text, and the Critic*, Edward Said articulates the sharp differences between Derrida and Foucault: "Derrida's criticism moves us *into* the text, Foucault's *in* and *out*" (183). For Said, Derrida's shortsighted focus on the nuances of textual artifacts finds a corrective in Foucault, who links these texts to the real world and matters of power and oppression. Even if Foucault's analyses wander toward the highly theoretical end of the spectrum, his analyses present the comforting reassurance that they can always be tied back to a "real world." In Foucault's work, written documents no longer circulate in a free-floating space but are instead seen as objects functioning within (and helping to produce) a social context. The transition from "text" to "archive" constitutes a shift in emphasis toward this broader context in which written material is embedded.

Indeed, this shift from "text" to "archive" constituted the major sticking point between Derrida and Foucault over the course of two decades. The tiff began shortly after the publication of Foucault's first major work, *The History of Madness*, a survey of the transformations of the titular topic during the "classical age." Derrida, a former student of Foucault's, presented an analysis of the book in his essay "Cogito and the History of Madness" at the College Philosophique in 1963. With Foucault in the audience, Derrida leveled a devastating critique of the presuppositions underwriting his mentor's work, suggesting that Foucault fell victim to the same gestures that he condemned Descartes for committing: "I would be tempted to consider Foucault's book a powerful . . . Cartesian gesture for the twentieth century" (55). Incensed by the treatment, Foucault stormed out of the conference but did not officially respond to Derrida's comments for nearly a decade when the second edition of the book was released in 1972. In an appendix to this version entitled "My Body, This Paper, This Fire," Foucault dismissed Derrida's myopic focus on those few pages in the massive volume that mentioned philosophical figures in Derrida's wheelhouse. For

Foucault, whatever strengths Derrida's analysis might possess, it is ultimately nothing more than "a historically well-determined little pedagogy"
that "inversely gives to the voice of the masters that unlimited sovereignty
that allows it indefinitely to re-say the text" (573). Foucault would make
much of Derrida's reliance on the work of prominent Descartes scholar
Martial Guéroult, suggesting that this betrayed Derrida's commitment to
an oppressive philosophical tradition. In the publication *Paideia* in Febru-
ary of that year, Foucault is even more to the point: "Derrida thinks that
he can capture the meaning of my book or its 'project' from the three
pages, the only three pages that are given over to the analysis of a text that
is recognised by the philosophical tradition" ("Reply" 575).[1] Foucault challenges Derrida's inability to think beyond the canon of accepted texts when
reconstructing a historical phenomenon. Even if Foucault were to have
fumbled his analysis of a canonical figure like Descartes, would that error
be enough to discredit the entirety of the project? Shouldn't other voices
make a compelling claim on our attentions?

Of course, each thinker's relationship to history and marginal figures is
a bit more complicated than their spat might initially suggest. While their
respective philosophical projects are by no means identical, the significant
overlap between them can easily be overshadowed. To say that Derrida
had no interest in history beyond canonical figures does a great disservice
to his work, and much of his later writing directly considers the status of
the marginal or dispossessed (including an analysis of the archive in *Archive
Fever*). Foucault may be an even more dynamic figure insofar as his work
exhibits an extraordinary range of competing impulses and investments.
One of the primary features of Foucault's work is a notion of genealogy
adopted from Nietzsche, wherein an assemblage of forces converge and
interact. What something "is" is nothing more than a collection of forces
that can be deployed in a number of contexts. This principle serves as both
a methodological point in his own work and a principle through which
we can understand his proliferation in critical discourse. When Foucault
outlines Nietzsche's concept of genealogy in the essay "Nietzsche, Genealogy, History," he does not offer a complete picture of Nietzsche so much as
mobilize particular forces in Nietzsche's corpus that help further his own
project. Like any other historical object, "Nietzsche" ultimately becomes
nothing more than the various forces that have taken possession of it over
time. It should come as no surprise, then, that "Foucault" also experiences
this same fate, his work seized by a number of critical camps that deploy his
ideas in diverse and often contradictory ways. Although Foucault's work
contains a dizzying array of emphases and objectives, for my purposes

here—even my assessment of the genealogy of Foucault's work will be a partial glimpse produced for specific ends—we might reduce this variety of forces to two principle impulses: "Foucault the archivist" and "Foucault the cartographer." I take these descriptions from Gilles Deleuze's seminal 1986 study *Foucault*, where he characterizes his deceased friend as both "a new archivist" and "a new cartographer." I make no claims of adhering to Deleuze's understanding of Foucault as archivist or cartographer. Instead, I deploy these terms for my own ends in diagnosing the disparate and often conflicting ways that Foucault has been incorporated into the American academy.[2]

The differences between the archival Foucault and the cartographer Foucault can be seen clearly in his essay "The Lives of Infamous Men," a preface for a book that was never published.

Foucault explains that the book is "an anthology of existences" consisting of "lives of a few lines or a few pages" that "convey not so much lessons to ponder as brief effects whose force fades almost at once" (279). Based on Foucault's description, the book is intended to embody what I am calling the "archival Foucault," an intense interest in the odd, the singular, and the peculiar for its own sake. Foucault writes that the process of selecting work for the book "was guided by nothing more substantial than my taste, my pleasure, an emotion, laughter, surprise, a certain dread, or some other feeling whose intensity I might have trouble justifying, now that the first moment of discovery has passed" (279). Foucault's interest in these long-deceased figures stems precisely from their resistance to being incorporated into a preexisting schematic and thereby being reduced to examples of "lessons to ponder." Indeed, the book was inspired by his wanderings through the Bibliothèque Nationale, where he spent much of his time simply wading through historical documents. At some level, the pieces in the anthology are included precisely because they defy explanation (even if only momentarily, since their impact "fades almost at once"). Foucault admits that the collection is one "compiled . . . without a clear purpose," explaining that "I resolved simply to assemble a certain number of texts, for the intensity they seem . . . to have" (280). Unlike Derrida, who would immediately feed these texts through a dense conceptual apparatus that would render them intelligible, Foucault wants to pause on the intensely affective moment in which these brief moments of writing defy a self-assured explanation.

And yet, as soon as this "archival Foucault" is fully articulated, a competing "cartographer Foucault" emerges to challenge it. Against his initial interest in the past for its own sake and his fascination with the ability of strange and marginal characters from history to disrupt long-held beliefs and assumptions, this other Foucault enthusiastically embraces system building and diagramming a range of conflicting forces that produce the effects he finds in these brief lives. During the first portion of "The Lives of Infamous Men," Foucault explains how the anthology constitutes a "rule-and-game-based book" insofar as there were a number of restrictions he imposed on himself in terms of what could be included. The pieces must not only address actual people who were both "obscure and ill-fated" but they needed to be "as brief as possible" (281). Furthermore, the actual written document itself must have participated in the fate of the individual (rather than simply describing that fate). Elaborating rules of limitation ultimately leads Foucault to constructing the constellation of social forces that would produce documents conforming to such criteria. Foucault details how these documents embody the introduction of sovereign power into the quotidian affairs of common people, since these documents are part of an apparatus by which individuals could seize "the mechanisms of sovereignty" and "divert its effects to one's own benefit" (288). As a result, "political sovereignty penetrated into the most elementary dimension of the social body" and a "whole political network became interwoven with the fabric of everyday life" (288). Much of the affective quality of the documents that Foucault enjoys so much stems from the unusual social circumstances surrounding these documents: "the petitioners for internment were lodged by illiterate or semiliterate persons of humble circumstance" and "with their meager skills . . . would compose as best they could the formulas or turns of phrase they believed to be required when one addressed the king or high officials" (290). The explanatory apparatus that Foucault generates in the latter half of the essay pushes against his opening gambit to allow these brief fragments simply to occupy a delicate, ineffable space.

While this latter set of concerns might seem to be more central to the general Foucauldian project, the first set of questions about the past and marginality would be foregrounded in the American criticism that claimed to be inspired by his work. Or, perhaps more appropriately, the split between Foucault the archivist and Foucault the cartographer serves as a useful shorthand for two basic conceptualizations circulating in English studies of how the socius is organized (and both of which cited French theory as a support for this writing). Generally speaking, the "archival" model corresponds to a liberal model of identity politics that pinpoints the state as the primary pivot for analysis. Envisioning the state as a largely homogenous entity that has long rejected difference, it demands that marginal groups and ideas be recognized and adequately represented within that system. The fundamental political gesture of work can be seen in its desire to "recover" lost voices that diversify and complicate the past and present. The "cartographic" model, meanwhile, while sharing much with the "archivist" model in approach, diverges in a number of crucial ways. Although it sees the state as an important operator within the socius, the cartographic model focuses on broader structural forces that function beyond the complete control of the state. While these forces are highly mobile and thrive on difference and reversibility, they do not promise political liberation—in fact, they are often more debilitating than the hierarchical power of the state. The cartographic model also cares less about diversity for its own sake (or as the end point of its analysis) than in using it as a springboard for further investigation. In other words, it understands the pivotal categories of the archival model as effects of this structure rather than as fundamental units. I want to stress that my use of "archival" here does not refer strictly to archival work as such. In fact, there is plenty of existing archival work in English studies that would be decidedly "cartographic."[3]

It remains an open question how to characterize the relationship between these two models. In many ways, they could be understood as completely incompatible or antagonistic; the model of identity politics unintentionally serves as a containment strategy that prevents examining the structural operations at work that produce undesirable power relations. Or they could be understood as complementary models that should be strategically combined or distinguished based on changing circumstances. Or one model could be seen as a preliminary or preparatory step for the other. Or critics can unknowingly oscillate between these two models from one moment to the next and generate strange synthetic models. My point here is not to decide the superiority of either of these models so much as it is to say that both circulate within contemporary academic criticism as ways of interpreting texts and archival materials and as ways of articulating the political effects that critics hope their work will produce.

The most conspicuous and influential critical movement within the social turn in literary studies, the New Historicism demonstrates how the archival and cartographic approaches intermingle in strange and unpredictable ways. Although both approaches can be located within work identifying itself as New Historicist, the archival model has tended to be emphasized. When Catherine Gallagher and Stephen Greenblatt, reluctant spokespeople for this critical movement (that refuses to consider itself a movement), engage with Foucault in their reflective work *Practicing New Historicism*, they examine "The Lives of Infamous Men" largely for the dilemmas presented in the opening pages and downplay the dynamics found in the elaborate analysis in the piece's second half. At just the moment that they are prompted to explore the other half of Foucault's essay, they abandon "The Lives of Infamous Men" and turn to the anecdote that opens *The Order of Things* so as to rehearse the same conceptual dilemmas through another text. The emphasis on these passages in Foucault at expense of other sections is a result of the New Historicists' investment in recovering the reality of past cultures and a corresponding realization that such efforts will, at best, be short-lived. Earlier in *Practicing New Historicism*, Gallagher and Greenblatt confess a desire for their criticism to recover "a confident conviction of reality" and experience a "touch of the real" (31). This complements Stephen Greenblatt's admission in *Shakespearean Negotiations* of his "desire to speak with the dead" (1). What the New Historicists find so compelling in Foucault is the endless cycle of being confronted by the singular strangeness of the past and ultimately "normalizing" this strangeness through an explanatory historical narrative. As Gallagher and Greenblatt explain, the New Historicists found in Foucault "an author who could acknowledge and reflect on the *pathos* of anecdotalism: the strong desire to preserve the energies of the anecdote by channeling them into historical explanation, which is followed by frustration and disappointment when the historical project stills and stifles the very energies that provoked it" (68). Gallagher and Greenblatt assert that Foucault "seemed to be living" the paradoxes of counterhistory "as an intense drama that all of us shared whenever we set out, as we constantly did, to capture the animation, the dynamism, of things that were bound to become inert and passive under our disciplinary gaze" (68). There is a "knot binding the desire to resurrect life and the power to end it" (70). From their perspective, Foucault cannot escape the realization that his own work is part of the power structure that began by condemning these marginal figures to death. Even though he wants to bring them to light and reveal unacknowledged marginal figures from the past, he recognizes that the desire to do so merely repeats the ways in which these individuals were brought under the gaze of power.

Although it would be difficult to deny that these concerns are not operating in Foucault's writing, his work seems primarily occupied with a different set of questions. Foucault's itinerary moves in an altogether different direction from the majority of New Historicists; the New Historicists' preoccupation with the dilemma of silencing the past in the attempt to recover it proves to be something of a provisional throat-clearing gesture within his work. Broadly varying statements throughout his corpus point to these differences. Take, for instance, the final moments in the introduction to *Discipline and Punish*, where he announces his intention of writing a history of the modern penitentiary system. "Why? Simply because I am interested in the past? No, if one means by that writing a history of the past in terms of the present" (31). Here, Foucault acknowledges the impossibility of ever transcending the limitations of one's own moment in order to accurately seize the past as it unfolded in its unique specificity and he appears unwilling to simply rehearse the endless failure to escape one's presentist biases. Foucault's project—what he calls a "history of the present" (31)—is admittedly "presentist." His explorations of past phenomenon exist only insofar as they help him better understand the specific arrangement of forces that structure the present day. This is the "cartographer" Foucault, a figure who relishes in constructing genealogies that include both discontinuities *and* continuities.

The reasons motivating Gallagher and Greenblatt's emphasis on the "archival" over the "cartographic"—a decisive reversal from that in Foucault—becomes clear once we see its connection to the social democratic values that they understand their work to be advancing. Their desire to have "an encounter with the singular, the specific, and the individual" has an unapologetically liberal political agenda behind it, one meant to promote difference against stifling conformity. Looking at the other inspirations for the New Historicism reveals that these critics saw their work operating within a larger political context where progressive, marginal social groups were battling a dominating, totalitarian power. For instance, their turn to the anecdote, meant to puncture the grand narratives of official history, correlates to the figure of Eric Auerbach. Their appreciation for his use of textual fragments to construct compelling analytic readings is necessarily connected to the political context in which his magnum opus, *Mimesis*, was composed. They argue that Auerbach's "informed appreciation of multiple styles bespeaks a kind of cultural catholicity, an openness to alternative ways of responding to the world" during a period when a war was raging and the enemy "would have consigned him to the gas chamber" (42). Auerbach's attention to difference and particular textual strategies for representing the world are placed within the much broader context of a fight against fascism. Gallagher and Greenblatt see their own work as a continuation of this fight, albeit in less dire circumstances. In the opening pages of *Practicing New Historicism*, they make clear that their work was inspired by the social movements of the 1960s, noting that women's studies served as a "model for new historicism in that it has inspired its adherents to identify new objects for study, bring those objects into the light of critical attention, and insist upon their legitimate place in the curriculum" (11). They regard the social movements of the 1960s as structurally analogous to the fight against totalitarianism during World War II—they want to preserve and promote previously marginalized pockets of difference against a homogenizing central power.

At the same time, however, New Historicists often work to extend the broader "cartographic" work found in Foucault's analyses. In fact, this cartographic work can be found in the writing of figures who also advance a notion of "archival" politics, thereby underscoring the important point that the relationship between the "archival" and the "cartographic" cannot be reduced to a simple antagonism or opposition. For instance, in the opening essay to H. Aram Veeser's 1989 collection *The New Historicism*, Greenblatt examines the impersonal structural forces that Foucault seems preoccupied with tracing. He writes that "capitalism has characteristically generated neither regimes in which all discourses seem coordinated, nor regimes in which they seem radically isolated or discontinuous, but regimes in which the drive towards differentiation and the drive towards monological organization operate simultaneously, or at least oscillate so rapidly as to create the impression of simultaneity" (6). From his perspective, the oscillation between these two regimes is "built into the poetics of everyday behavior in America," suggesting that he too, like Foucault, is concerned with the broader structural dynamics that would produce the strange idiosyncratic personalities that his "archival" work is intent on recovering.

But in many cases, a mix between the archival and cartographic forms produces a strange mixture wherein the state is ascribed more power than it deserves. New Historicism's tendency to read the cartographic model through the lens of the archival model explains its peculiar investment in "co-optation," a concept ostensibly derived from Foucault. As Veeser articulates in the introduction to his collection, these "key assumptions continually reappear and bind together practitioners" of the titular critical practice: "that every act of unmasking, critique, and opposition uses the tools it condemns and risks falling prey to the practices it exposes" and—what may amount to a simple rephrasing of the first point—"that a critical method and a language adequate to describe culture under capitalism participate in the economy they describe" (xi). This formulation that regards co-optation as an unavoidable ontological reality takes certain positions in Foucault's corpus and combines them with a preexisting preoccupation with state power. Taking Foucault's dictum that there is no "outside" to power, New Historicism reads this as a case of an inevitable appropriation of the energies of the margins that will be diluted through contact with a homogenizing power. Gerald Graff articulates the specific dynamics of this process later in Veeser's collection, explaining that New

Historicism outlines how "societies exert control over their subjects not just by imposing constraints on them but by predetermining the ways they attempt to rebel against those constraints, by co-opting their strategies of dissent" (168–169). What Graff's cogent formulation reveals is the degree to which "co-optation" assumes a starting point of authenticity that is then corrupted (typically unknowingly). Frank Lentricchia's analysis later in the volume further underlines the degree to which Foucault is seized by the New Historicists and fashioned into a thinker of an inescapable totalitarian power. He writes that "Greenblatt's account of the 'I,' like Foucault's, will dramatize its entrapment in a totalitarian narrative coincidental with the emergence of the modern world as dystopian fruition" (235). As Lentricchia's subsequent sentence makes explicit, Foucault is equated to an updated version of the paranoid musings found in George Orwell's *1984*. While I find Lentricchia's assessment compelling in its generalities, his conflation of Foucault and Greenblatt remains problematic.

In the first volume of *The History of Sexuality*, Foucault dispels this version of power relations that Lentricchia ascribes to him. He writes that "power is everywhere; not because it embraces everything, but because it comes from everywhere" (93). He clarifies the point: "Should it be said that one is always 'inside' power, there is no 'escaping' it, there is no absolute outside where it is concerned . . . [that] power is the ruse of history, always emerging the winner?" (95). Foucault clearly rejects this formulation. Indeed, his analysis of power, which he insists cannot be reduced to an "institution" or "structure," seems to be interested in moving beyond the sovereign model of the state to a distributed form of relations that cannot be directly tied back to a central authority. Meanwhile, during his analysis of the Panopticon in *Discipline and Punish*, he anticipates Lentricchia's critique a decade later. Against the New Historicists (and their critics) who see it as the pinnacle of the totalitarian state, Foucault stresses that it should not be understood as a "dream building" but instead as "the diagram of a mechanism of power reduced to its ideal form" (205). The Panopticon should not be taken as a general metaphor for diagnosing the social world at large but instead a particular apparatus that works in varying degrees of intensity in localized sites. But it is difficult to read Foucault in this manner if one begins with certain assumptions about the centrality of the state as the dominant form of power in the contemporary world.

At this point, I will adopt a signature move from New Historicism to further contextualize that critical camp's emergence in literary criticism. As Gallagher and Greenblatt make clear in *Practicing the New Historicism*, one of the chief gestures in their writing involves incorporating literary works that had been previously overlooked and crowning them as "major achievements" (10). While Gallagher and Greenblatt's admit that their initial interest may have resided in canonical figures, these new voices make clear that the literary "achievements that have seemed like entirely isolated monuments are disclosed to have a more complex interrelation with other texts by 'minor' authors'" (10). By their account, their critical work "helps raise questions about originality in art and about the status of 'genius' as an explanatory term, along with the status of the distinction between 'major' and 'minor'" (10). What if this same maneuver were applied to *critical texts* as well as *literary texts*? Using their own interpretive protocols, one of the first steps toward properly understanding the New Historicism (and the social turn within English studies more broadly) would involve putting its central documents in conversation with less prestigious work circulating within the same general economy of written material. Although Gallagher and Greenblatt problematize the notion of genius that attaches itself to the traditional canonical text, their very problematization often receives the same sort of breathless deferential treatment afforded these quasi-divine writings. "New Historicism" has, in many real ways, been canonized much like the writing their criticism works against reifying. What might Gallagher and Greenblatt, paragons of elite coastal universities, and their work look like when situated next to less distinguished criticism composed in the American heartland and rustbelt during the same period?

The Archival Impulse in English Studies

Within English studies, James Berlin's work emerged at the same time as the New Historicism and helps complicate the standard narrative of the discipline. Take this programmatic statement about the direction of the discipline:

> Rather than organizing its activities around the preservation and maintenance of a sacred canon of literary texts, it would focus on the production, distribution, exchange, and reception of textuality, in general and specific cases, both in the past and present. English studies would thus explore the role of signifying practices in the ongoing life of societies—stated more specifically, in their relations to economic, social, political, and cultural arrangements. (113)

While one might be tempted, given the preceding analysis, to attribute this statement to Gallagher or Greenblatt, it actually can be found in Berlin's *Rhetorics, Poetics, and Cultures*. Although this work was not published until

1996, two years after Berlin's untimely death, it can be considered a summation of work that Berlin had been producing since the early 1980s. Although his gradate work at the University of Michigan focused on Victorian literature, Berlin's professional research agenda focused on the history of rhetorical education in American universities and rhetoric's role in contemporary debates in college curricula. Beginning with 1982's *College English* article "Contemporary Composition: The Major Pedagogical Theories" and extending through his major publications, 1984's *Writing Instruction in Nineteenth-Century American Colleges* and 1987's *Rhetoric and Reality: Writing Instruction in American Colleges, 1900–1985*, Berlin sounds a refrain that shares much with someone like Greenblatt, whose major pieces of New Historicism, 1980's *Renaissance Self-Fashioning* and 1988's *Shakespearean Negotiations*, bookended the same decade.

Much like the New Historicists, Berlin draws upon Foucault to anchor his project, and while his reading of Foucault is split between the philosopher's "cartographic" and "archival" dimensions, his work ultimately emphasizes the latter features. In the introduction to *Rhetoric and Reality*, Berlin counts Foucault, along with Kenneth Burke and Hayden White, as his main theoretical inspirations. Berlin's most extensive treatment of Foucault can be found in *Rhetorics, Poetics, and Cultures*, where he characterizes Foucault and Jean François Lyotard as "the two most conspicuous figures" in the challenge against "Enlightenment claims for the power of reason in arriving at universal truths" (66). From Berlin's perspective, Foucault offers a version of history that eschews any "confidence in subjects as completely free makers of history and in reason as the principle undergirding human action" (66). His description of Foucault's project as a documentation of how individuals serve as "instruments of impersonal institutions" (67) hints that he may be more invested in a structural, "cartographic" approach than an "archival" one. Yet, in the next breath, Berlin swerves away from the implications of these insights. He claims that Foucault "is particularly interested in exploring those historical events that represent resistance to the dominant power-knowledge formations, stories of the victims of history that have been ignored. Here the coherent narratives of conventional histories are especially repudiated" (67). The rest of his work seems informed by this final assessment, enlisting Foucault to undermine "dominant power-knowledge formations" like the "objective rhetoric" of current-traditional pedagogies that cast their own interested perspectives as universal truths.

Indeed, Berlin mobilizes those threads within Foucault's work that contribute to the promotion of a broad social democratic movement. Berlin's particular formation of Foucault can be pinpointed more easily if we look to the main source through which he understands Foucault: Göran Therborn's *The Ideology of Power and the Power of Ideology*. Berlin explains in "Rhetoric and Ideology in the Writing Class" that Therborn's analysis insightfully weaves together the strengths of both Althusser and Foucault while discarding their weaknesses. Berlin finds Therborn's reading of Althusser attractive because it rejects the claims of scientific objectivity of Marxism found throughout his work. He agrees with Therborn that it is not a choice "between scientific truth and ideology, but between competing ideologies, competing discursive interpretations" (478). Meanwhile, Therborn adopts Foucault's analysis of the "micropolitics of power" without having to situate subjects "within a seamless web of inescapable, wholly determinative power relations." As a result, "power can be identified and resisted in a meaningful way" (478). In Berlin's endorsement of Therborn and his specific deployment of Foucault, we hear echoes of Lentricchia's dismissal of New Historicism and Foucault as a totalitarian cage that allows no room for resistance. Refusing to discard him entirely, however, Berlin offers a reparative reading of Foucault. The opening pages of "Rhetoric and Ideology in the Writing Class" reveal that this reparative reading treats Foucault as a supplement to Althusser, a way of allowing the ideology of state apparatuses to infiltrate everyday language and activities.

If Berlin actualizes the "archival" dimensions of Foucault's thought at the thematic level in his work, he actualizes the "cartographic" features at the formal or methodological level. Departing from the New Historicists, his conception of history writing unabashedly foregrounds its unavoidably "presentist" orientation. In the introduction to *Rhetoric and Reality*, Berlin responds to Robert J. Connors's objections that his first book failed to be an objective account of writing instruction in American colleges in the nineteenth century. Berlin denies Connors's assumption "that it is possible to locate a neutral space, a position from which one can act as an unbiased observer in order to record a transcendental object, the historical thing-in-itself" (17). Rather than simply rehearsing the failure to seize the past in all its radical alterity like the New Historicists, Berlin foregrounds his limited perspective and thereby provides an alternative rationale for conducting historical research. As he explains in the opening moments of "Rhetoric and Ideology in the Writing Class," his surveys of rhetorical education in American universities are meant to intervene in the present moment. The competing rhetorical approaches to textual consumption and production that he outlines—his taxonomy comprises objective rhetoric, subjectivist rhetoric, and transactional (later called social-epistemic) rhetoric—are not objective phenomenon but provisional categories meant to facilitate a practical agenda. If Berlin's disciplinary histories trace the fates of these three different modes of rhetoric, Berlin does not hesitate to announce that his narrative is motivated by a desire to promote social-epistemic rhetoric. While all three rhetorics operate at any given moment in history, one tends to be dominant (typically, it has been objective rhetoric), and Berlin envisions his narrative as a way of mapping the present moment and providing a justification for endorsing social-epistemic rhetoric. Berlin admits that he is "arguing from ideology" and that his support of social-epistemic rhetoric "provides the ground of my critique of its alternatives" (478).

If Berlin's histories are deliberately practical analyses meant to inspire change in the present, one feature of these works that warrants further exploration is Berlin's conceptualization of contemporary literary studies. In *Rhetorics, Poetics, and Cultures*, Berlin argues, "English studies was founded on a set of hierarchical binary oppositions in which literary texts were given an idealized status approaching the sacred" (xiv). To be sure, this characterization works fairly well in terms of assessing critical conceptions of the literary work earlier in the century. Several pages later, Berlin maintains that these oppositions still adhere in the present moment: "all that is important and central in the study of discourse falls within the domain of literary texts and all that is unimportant and marginal falls within the realm of rhetoric" (3). But as my previous analysis of Gallagher and Greenblatt illustrated, literary studies had already made internal steps toward problematizing the sacredness of the literary text and placing it on the same social plane as other texts. When Berlin insists that "workers in rhetoric . . . find themselves aligned with department colleagues in literary theory and cultural studies" in "challenging the dominant hierarchies of texts and tasks in the discipline" (xvi) he posits fairly clear separations between rhetoric, literary studies, and theory/cultural studies. In doing so, however, Berlin seems to overlook the degree to which theory had been integrated into the everyday workings of literary studies. Berlin wants rhetoric and theory to join forces against the worst tendencies in literary studies, but his proposal overlooks an emerging consensus throughout the discourse. Rather than point out the inaccuracy of Berlin's claim, I suggest we instead understand the statement as a savvy tactical move.

We might understand Berlin's decision as a way of situating the emerging discourse of Rhetoric and Composition as a marginalized discourse warranting closer attention. If the "social turn" in English studies was generally oriented around recognizing and incorporating the marginal and the different, Rhetoric and Composition could strengthen the case for greater visibility and influence in English studies by positioning *itself* as a marginal and different entity. Rhetoric and Composition, which was still in a position of defining itself as a field and consolidating its strengths, drew upon fundamental maneuvers from the social movements of the 1960s to lend an additional degree of importance or authority to the work that was being generated during this time. Berlin's decision to cast Rhetoric and Composition in this light is less surprising when we learn that his books are among the first monographs of the field. Although a few important full-length books on composition (most notably Janet Emig's *The Composing Processes of Twelfth Graders* and Mina Shaughnessy's *Errors and Expectations*) had been published in the 1970s, it was not until early in the following decade that the field began producing scholarly monographs en masse. Scanning through the book review section of *College Composition and Communication* reveals a decisive shift in the early 1980s from solely reviewing composition textbooks to mostly reviewing scholarly monographs on writing and rhetoric. Southern Illinois University Press's series "Studies in Writing and Rhetoric," which began in 1984 with five titles including Berlin's *Writing Instruction in Nineteenth-Century Colleges*, marks the beginning of a concerted effort to showcase innovative work in the burgeoning field. In order to acquire credibility and cultural capital to improve its standing in the discipline, this discourse had to fortify its foundations. The most obvious way Rhetoric and Composition accomplished this goal was by connecting itself to rhetoric, a tradition dating back to the ancient Greeks (far longer than any literary tradition). But it also did so by asserting that the field had already long been in existence and had simply been overlooked. At some level, the field required a quickly evaporating version of literary studies (one oriented around sacred texts) as a foil to solidify its own standing.

As a result, histories of composition studies proliferated during this period and have become a staple of the discourse. One of the field's most important early composition historians, Robert J. Connors offers a compelling explanation of this trend. Indeed, in addition to producing specific analyses of particular moments and movements within the history of composition studies, Connors should be counted as one of the field's earliest thinkers on the value of writing history for the field of Rhetoric and Composition. In his essay "Composition History and Disciplinarity," he documents the growth of historical accounts of Rhetoric and Composition, including the groundbreaking work of Kate Adams, James Berlin, Sharon Crowley, Nan Johnson, Tom Miller, David Russell, and Bill Woods. While Connors claims that many of these figures wrote histories "simply because they were fascinated by it" (411) he also asserts that "we were also writing history in order to create ourselves as members of a discipline . . . [and] unify it" (412). Connors clarifies this position in the essay "Dreams and Play: Historical Method and Methodology," declaring that the act of writing history is "the telling of stories about the tribe that make the tribe real" (234). From his perspective, "the recovery of composition history" is "so important" because in "telling the stories of our fathers and our mothers . . . we are legitimating ourselves through legitimating them" (234).

The double meaning in the following book titles by specialists in Rhetoric and Composition confirms Connors's claims: *Rhetoric at the Margins*, *Writing from the Margins*, and *Writing on the Margins*. Beyond the obvious fact that the concept of marginality assumes a prominent role in the discourse, these titles all suggest the close connection forged between the subject matter being analyzed and the investigator conducting the analysis. In the case of the first book, David Gold's *Rhetoric at the Margins*, which explores writing instruction at three small colleges during the late nineteenth and early twentieth centuries, the title is meant to refer to the instructional practices at schools that serve minorities who are marginalized both from society at large and from "elite" educational institutions (Gold's book examines one African American college, a women's college, and a normal college for working-class students). But the title might also be read as a description of the author of said analyses—the field of Rhetoric and Composition is "at the margins" of English studies. An implicit connection is made between unearthing the lost voices of the past and the field's current disciplinary status. By documenting marginalized figures and incorporating them into the growing history of Rhetoric and Composition, not only will these historical figures escape their marginalized position. Additionally, the discourse that has brought these figures to light will also assume a more centralized role within English studies insofar as the account will further solidify Rhetoric and Composition's own history, thereby granting it more legitimacy as an academic area of interest. A similar dynamic operates in a title like Jessica Enoch's *Refiguring Rhetorical Education*. In documenting the teaching practices of female instructors of African Americans, Native Americans, and Chicano/a students from 1865 to 1911, Enoch hopes to bring to light the innovative teaching practices of neglected marginal figures from the past. She also envisions her work as a way of contributing to current efforts "to revitalize rhetorical education in the twenty-first century" (11). In refiguring the rhetorical educational practices of the past, Enoch aims to simultaneously refigure the status of Rhetoric and Composition today. The discipline's strategy might best be encapsulated in the title of Sheryl Fontaine and Susan Hunter's 1993 edited collection *Writing Ourselves into the Story: Unheard Voices from Composition Studies.*[4]

In fact, the field is so united around the concept of marginalization that one might see the competing modes of historiography in composition studies as simply two sides to the same coin. In his essay "Writing the History of Our Discipline," Connors maintains that revisionist historiography in Rhetoric and Composition has divided into two competing camps: "those who seek to promote a specific program or perspective, and those who point out the incompleteness, potential for totalization, or naiveté of any specific program or perspective" (216). Connors counts Sharon Crowley, Jan Swearingen, James Berlin, and Wallace Douglas in the first group and Victor Vitanza, John Schilb, and Susan Jarratt in the second group. Although certain emphases and values obviously separate these groups, closer inspection suggests that they share an underlying foundation. If the first group engages in "recovering heretofore marginal figures in rhetorical history" (216) while the second group problematize the act of writing history by showing "the undecidablity of meaning in texts" (217), both parties seem equally committed to challenging a notion of totalization. While this goal is made more explicit in the latter camp, particularly in the work of Vitanza, the former camp's focus on marginalized figures, while making objective claims, does so in the service of overturning the existing "grand narratives" of English studies that exclude composition. So long as first group's recovery of marginalized figures remains an ongoing process that continually revises its own insights, it can be considered to largely conform to the second group. In this respect, beneath the seeming antagonism among its various practitioners, the historians share an implicit attachment to marginalization that orients their various research investigations.

Examining Rhetoric and Composition's emphasis on marginalization serves as a useful way of exploring tensions that the field has never been able to escape. Wanting to achieve the status of a respected area of study, Rhetoric and Composition has often had to indulge in the qualities and practices that it finds most problematic. Connors's ambivalence about the growing success of Rhetoric and Composition as an area of research is symptomatic of a fundamental tension structuring the field: "I know I am not the only one . . . who has viewed the growing success and status—what I think of as the 'MLA-ization'—of the field with strongly conflicted feelings. We entered composition work out of a deep dissatisfaction with the fatuity of overly specialized and theoretical literary studies—but we brought more baggage from that world than we meant to" (420). Against Connors, who seems to regard this "MLA-ization" as an unfortunate accident that could have been avoided with more vigilance, I would argue that the turn toward specialization and theorization is a necessary condition for the field to emerge and gain respect at all, since some form of theoretical problematization is what founds a research area in the first place. The field's numerous research publications lamenting the academy's focus on research underscores this point (Spellmeyer's article from my introduction serves as a paradigmatic example). While making compelling arguments that teaching and service constitute important forms of intellectual work that should be counted toward tenure and promotion, this writing cannot escape its own formal character—that is, as scholarly research—that undermines some of its critical thrust.

A related tension organizes the field's commitment to a notion of politics that uses the concepts of recognition and respect as a way to assess all structural issues. By necessity, it has to lean toward the "archival" rather than the "cartographic." This is not the fault of any of its individual practitioners so much as it is an indication of the contradictions governing the discourse. At some level, Rhetoric and Composition would be remarkably well positioned to address the structural issues that create exploitative labor practices, since it confronts them more directly than literary studies. However, it has tended to interpret this exploitation in terms of respect and recognition (a matter of persuading a powerful and homogenous center to appreciate different or marginal practices like itself) because the discourse of Rhetoric and Composition is actually distinct from those suffering from structural inequalities. In other words, the demand for "respect" and "recognition" has been an overriding concern in the vast majority of scholarship in Rhetoric and Composition since that is the terrain on which it can justify the study of writing as a research agenda to its colleagues in the rest of the department. According to this argument, rhetoric and writing are not respected as much as literary studies and the way to end the exploitative labor seen in composition teaching is to foreground the intellectual depth of research in this area. Understanding politics largely in terms of inclusion and exclusion, Rhetoric and Composition argues that it has been excluded because it is different from literary studies and only by highlighting its unique contributions to intellectual study will the exploitation of its practitioners be addressed. Unfortunately, Rhetoric and Composition's desire to be represented and respected as a field of intellectual inquiry conflicts with its capacity to illuminate the structural labor inequalities that plague the discipline. Merely "respecting" the research discourse that investigates writing practices will not automatically lead to equality among all those who teach in an English department. Similarly,

the exploitation of cheap adjunct labor cannot be directly connected to issues of recognition and respect, since merely respecting the composition
teacher (and his or her students) will not cleanly translate into the elimination of their exploitation.[5]

I would like to stress here that I am generalizing about the field. There
are a significant number of critics who have articulated a similar version
of what I am advancing. But it bears repeating that a rights-based politics
of recognition always presents itself as an attractive option for diagnosing the ills plaguing Rhetoric and Composition, even among those who
at some level recognize its limitations. Take, for instance, Joseph Harris's
article "Meet the New Boss, Same as the Old Boss: Class Consciousness in
Composition," published in *College Composition and Communication* in 2000.
Here, he cogently points out that attention is usually shifted "away from
present and real labor practices—who does what work for what pay—
and toward questions about the potential disciplinary status of composition" (56). From his perspective, "we need to distinguish between questions of disciplinary status and working conditions," recognizing that "the
two issues are connected but not identical" (57). But while he distinguishes
between these two concerns, he quietly imports useful concepts from one
arena in order to fix the other, arguing that "what teachers want" in addition to reasonable pay and work conditions is "to be treated with respect
as colleagues" (57). Responding to this assertion, Marc Bousquet corrects
Harris by explaining that "what a large sector of composition labor . . .
'really wants,' is not to be '*treated . . . as* colleagues,' but instead to *be* colleagues" (*How* 182). The term that Bousquet excises from his quotation of
Harris—"respect"—actually provides the key for approaching some substantial issues within the political imaginary in contemporary composition
studies.

The Administrative Suture

The previous section adopted a fundamental gesture of New Historicism
to contextualize the New Historicism itself, situating the work of Gallagher and Greenblatt by putting it in dialogue with the work of James Berlin and other historians of composition. This section extends that gesture
further. As Gallagher and Greenblatt explain, New Historicism does not
simply bring noncanonical literary works into conversation with canonical
literary works; it also incorporates texts that would not be considered literary. Novels, poems, and plays can only be fully understood if they are
placed alongside legal documents, business plans, and other decidedly

nonliterary texts. Retaining the loose analogy between literary works and critical works, my discussion of the social turn in English studies should, in following the spirit of the New Historicism, also examine writing that would not be considered critical scholarship but that nevertheless circulates within the same network of textual artifacts and plays a decisive role in how we interpret these critical texts. Speaking more concretely, I explore how the scholarship of the social turn in English studies should not be separated from broader changes in the university during this period and the administrative discourse that has accompanied these changes.

Donna Strickland's 2011 *The Managerial Unconscious in the History of Composition Studies*, a revisionary history of the field of Rhetoric and Composition, serves as a useful starting point for examining the interaction between "critical" and "non-critical" texts since her analysis addresses the intersection of disciplinary scholarship with institutional demands. Detailing pivotal moments in Rhetoric and Composition's institutional development, most notably the founding of the Conference on College Composition and Communication (CCCC) in 1949 and the establishment of the Council of Writing Program Administrators (WPA) in 1977, Strickland asserts that historians of the field have not fully appreciated the importance of these professional organizations. From her perspective, these organizations reveal that composition specialists have long been governed by a managerial impulse. While most (if not all) English professors split their time among research, teaching, and administrative duties, Strickland's analysis stresses that composition specialists' research and teaching interests have a unique relationship with these administrative tasks. Although they freely teach their own courses and conduct research about liberatory pedagogical strategies, they also impose orders on an underclass of precarious untenured adjunct instructors. The gap between its professed values and its daily administrative practices produces a schizophrenic experience for many working in the field. As Strickland explains, "to profess composition . . . is to occupy a position unlike most other professors of English" insofar as it "is to study one thing and to do quite another" (2). Strickland wisely notes how the "social turn" in the 1980s and 1990s—her primary target is none other than James Berlin—which advanced a liberatory pedagogy valorizing equality and democratic participation, possesses an ironic subtext when put in dialogue with the increasing hierarchical bureaucratization of the labor force teaching this material. Rhetoric and Composition is split between widespread espousals of democracy as a value and its increasing scarcity as an actual practice in the field.

Strickland's analysis suggests that this gap is being closed, but not in a way that most would consider desirable. Scholarship in Rhetoric and Composition is becoming increasingly organized according to these administrative demands—or, perhaps more appropriately, administrative strategizing has begun to count as a form of scholarship—thereby dissolving the once sturdy boundaries between these two spheres. The founding of the WPA in 1977 marks the period when scholarship with a decidedly administrative tenor would assume a legitimate position within the institution. Although the founding of the CCCC in 1949 was designed to support composition professionals, most of the research produced by these scholars was a step removed from the administrative duties they were expected to perform. As Strickland points out, "what seems surprising is that composition professionals felt, some twenty-five years after the founding of the CCCC, the need for a new organization devoted exclusively to administration" (76). After all, as her earlier analysis revealed, "the CCCC itself had come into being to meet the needs of composition professionals, which more often than not meant administrators rather than simply teachers" (76). The founding of both the WPA and its journal *WPA: Writing Program Administration* signal a shift whereby one's research agenda could explicitly focus (at least in part) on one's administrative responsibilities. Not only a blurring of the boundaries between scholarship and administration, the emergence of what we might call "administrative scholarship" hints at a shift in priority away from scholarship and toward administration. Rather than being conducted for its own sake, scholarship is conducted in the service of more efficient administrative service. While admittedly a small fraction of the scholarship produced within English studies, "administrative scholarship" has continued to grow, evident in the emergence of scholarship on the assessment of college writing.[6]

Published only a month after *The Managerial Unconscious*, Benjamin Ginsberg's 2011 *The Fall of the Faculty* not only provides a compelling narrative of the sweeping changes to higher education over the past several decades but also includes a helpful account of the discursive regime that has emerged to facilitate this transformation. His tale recounts the slow transfer of power in the university away from the faculty and into the hands of a ballooning administration. As Ginsberg points out, while the growth of full-time faculty has barely kept pace with the growth of the student population, administrative positions have increased by over 80 percent (and administrative staff positions have increased by 240 percent). While the faculty-to-student ratio has remained basically unchanged between 1975 and 2005, the administrator-to-student ratio has shrunk drastically: from 1 administrator for every 84 students to 1 administrator for every 68 students. Ginsberg writes that "as colleges and universities had more money to spend they chose not to spend it on expanding their instructional resources, i.e., faculty. They chose, instead, to enhance their administrative and staff resources" (26–27). From his perspective, the growth in university administration has led to a decline in the power of the faculty to influence policy and make decisions. An "army of professional staffers" has become "the bulwark of administrative power in the contemporary university"; before they created this army, "administrators were forced to rely on the cooperation of the faculty to carry out tasks ranging from admissions through planning" (25).

The administrative takeover of higher education has stifled diversity in two important ways. Most obviously, it has centralized decision making and transformed the faculty into employees fulfilling the whims of their administrative superiors. Furthermore, the actual policy initiatives inaugurated by administrations have a strikingly similar feel regardless of the institution. As Ginsberg explains, professors tend to "advance their careers by advancing ideas different from and superior to those of their professional colleagues. The same is most definitely not true of administrators. In my four decades in the academy I have seldom heard an administrator voice an idea that diverged much from those concurrently being articulated by virtually every other administrator. Imitation seems to be the norm in the world of higher education administration" (135). Sometimes this imitation borders on outright plagiarism, and Ginsberg's analysis of contemporary universities' "strategic plans" illustrates a striking case of this problem. "Similar phrases and paragraphs can be found in many plans," Ginsberg explains, describing a case where the chancellor of Southern Illinois University was forced to resign when it was discovered that he had copied portions of Texas A&M University's strategic plan. Ironically enough, administrative plagiarism is very common in "diversity planning" documents. Johns Hopkins University's 2008 "Commission on Equity, Civility, and Respect" ultimately generated policy recommendations "remarkably similar in character" to those made by the University of Virginia several years before (113). There is a lack of diversity when it comes to statements about diversity within the administrative ranks of the university.

In *The University in Ruins*, Bill Readings proposes an alternative to this top-heavy managerial form. In the eighth chapter of the book, Readings explains that he wants to articulate a new function for the University, one distinct from "the vast majority of those who" articulate "either nostalgic calls for a return to the Humboldtian ideals of modular community and social functioning, or technocratic demands that the University embrace its corporate identity and become more productive, more efficient" (125). Rejecting both of these options, Readings argues that the university should become a site where knowledge is produced and circulated without being tied to a "notion of identity or unity" (127). He declares that "we should seek to turn the deferentialization that is characteristic of the posthistorical University to good advantage. That is to say, we should try to think what it may mean to have a University that has no idea, that does not derive its name from an etymological confusion of unity and universality" (122). From his perspective, the university must be a place where questions are never settled conclusively but are instead constantly discussed and reassessed. The question of value should always be central to the university, particularly the value of the university itself. Readings envisions a university where those in it "have to speak amongst themselves and to others in terms that acknowledge the complexity of the problem of quality" (132). Any judgment about the purpose or value of the university must itself be judged (and this judgment must be judged in turn, ad infinitum), such that any metrics used to evaluate performance will always remain provisional tools at best. Readings detests the idea that a completely "objective" metric could ever be devised that would settle the question of value once and for all, noting that a huge gap exists between "accounting" and "accountability."

Readings's analysis shares much with the work of Alain Badiou, who in *Manifesto for Philosophy* makes an impassioned plea for the practice of philosophy to root itself in dissensus. Badiou argues that philosophical thinking arrives at knowledge through four distinct and incompatible "truth procedures": poetry, politics, math, and love. Each of these procedures arrives at knowledge through a different set of questions that cannot be reduced to the other three. Arguing that philosophy requires all four truth procedures in order to remain vibrant, Badiou warns that often one of these truth procedures takes precedence over the others so that philosophy becomes completely tethered to a single form of inquiry. He calls this situation a "suture" and writes that "philosophy is placed in suspension every time it presents itself as being sutured to one of its conditions" (61). Badiou regards much of twentieth-century philosophical thought as being sutured to the poetic truth procedure, most evident in the work of Martin Heidegger and his followers. Badiou's "manifesto" for philosophy amounts to "desuturing" it from the poetic truth procedure so that it can reconnect once again to politics, math, and love. Although Badiou may undercut his own argument by ultimately calling for a new suture for philosophy—this time math rather than poetry—the basic model and vocabulary that he provides are enormously helpful in thinking through a site rooted in perpetual dissensus.

Indeed, Readings's notion of the university as "a locus of dissensus" resonates strongly with Badiou's conceptual schema insofar as we replace "philosophy" with the "university." As Readings explains, the contemporary university is composed of three distinct functions: research, teaching, and administration. From his perspective, the University of Excellence is the name for a university governed by what we might call an "administrative suture." As Readings explains, "the University of Excellence is one in which a general principle of administration replaces the dialectic of teaching and research, so that teaching and research, as aspects of professional life, are subsumed under administration" (125). The logic of accounting that underwrites the administrative suture shapes the practices of both teaching and research. For instance, student evaluations of courses typically work according to a fixed scale that makes the question of "excellent teaching" a matter of straightforward calculation. Questions like "did the professor respect the syllabus?" and even broader ones like "did you think this was a good course?" contain a number a problematic assumptions. Concerning the first question, for instance, Readings wonders whether a course can be judged poorly if the instructor departs from the syllabus after realizing its material "seems pitched at the wrong level for the class" (131). Concerning the second question, Readings asks us to doubt "whether student pleasure is the absolute criterion of value" since successful "learning may be a painful experience" in certain circumstances (131). Likewise, the value of faculty research ends up being determined by rather inflexible scales that are ultimately decided and monitored by a centralized administration.

Readings doesn't simply want to replace one suture with another (something that Badiou's analysis lacks). Later in the book, he sees through calls to strike down elitist professors and thereby make education more accessible and egalitarian as a simple reversal of the status quo: "to mount an attack on the professors' authority, on the professor as the transcendent subject of the educational process, must not simply be to seek to replace the professor by the student" (163). Readings emphasizes that the main focus should be resistance to closure within the university, a fate that arises whenever one of the groups of constituents of the university seizes enough authority to ignore the others. Readings imagines a scenario where all three major stakeholders in the university—students, professors, and administrators—are all constantly held accountable for both the valuations of their own practices as well as their valuations of the others' practices (and the valuations of these valuations). He argues that students, rather than filling out a predetermined course evaluations at the end of the semester, should be asked to produce their own criteria for evaluating the course as well as offering a justification for said criteria. University administrators should not simply collect and synthesize these judgments but also be required to produce evaluations themselves, crafting and defending criteria to judge the quality of the university instead of composing "banal and cliché-ridden mission statements . . . and then quantify[ing] how far they have lived up to them" (133). Readings admits that "this will mean a lot of work for University presidents" but that these forms of "evaluation, judgment and self-questioning *are* the real business of the University" (133).

In this respect, Readings clearly differs from Ginsberg, who concludes *The Fall of the Faculty* by simply replacing an administrative suture with a faculty one. He maintains that the university should be run according to the vision of the faculty; students and administrators should be beholden to the decisions made by this informed and powerful sector of the university. Ginsberg totally resists the shaping of curriculum based on student concerns or interests: "few students actually arrive on campus with preferences that should be taken seriously" (171). From his perspective, "professors quite reasonably believe that they are better qualified than students to decide what the latter should learn" (171). At first blush, Ginsberg's arguments are difficult not to endorse, since they provide a necessary antidote to the consumer model of education that has transformed higher education in recent years into largely "employment or career preparation" with "a hefty dollop of clubs, sports, and other activities" (171). At the same time, however, Ginsberg's doubling down on faculty autonomy is problematic when one recalls that the student movements of the 1960s initiated the push for diversity within the curriculum. Replacing one form of hierarchical power with another does not fix the problem since it is unchecked power in itself that leads to unnecessary growth, waste, and fraud. The university needs (and thrives on) a series of checks and balances among the students, faculty, and administrators, all of whom approach the university from unique perspectives that are valuable but limited (of course, Ginsberg's emphasis on the faculty regaining control of the university is premised on the idea that the faculty will become indistinguishable from the administration as they once were, as those multiple functions will be occupied by individuals rather than reified into discrete positions without any overlap (the full-time administrator with no research agenda as a professor)).

The concept of the suture can also be usefully deployed at the disciplinary level. If the university writ large involves a struggle among faculty, students, and administrators for supremacy, the discipline reformulates this contest in terms of how research, teaching, and administration are prioritized. Much like the University in its entirety, departments should ideally avoid privileging one of these practices at the expense of the others. In reality, of course, as numerous complaints from both inside and outside the university have made clear, research is championed over the other two functions, effectively producing a "research suture" within departments to accompany the "administrative suture" of the university more generally. While it remains up for debate whether the first suture helped to produce the latter, or vice versa—in all likelihood, they were co-constitutive—I am more concerned with the effects produced when these two sutures converge. More specifically, I argue that Rhetoric and Composition as a discourse should be understood as an outcome of the confrontation of the research and administrative sutures. As Strickland's analysis in *The Managerial Unconscious* makes clear, tenure-track positions within Rhetoric and Composition were largely a response to the growing need for administrative and managerial work within the department, namely the supervision of adjunct labor. If managerial tasks constituted the primary purpose for these new hires, they would not lessen the demand to publish that typically accompanies tenure-track positions.

Composition scholarship is therefore constantly trying to reconcile the demand to publish with high volumes of administrative work, thereby producing a number of unusual research agendas. On the one hand, we have work like the aforementioned "administrative scholarship," which could be interpreted as largely indistinguishable from bureaucratic documents like strategic plans or progress report, since it is so closely related to the daily workings of the department. On the other hand, we have scholarship seeking to problematize the borders separating department service from intellectual work. If Rhetoric and Composition has historically been undervalued because it focuses more on teaching and administration than on research, some of its specialists have sought to correct this imbalance by using their research as a means of outlining how administrative duties should be understood as a form of intellectual work and thereby be reevaluated more favorably for tenure and promotion. Take, for instance, Shirley K. Rose and Irwin Wesier's twin volumes *The Writing Program Administrator as Researcher* (1999) and *The Writing Program Administrator as Theorist* (2002) or Gary A. Olson's edited collection *Rhetoric and Composition as Intellectual Work* (2002). While this scholarship has thoughtfully aimed to reconfigure the borders that separate research, teaching, and administration, this work has done little to slow the publish-or-perish model that makes a substantial research agenda a high priority for tenured faculty in Rhetoric and Composition. In fact, it serves as the fiercest articulation of the stranglehold of the "research suture" insofar as its existence undermines its explicitly stated goals—that is, it participates in the publish-or-perish model despite its attempt to think outside its logic. I would like to argue that the social turn within English studies, particularly the version advanced within Rhetoric and Composition, should also be read by situating it along this uneasy border between a department's "research suture" and the university's "administrative suture." The drive to make composition studies more legitimate—and one of the ways that composition studies articulates its importance is by providing a more inclusive and accessible pedagogy that literary studies lacks—may necessitate an unintentional (and perhaps unavoidable) turn against the values that it most dearly cherishes.

One underlying theme throughout Ginsberg's *The Fall of the Faculty* that warrants more attention is how administrative rhetoric has adopted commendable values and principles and deployed them for questionable ends. Ginsberg specifically emphasizes how the demand for diversity, part of the broader 1960s social movements, was taken up by administrators as a way to wrest power away from the faculty.[7] "Administrators will always seek to use our principles against us," Ginsberg warns, arguing that their efforts to do so "should be resisted even though administrators and some credulous colleagues will declare that such opposition indicates a lack of proper political commitment" (213). One specific phrase that demands further analysis is the phrase "outside the classroom," which Ginsberg explains has become "an administrative mantra" in recent years (20). While administrators claim that attending college involves more than coursework and that engaging in extracurricular experiences plays an integral role in creating well rounded, fulfilled, and socially committed graduates, Ginsberg remains suspicious of these efforts and mocks the "event planning" training and other relatively trivial activities that administrators promote. From his perspective, "the phrase *outside the classroom* usually signals an effort by administrators to shift budgetary priorities from teaching, which the faculty controls, to other activities where . . . faculty claims of expertise are weaker and administrators have an opportunity to expand their bureaucratic domains" (12). Interestingly enough, however, conducting a brief genealogy of the phrase "outside the classroom" reveals that it actually originated in some ways *within the classroom*, beginning as a form of self-critique that was ultimately seized for drastically different purposes.

The word "classroom" initially operated as a synecdoche for the forms of disciplinary knowledge legitimized by the institution; the attempt to move "outside the classroom" involved questioning these existing disciplinary specializations. The turn to "local" and "minor" knowledge that helped to establish interdisciplinary programs like ethnic and women's studies could be seen as an impulse to move "outside the classroom" insofar as these forms of knowledge had never held a place within higher education. Although this impulse to move "outside the classroom" may not have been initiated within the classroom, its effects were ultimately located there. In other words, while external pressure—"outside the classroom"— was required to make higher education more democratic by serving and studying previously ignored constituencies, the result of this external pressure was a transformation of a curriculum firmly situated within an existing institutional space. Using English studies as an example, we can see that the concept of the "classroom" can be traced to the literary canon, which necessarily enshrines certain texts while discrediting others. A variety of forces converged to prompt a desire to move *beyond* or *outside* this restricted territory to discover and include other literary works. Reflecting on its practices, English studies aimed to be more inclusive and expand the range of texts that it circulated and analyzed. But this initial move beyond the classroom ultimately became a return to it, since texts previously outside of the domain of the institution's purview would not simply play a role in transforming its curriculum but also in fortifying the institution in which this curriculum was disseminated.

But the gesture to move "outside the classroom" was also taken more literally—that is, as a challenge to the institution's investment in existing educational strategies. Rather than reforming higher education by adding or subtracting material in the classroom, it has involved restructuring education in much more fundamental ways, beginning with the modification of teaching practices and extending to the reconfiguration of the institution's relationship to the broader public. Rhetoric and Composition has played a pivotal role in questioning traditional forms of classroom instruction. Some of these reforms have been relatively minor, like its nearly ubiquitous emphasis on constructing a "student-centered classroom." But small changes like these are part of a much larger effort to rethink higher education's relationship to the public it serves. As Christian Weisser explains in his 2002 *Moving Beyond Academic Discourse: Composition Studies and the Public Sphere*, the desire to transcend disciplinary concerns so as to impact the social world more directly is a defining feature of contemporary composition studies:

> For many compositionists, the classroom—or, more specifically, the
> writing course—has emerged as a microcosm of the public sphere,
> as our point of contact with the "real" world out there somewhere.
> This point of contact is something that distinguishes composition
> from many other academic disciplines; our close and personal connec-
> tions with students differentiate our work from the "merely academic"
> pursuits of our colleagues down the hall. If we believe that power is
> entrenched in discourse and that language is an instrumental tool in
> shaping knowledge and reality, we could, by extension, assume that the
> work that we do can have real implications in the world. (43)

The "colleagues down the hall" that Weisser gestures to are clearly those
working in literary studies whose very subject matter, he would argue, presupposes and reinforces hierarchical social arrangements. From his perspective, traditional forms of teaching grant all authority to the instructor
and none to the students, thereby ensuring the perpetuation of oppressive
power relations both within the classroom and society more generally. In-
sulated academic discourse becomes a problem since it divorces itself from
the pressing social matters that education is ostensibly meant to address.
It is no surprise, then, that Rhetoric and Composition has made it a priority to transcend the limitation of the classroom altogether and connect
to society directly. Rhetoric and Composition doesn't want to prepare its
students for entry into the real world following graduation but to make
them interact and change the world while being educated. Weisser ven-
tures that "'public writing' and 'service-learning in composition' . . . might
very well become the next dominant focal point around which the teaching of college writing is theorized and imagined" (42). Weisser notes that
the turn toward the "the writing classroom and public discourse" must be
understood as "the progeny" of radical democratic theories of pedagogy
embraced in composition studies (26). Weisser's analysis alludes to the fact
that radical pedagogy was itself an effect of student-centered pedagogical
practices that constituted an attractive alternative to the traditional literature classroom: "these theories argued for greater attention to the writing
that was being produced by students and less attention to the consumption
of great works of literature" (11).

But if Rhetoric and Composition is firmly committed to achieving social
justice through the promotion of a democratic politics, the discourse has
also contributed to precisely the opposite effect in a sphere that it all too
often overlooks—that is, the university itself. While Rhetoric and Composition has leveled the most full-throated defenses of democracy in the

classroom, in the discipline of English studies, and in society more generally, its efforts to produce these admirable goals have sometimes contributed to the increased hierarchization of the university. The phrase "outside the classroom" has been generally linked to both a revision of the canon within the traditional literary studies as well as to a mode of engaging students with discourses outside the university altogether, but its circulation within university administrative discourse constitutes a third space in between the micro-level of the classroom or department and the macro-level of "society" or "the real world" that must be acknowledged. In all three spheres, the metaphor of expansion or of transcending an existing set of constraints is configured as participating in a project of social justice. It would seem that the same phrase or concept unites the figures in these different areas. As Ginsberg's experience suggests, however, the same phrase can be deployed for diametrically opposed ends:

> Many of the new administrators would like to redefine . . . the mission
> of the university to enhance the centrality of their own roles. . . . This
> point was brought home to me when I served as one of the few faculty
> members of a search committee organized to find a new director of
> admissions. The dean who chaired the committee . . . informed us that
> while some people might think that the admissions process entailed
> bringing students to the campus to work with the faculty, this was a
> mistaken notion. There were, he intoned, many "stakeholders" in the
> admissions process who should have a voice in admissions decisions
> and the selection of an admissions director. When I inquired who these
> might be besides, of course, the coach of our often-national championship lacrosse team, he mentioned the counseling staff, the librarians,
> the residence hall staff, the dining hall staff, and many others. A good
> deal of education occurred "outside the classroom," he declared. . . .
> I suggested that students did not come to Hopkins to work with our
> dining services personnel, our counselors, or even our distinguished
> administrators, but my objection was dismissed. This dean was determined to redefine the purposes of the university in terms that inflated
> the importance of his own place in it. (20)

Whereas the demand to move beyond the existing canon or academic discourse altogether was a part of an effort to be more inclusive and less hierarchical, the same phrase has been mobilized to weaken democratic and participatory formations and make them more hierarchical (although this is done under the auspices of making the university more inclusive). If the move to go outside or beyond the existing set of texts or practices was used to strengthen the academic disciplines from within, this same gesture has been used to undermine the influence these same academic disciplines exert on the affairs of the university. This is not to denigrate all service learning or "outside the classroom" initiatives so much as it is to say that these practices may work against their explicitly stated goals if we recognize them functioning within multiple contexts or spaces simultaneously.

A different model is needed for understanding how these counterintuitive effects can be produced. The "archival" form of politics seems to subscribe to a "domino theory" of social change. According to this model, if a small space like a classroom can be made democratic, that can create a ripple effect that will ultimately transform the university and the broader public into a more democratic space as well. Unfortunately, history has shown that the democratization of one space can actually contribute to the hierarchization of adjacent spaces (which can in turn lead to the de-democratization of that initial space). In the introduction to *A Thousand Plateaus*, Deleuze and Guattari offer an alternative understanding of how democratic and hierarchical formations interact. Here, they outline the differences between two competing models of organization: the hierarchical model of the tree (with its corresponding roots) and the nonhierarchical distributed model of the rhizome. Although it would be easy to envision these as two totally disparate and competing models in which one would have to choose sides, Deleuze and Guattari point out that "the root-tree and canal-rhizome are not two opposed models" (20). Instead, they co-constitute one another. If the tree "operates as a transcendent model and tracing," it nevertheless "engenders its own escapes"; if the rhizome "operates as an immanent process that overturns the model and outlines a map," it also "constitutes its own hierarchies" and "gives rise to a despotic channel" (20). As they explain, "there are knots of arborescence in rhizomes, and rhizomatic offshoots in roots. Moreover, there are despotic formations of immanence and channelization specific to rhizomes, just as there are anarchic deformations in the transcendent system of trees, aerial roots, and subterranean stems" (20). For Deleuze and Guattari, one should attend to the general process that produces the interconnection between these two modes of organizing space, "a model that is perpetually in construction or collapsing" but nevertheless "prolonging itself, breaking off and starting up again" (20). Deleuze and Guattari's understanding of the relationship between hierarchical and rhizomatic formations suggests a more complex dynamic between democratic spaces both within and outside the university, since they challenge the belief that the democratization of a small space (like a classroom or university department) will serve as a launching pad for broader democratic uprisings in society more generally. In fact, their analysis points out that these democratizing movements can actually help to produce hierarchical formations in adjacent spaces.

The Fall of the Faculty provides a vivid example to illustrate how practices in one social space can produce unintended consequences in adjacent social spaces. At one point in the book, Ginsberg details how university administrations have increased their power through their relationships with various institutes and centers on campus, most notably race and gender studies programs. While admiring the commendable goals underwriting these programs, Ginsberg notes that the relatively low enrollments in these programs has led to its directors "constantly having to defend its share of the school's budget against rival claimants with demonstrably more student need" (105). As a result, "Africana studies and similar programs [have] a stake in supporting the college presidents, provosts, or deans from whom it has received its largesse and on whose sufferance it depends" (105). He cites an infamous case at the Du Bois Institute at Harvard to support his argument. During his tenure as Harvard's president, Larry Summers committed so many egregious administrative errors that the faculty called for his resignation. Henry Louis Gates was "seldom if ever" (106) critical of Summers, however, even though the president had been highly critical of Gates's colleague Cornel West and precipitated West's departure for Princeton. As Ginsberg explains, "despite Summers's alleged mistreatment of an important black faculty member, the university's president and the chair of Afro-American studies had negotiated a mutually satisfactory renewal of their previous accommodation" (106).

Although Ginsberg's book does not explore this aspect of the incident, it is important to point out that both Cornel West and Henry Louis Gates are prominent public intellectuals who have sought to disseminate their work beyond the confines of the university. The creation of the Du Bois Institute, while situated within the university, should be understood as an extension of their work in public outreach; the Du Bois Institute's website claims that the center aims "to increase public awareness and understanding of this vital field of study" ("W.E.B. Du Bois Research Institute"). But if the Institute serves as a point within the university to enact positive change in society more broadly, we should also be attentive to the ways in which it can produce negative effects within the university that it never intended. The Institute should be understood as a nodal point operating simultaneously within the university and the general public. While the Institute has undoubtedly accomplished much important work in terms of raising awareness in the public consciousness surrounding issues of racial equality and social justice in the hope of producing a more democratic society, the hidden cost of achieving these goals has been to potentially make the space of the university *less* democratic by further shifting the balance of power toward the administration and away from the faculty.

Composition programs and their directors face these irresolvable problems on a more frequent basis than many other academics insofar as their work, which affects a wide swath of the university community, by necessity has more oversight and interaction with the university's central administration.[8] The same forms of dependency and symbiotic relationships that Ginsberg identifies between the Du Bois Institute and President Summers would be less avoidable for composition program directors because their work tends to extend beyond the confines of the English department, thereby necessitating a greater degree of assistance through nondepartmental administrative units.

The close contact between university administration and Rhetoric and Composition can be rather easily teased out in the title of Emily Isaac's "The Emergence of Centers for Writing Excellence," published in the edited collection *Before and After the Tutorial: Writing Centers and Institutional Relationships*. The discourse of excellence that Readings identifies as inseparable from contemporary university administrative practice has smuggled itself into the vocabulary of Rhetoric and Composition and its attendant facilities. Near the conclusion of her piece, she recommends "the CWE [Center for Writing Excellence] director and budget should . . . be independent of an academic or other department, *reporting directly to a high-level administrator* such as the provost. Further, although clearly there are successful centers that do not follow this approach, given that the CWE needs faculty interest and engagement to be effective in affecting the lives of every student, the CWE should be tied to the academic side of campus. Many faculty will not see a center located in student support services as a place where they can get support for their teaching and writing" (142, my emphasis). Her recommendations confirm that the work of Rhetoric and Composition is increasingly occupying a precarious liminal space within the university that is considered simultaneously "academic" and "outside the classroom" since it is not under the control of a traditional department.

Isaac acknowledges Readings's work, but the lessons she draws from *The University in Ruins* are telling. She considers the risks involved in assuming the corporate language of "excellence" in order to promote writing studies in the university. From her perspective, "writing people can and should give up their fear of *appearing* un-English, un-academic or anti-intellectual in choosing to use the language of the dominant culture (and yes, that is often corporate culture) because it's the very language that will allow us to reach much-need and desired public *and* student alliances" (133). She deftly recognizes the rhetorical situation in which her work is embedded and suggests that her goals are dependent on having her wider audience identify with her cause—"the language of excellence attempts to speak the language of administrators, potential donors, non-humanities faculty, and the general public" (134–135). But the notion of language that she advances in doing so warrants further exploration. Indeed, there is nothing "anti-intellectual" about adopting the language of the dominant culture, as if language were a possession that one had to purchase wholesale. As Foucault explains in *The History of Sexuality*, "there is not, on the one side, a discourse of power, and opposite it, another discourse that runs counter to it . . . [discourses] can, on the contrary, circulate without changing their form from one strategy to another, opposing strategy" (101–102). And, in fact, Readings attempts in *The University in Ruins* to recuperate certain strands of the rhetoric of excellence and deploy them for different ends.

But this inherent flexibility of language should not be read as automatically liberating. Preoccupied with the costs of adopting the discourse of excellence, Isaac's analysis misses the fact that the greater political risk actually emerges from the other direction—namely, when other parties use the same primary signifiers with which one most clearly identifies. When interacting with these groups, it is tempting to assume that a shared language translates into common beliefs and goals. Given the lasting memory of the infamous "affair at U.T.," where university administrators stymied the attempts of the composition director to create a first-year writing course at the University of Texas revolving around questions of difference and diversity, it might be difficult not to embrace university administrations that explicitly encourage diversity and "outside the classroom" initiatives.[9] Since these administrators share the same signifiers as activists in Rhetoric and Composition, the university administration understandably appears as a fitting ally in producing positive social change, particularly since Rhetoric and Composition has understood its colleagues in literary studies as not only indifferent but actively resistant to such work. The excitement of finding an ally elsewhere in the university can obscure the fact that phrases like "diversity" or "outside the classroom" can be used for drastically different purposes without violating some fundamental authenticity attached to those terms.

In closing, I want to stress that my analysis is not meant as a finger-wagging critique of the Du Bois Institute or WPAs or Rhetoric and Composition in general. These various individuals and collectivities all have commendable values and their actions are usually underwritten with the best intentions. Instead, my analysis has attempted to outline the unavoidable risks involved in any practical action, risks that are only more difficult to avoid in the kind of increasingly decentered structure that characterizes our contemporary moment where the interiorized intentionality of subjects matters less than the unexpected consequences of their external actions. This distinction returns us to the crucial tensions between "archival" and "cartographic" politics (always keeping in mind that these two modes are not in direct opposition to one another). One way of articulating the differences between these two approaches is revisiting the notion of an "unconscious" that Strickland uses in *The Managerial Unconscious in the History of Composition Studies*. In her review of Strickland's book, Shirley K. Rose (editor of two volumes on Writing Program Administration as theoretical research) questions the notion that a "managerial unconscious" is the best way to understand the actions of leading figures in the history of composition studies including James Berlin. "How might we understand their rhetoric differently," she asks, "if we read it as strategic action, rather than the product of a 'managerial unconscious'?" ("WPA Within" 225). From her perspective, composition directors and administrators were not subjected to pernicious psychic forces that compelled them to dominate others; instead, they should be regarded as activists "engaged in community organizing" who understood that the professionalization of composition "was, at the time, the only argument that could be effectively made for systematically developing the necessary body of knowledge of teaching composition" (225). A different conception of an unconscious would complicate Rose's assurances without reverting to Strickland's problematic conception. As Foucault once explained, "people know what they do; they frequently know why they do what they do; but what they don't know is what they do does" (quoted in Dreyfus and Rabinow, *Michel Foucault: Beyond Structuralism and Hermeneutics*, 187). But it is precisely this murky region where one does not know what one's "doing does" that Fredric Jameson called the "political unconscious," a concept that proved to be the main sticking point in his debate with Kenneth Burke in 1978. The managerial unconscious in composition studies cannot be located so much within the subjectivities of its practitioners, like in a reductive Freudian model. Instead, it must be located in the unintended consequences of the actions produced by composition specialists that can only be unearthed through broader structural analyses.

The map constructed in this chapter has attempted to produce a broader structural analysis of the "political unconscious" within English studies during the social turn. If it began by documenting the translation of theory into a multicultural "archival" politics, it ends by showing how the fundamental nature of appropriation that unites many of the key thinkers of French theory (Foucault's genealogy served as the primary example, but a similar analysis could have been conducted using Derrida's trace structure or Deleuze's notion of multiplicity) provides a useful set of tools for showing how the "archival" politics of English studies, found in its most intense form in Rhetoric and Composition, was itself appropriated for very different purposes within the contemporary university. "Cartographic" politics was appropriated and became "archival" politics, which itself was appropriated for very different ends, thereby becoming a compelling illustration of "cartographic" politics. Or, using Foucault as a specific example, genealogy was appropriated into a version of democratic identity politics that was itself ultimately appropriated to serve decidedly undemocratic ends; Foucault's notion of genealogy helps us better understand how that appropriation works.

CHAPTER 4

Toward an Aesthetics without Literature

The previous chapter documented Rhetoric and Composition's antagonistic attitude toward literary studies that, while justified in certain respects, blinded its practitioners from fully grasping their field's current role within the university. The field's commitment to an "archival politics" has prevented it from seeing the full range of forces both inside and outside of the discipline that have configured it over half a century. The chapter concluded with the problematic convergence of Rhetoric and Composition and the discourse of university administrators, a convergence that Donna Strickland's *The Managerial Unconscious* intimates has long existed. In this chapter, I want to extend the previous analysis by examining the kinds of pedagogical reforms that correspond to the complicated dynamics among literary studies, literary theory, Rhetoric and Composition, and the increasingly corporate university.

As a way of doing so, I examine two important critical works published in the early 1990s that have become touchstones within English studies: Susan Miller's 1991 *Textual Carnivals* and John Guillory's 1993 *Cultural Capital*. *Textual Carnivals* won three prominent book awards (the Modern Language Association's Mina P. Shaughnessy Prize, the Conference on College Composition and Communication's Outstanding Book Award, and the Association of Teachers of Advanced Composition's W. Ross Winterowd Award), while *Cultural Capital* won the René Wellek Prize from the American Comparative Literature Association. Over the last two decades, both books have received hundreds of citations and have solidified the reputations of their authors. Beyond being published at roughly the same moment and subsequently showered with accolades, both books attempt to theorize the entirety of English studies in the contemporary university and its future direction. *Textual Carnivals* presents a sustained analysis of the history between literary studies and composition studies, and while *Cultural Capital* does not invest much of its energy exploring the specifics of composition studies, this discourse nevertheless makes a significant appearance at crucial moments in his argument. In many ways, *Textual Carnivals* and *Cultural Capital* might also be conceived of as fairly early texts addressing what is now commonly known as "the crisis in the humanities."

Given all these similarities, it is striking how differently Miller and Guillory assess the state of English at the end of the twentieth century. Whereas Miller's *Textual Carnivals* conceives of composition's low status as an unavoidable effect of its relationship to literary studies, Guillory's *Cultural Capital* regards composition as the new center of English studies, replacing an obsolete literary studies. I argue that Miller's account differs so drastically from Guillory's because she understands composition's status within the university as wholly determined by its connection with literary studies rather than a host of additional forces. Her subsequent rejection of literary studies leads her to embrace an ideology of immediate practicality that may actually work against her explicitly articulated progressive agenda. Not only does this ideology dovetail with the short-term logics of contemporary capitalism that underwrite the university but it also threatens the long-term viability of English studies by reducing its curriculum to a set of fairly mechanical service courses. To avoid this path, the discipline should retain a notion of aesthetics that is distinct from the concept of literature that I develop out of the final chapter of Guillory's book.

Conflicting Accounts of the Discipline's Trajectory

In *Textual Carnivals*, Susan Miller argues that composition studies in the contemporary university must be understood as a recent invention. She rejects the idea that composition studies simply continues a long tradition of writing instruction dating back to ancient Greece. Rather than a point on a seamless continuum between past and present, composition studies is a historical event. Failing to recognize the discourse's historical specificity may have relatively minor consequences like preserving obsolete pedagogical methods. Miller explains that composition scholars who have linked themselves to the rhetorical tradition (which is rooted in oral delivery) may overlook emerging writing technologies that call into question the usefulness of these ancient techniques in the contemporary world: "neoclassical historians do not account for this technology or for new ways of publishing and reading that have inevitably recentered 'rhetoric' in a series of actual changes in its doctrines" (40). But Miller's critique of the ostensible union between composition and neoclassical rhetoric extends beyond pointing out ineffective pedagogy. From her perspective, positing this union also obscures the existence of certain social inequalities and, in some respects, perpetuates them. Only by emphasizing "the actual historical discontinuity with earlier curricula that composition courses embody" will critics ever be able to effectively challenge this system of inequality (44). For Miller, the turn to neoclassical rhetoric by many composition scholars is merely a symptom of a much broader trend—it is an unexpected offshoot of the codependent relationship between composition and literary studies that sustains social hierarchies both inside and outside the university.

Drawing upon the work of Peter Stallybrass and Allon White's *The Politics and Poetics of Transgression*, Miller asserts that composition studies constitutes a carnivalesque discourse that reveals the interconnections between powerful and marginal populations. Miller argues that literary studies, which has long been the discourse of an elite class, has required nonliterary writing as an "other" through which it defines itself. In the contemporary university, composition has played this role of "other." As Miller explains, "literary authorship could be openly compared to the inadequacies of popular writing and especially to inadequate student authorship . . . institutionalized writing-as-composition could be implicitly demeaned as unequal to writing from the advanced elect" (54–55). Without the marginal discourse of composition studies, the very concept of literature on which literary studies depends would fail to cohere. Conversely, those teaching or enrolled in composition were able to measure their inferiority by their distance from those engaged in literary studies. Composition studies was created as a way of ensuring that the vast majority of college students feel unworthy of belonging to this elite and powerful class and thereby willingly accept a lower, denigrated station within society. Miller writes that the dynamic between literature and composition reenacts earlier discriminatory practices that kept all but upper-class boys out of Harvard and Yale in the early nineteenth century. . . . At the "new" Harvard and at its public imitations across the country, ostensibly founded to educate contemporary students differently, composition has provided a continuing way to separate the unpredestined from those who belong . . . by convincing large numbers of native speakers and otherwise accomplished citizens that they are "not good at English." By helping to make this inadequacy the tenor of academic textual production and by providing a way to distinguish insiders from outsiders, institutions of writing instruction have willingly marginalized the majority of students. (74–75)

A social process that once was more immediately visible (only a small fraction of students were ever even allowed entry in Harvard and Yale in the nineteenth century) has now been incorporated into the structure of the school curriculum, helping to preserve and reinforce social inequalities.

Given her rejection of the neoclassical rhetoricians due to their lack of historical inattentiveness, Miller's own understanding of the specific historical coordinates of composition studies in the second half of the twentieth century proves surprisingly problematic. In many respects, her account of composition becomes just as ahistorical as the ones she criticizes and the coherence of the account begins to unravel when inspected more closely. For starters, one might wonder about the effectiveness of including young adults in higher education as a means of ensuring their exclusion from the powerful upper class when this exclusion was previously achieved simply by excluding them from higher education altogether. Also problematic is how Miller's account of composition studies treats literacy as a form of ideological indoctrination; for her, governing and controlling populations largely involves shaping the way that they think about a particular topic. Miller maintains that the composition curriculum has been invested in a project of "spiritual regulation, a process of assuring a well-behaved, cooperative body politic" (28). She targets literary studies for creating a sense of helplessness and passivity on the part of the students in composition courses. By ignoring literary works' conditions of production, literary studies posits that these writings were divinely inspired and required no preparation or revision: the "history of 'literature' must by definition be told as a history of *authorship* and of the authorized voice, whose origins, successes, and privileges are not bound to the material circumstances of either readers or writers" (27). As a result, students who struggle with writing convince themselves that they do not possess the innate talents necessary to make consequential contributions in society, concluding that these tasks are better left to an elite class which does possess said innate gifts. But if this were how the process of social distinction and exclusion functioned, wouldn't it be just as effective (if not more so) to place less talented writers in literature classes, forcing them to confront the inadequacies of their own writing more directly, than to experience that inadequacy secondhand by being excluded from these courses? At the very least, enrollment in either composition or literature courses would ultimately achieve the same desired effect.

It would seem that Miller fails to take her own recommendations seriously and follow through on the compelling logic that she uses to diagnose the concept of "literature." While Miller stresses the material conditions that are necessary to the production of any written text, she actually fails to address the historical specificity of contemporary writing instruction, beginning with a misunderstanding of the educational system itself. While schools have long played a role in the formation of social classes, it would be a mistake to see all of the social classes inscribed within them, as if each institution replicated the broader class dynamics of society within its institutional walls. In other words, it is not immediately apparent why a lower class would necessarily be included within the university, even in a demeaned position. Throughout *Textual Carnivals*, Miller continually conflates the university and the nation, seeing the former as a small-scale replica of the latter. She writes that composition was "set up to be a *national* course in silence" that "stripped from new students and *a nation* of unschooled potential writers their needs and desires to create significant pieces of writing" (55, my emphasis). Here, the students entering the school are conceptualized as direct representatives of a nation and in doing so, Miller reads the school as a reflection of society more broadly rather than attending to the specificity of the school itself. At several important moments in the text, Miller compares composition's struggle for recognition to other broader social struggles and therefore participates in the same gestures that I analyzed earlier in Chapter 3. In doing so, Miller mistakes the university as representative of the entire school system and the school system as representative of broader social dynamics, resulting in her comparison of composition studies to an exploited lower class.

Miller's conflation brings her into sharp disagreement with John Guillory, who in *Cultural Capital* warns against confusing the school system and the nation in which that school is located. His book begins with a study over recent conflicts concerning the literary canon and its exclusion of marginalized voices from an elite "Western culture." The major blind spot of all the participants in the canon debate, he maintains, is the educational system itself. Writing is not a universal medium possessed by all but has instead historically been restricted to certain segments of the population through access to the education. Those arguing for "nonhegemonic" figures to be added to the canon fail to realize that the exclusion of minorities occurs at the level of access to writing itself, not to the content disseminated in the school. For example, there are fewer women in the canon less because of some current prejudice against them and more because so few women were even granted access to literacy in previous centuries, making texts by women writers much more rare. As Guillory points out, a "critique which is confined to the level of consumption must necessarily misrepresent the historicity of literary production, the systemic effects of the *educational system* in the determination of who writes and who reads, as well as what gets read, and in what contexts" (19). While by no means identical to Guillory's targets, Miller similarly leaps over the crucial function of the school itself when she emphasizes the differences between the composition and literary curriculum.

The sharp differences between Miller and Guillory become even clearer when comparing their respective treatments of the concept of "remediation." For Miller, remediation refers to the process of convincing students of their own inadequacies as writers and thereby reinforcing inequality among students. It is inevitably a word directed at the individual, isolating him or her and pointing out their unavoidable internal flaws—the school simply identifies these flaws and responds to the student accordingly. Remediation stigmatizes the individual and prompts them to believe in some inherent flaws of which they may have only been dimly aware. But Guillory rejects this formulation of "remediation" in an essay produced several years after *Cultural Capital*, explaining that while it "has been rejected by most recent teachers of composition as stigmatizing, remediation properly understood has nothing to do with the innate abilities or disabilities of students. It refers to a demonstrable social fact: the gap between the competence produced at the top of the secondary level and the competence demanded at the bottom of the tertiary level. This structural gap represents a failure of the system, not of students" ("System" 1157). Against someone like Miller, who sees the creation of composition as a deliberate tactic at stigmatizing individuals and keeping them in a "low" position within society, Guillory argues that remediation is an inevitable fact of tertiary education insofar as secondary education remains a fragmented and uneven endeavor. Since the curricula of the secondary schools and the universities have never been coordinated—a situation that has arisen for a number of reasons—remediation has always been an unavoidable fact of life in the university. It is only because a four-year college degree has increasingly come to be regarded as the natural next step after high school that remediation has become so noticeable in the last few decades.

Miller and Guillory's divergent understandings of remediation only begin to gesture toward their much larger differences concerning the current state of English studies in the contemporary university. The differences are so startling that one could be forgiven for thinking that the two critics occupied completely separate worlds. And while a substantial distance (both literal and metaphorical) exists between Guillory's Harvard University and Miller's University of Utah, the general nature of their accounts transcends any idiosyncrasies specific to these critics' home institutions. In other words, both Miller and Guillory are offering a "big picture" view of the discipline as it nears the end of the twentieth century, and their assessments of composition and literary studies' respective future prospects are almost diametrically opposed. After reading *Textual Carnivals*, one has the impression that literary studies remains a mighty monolith that has never been questioned, let alone experienced its foundations being dramatically shaken. In fact, one of the motivating principles behind the book is to expose the "entrenched investment in literature" that typically goes unnoticed (19). While Guillory's *Cultural Capital* begins by documenting a fierce intellectual contest about the canon that would only seem possible if the discipline's underlying belief in "literature" were still stable, it ends by stating that the participants in this debate will eventually be stranded "on an ever shrinking island within the university" (45). Far from invincible, literary studies is in very real danger of becoming extinct.

Meanwhile, if Miller characterizes composition teachers and students as a pitiable group of outcasts who deserve more respect and ultimately equality with their counterparts in literary studies, Guillory suggests that they are already usurping their colleagues as the predominant group of literacy training in the educational system in the United States. He argues that "the function of producing in a segment of the populace a minimal degree of linguistic uniformity (in ideological terms, 'competence') has been given over to the field of composition, which has developed a nonfictional prose syllabus specific to its function, a syllabus which seems to have no necessary relation to the study of literature" (263–264). So while Miller regards literary studies as the discourse of an elite whose privilege continues to go unchecked, Guillory's account of English studies hints that this elite group's days are nearing an end—or, at the very least, that they no longer possess the same power or influence that they once did.

Put slightly differently, each account argues that English studies is moving in the opposite direction. Miller declares that "the existence of composition within English permits literature to displace and translate an older social identity onto only one of its parts. Composition is a site for residues and traces from earlier literary identities that first coded English as 'female' among 'hard' disciplines" (139). Composition becomes the site where the weaknesses of literary studies are externalized and chastised so as to protect itself from external critiques of irrelevance or ineffectiveness. But for Guillory, the transfer of power is working in the opposite direction, with composition as the veritable replacement of literary studies. Literary studies is, in fact, the residue and trace of an earlier disciplinary identity. It has become the site of precious affective experience that is increasingly marginal within the profit-driven corporate university, while composition has begun to receive respect from constituents both inside and outside of the university as more practical and immediately useful. So whereas Miller regards a basic holding pattern within English studies, where reform and resistance efforts are, if anything, only strengthening literary studies, Guillory sees a tectonic shift occurring wherein a once-powerful paradigm is quickly but quietly being eclipsed. Why then Miller does insist on stressing the degradation of composition studies at its very moment of ascendancy within the university? As Guillory points out, "at the present moment, the nation-state still requires a relatively homogenous language to administer its citizenry, but it no longer requires that a distinctive practice of that language identify a culturally homogeneous bourgeoisie" (263). Composition fulfills this need quite adequately, rendering literary studies as an anachronistic endeavor whose endpoint has come into clear view on the horizon. If Miller's analysis can be registered as a rallying cry for radical change within the discipline, why does it fail to emphasize the support that composition has been gaining outside the discipline?

Reversing the trajectory of Miller's argument, where literary studies requires composition studies to make clear the privileged nature of its own discourse, composition studies now uses an old version of literary studies to make itself appear to be in the position of the "silent" masses who have finally been given a voice. *Textual Carnivals* derives the force of its argument using a concept of literature that even those in literary studies have largely abandoned. She argues that literary study must be divorced from the conditions of its production: "its particular mission, development, and character are devoted to displacing the inevitably ordinary circumstances around the texts it chooses to call extraordinary . . . literary study logically must be dissociated from textual production" (27). But much like James

Berlin, Miller does not recognize that literary studies has begun an earnest effort to undermine the very concept of literature. Miller seems to be fighting a useless war against a nearly dead enemy, a choice that makes sense only when one attends to the additional effects this war might have.

I would argue that composition studies needs this bogeyman of literary studies as a way of securing its own status as a universal discourse. As Guillory argues, the emergence of composition "marks the appearance of a new social formation for the university, the task of providing the future technobureaucratic elite with precisely and only the linguistic competence necessary for the performance of its specialized functions" (263–264). Composition is nothing other than the production of a "new kind of 'oral performance'" that proves to be "the speech of the professional-managerial classes, the administrators and bureaucrats; and it is employed *in its place*, the 'office.' It is not 'everyday' language" (80). Guillory's analysis hints that the transition from "literature" to "composition" should not be understood according to the model of the proletariat seizing power from the ruling class. Instead, it should be understood as a transition from an old moneyed bourgeoisie culture to a growing technobureaucratic culture, or, put slightly differently, a transition of power within the university from *cultural* conservatives to *economic* conservatives. Of course, if composition is nothing more than the discourse of a new "technobureaucratic elite," its claims to universality, its capacity to speak for all, would become an obvious problem. Guillory maintains that although this new culture is no more universal than the one it replaced, it nevertheless still makes these claims: "in taking over the social function of producing a distinction between a basic and a more elite language, composition takes on as well the ideological identity of that sociolect, its pretension to universality, its status as the medium of political discourse" (80). This may help explain not only why composition makes an effort to link itself to the rhetorical tradition, since its connection to deliberative democracy produces an aura of universality that this emerging culture requires, but also why it continually beats the dead horse of a stodgy conception of "literature" since this reinforces its own pretensions toward universality.

While the values that composition champions may ostensibly be understood as politically progressive since they aspire to universality, Guillory's suggestion that they are merely the values of the business-managerial class invites us to explore how these values might serve ends other than those advertised. Take, for instance, a common attitude adopted by composition scholars concerning the practice of reading—and, to a certain extent, thinking or contemplation—which they have coded as the tool of the dominant

class. In 2009, former NCTE President Kathleen Blake Yancey, outlining
the prospects of "writing in the 21st century," argues "writing has never
been accorded the cultural respect or the support that reading has enjoyed,
in part because through reading, society could control its citizens, whereas
through writing, citizens might exercise their own control" (2). Within
her piece, Yancey approvingly cites the work of E. Jennifer Monaghan and
E. Wendy Saul, who have concluded that "society has focused on children
as readers" rather than as writers because social reproduction depended
on "obedience to the law" rather than "creative individuality"; from their
perspective, it is only "by requiring children to read the writings of adults
that society has consistently attempted to transmit its values" (90–91). For
Yancey, Monaghan and Saul, and others, the study of literature or theory
amounts to a decided disengagement with the political; even if literary
studies addresses political topics or gives voice to marginal figures, it does
not directly engage in political processes. The practice of reading itself,
then, reinforces politically conservative energies insofar as it does nothing
to intervene in the world. At best, even if it points out political atrocities,
it stops short of actually doing anything about them. At worst, it is one
of the most effective tools for reinforcing the status quo and maintaining
social inequalities. The act of writing, meanwhile, is coded as a politically
progressive force insofar as it is a productive tool for engaging in practical
matters. Rather than simply thinking about and interpreting the world, it
strives to change it. Many in composition seem to have adopted Marx's
eleventh Thesis on Feuerbach as their mantra, modifying it only slightly:
"The [literary critics and theorists] have only *interpreted* the world, in various ways; the point, however, is to *change* it" (145).

But as numerous literary and cultural theorists have noted, we are living
in an era where this demand for immediate action is inescapable and might
be characterized as the paradigmatic conservative political and economic
gesture of our time. Slavoj Žižek has pointed out that the pervading impulse today is "Don't just talk, do something!" only to add that "the problem lately has been that we have been doing too much . . . Perhaps it is time
to step back, think and say the right thing" (*First* 11). In much of his recent
work, particularly *For a New Critique of Political Economy*, Bernard Stiegler
links the attenuation of contemporary attention spans to late capitalism's
short-term orientation that dooms the latter's long-term prospects. Meanwhile, Jodi Dean's analysis of "communicative capitalism" underscores how
critical debate sponsored through new networked media actually amounts
to the foreclosure of politics rather than its reinvigoration. And Fredric
Jameson has articulated his frustrations with questions about the political

ramifications of his literary analysis, bemoaning the demand for immediate action implicit in the inquiry: "it is worth asking ourselves what the mirage of the great single-function political 'line' or strategy draws its power from. And I think, particularly for intellectuals, this mirage comes from impatience with the mediated, with the long term; it gets its power from the desire (quite proper to a business society, by the way) to show immediate results, to feel some ego satisfaction, to make the tangible mark right now. That is a pleasant luxury, a wonderful gratification, but it is not for us" (16). As Jameson's remarks underscore, what may appear as a politically progressive agenda of immediate action may actually be hard to disassociate from the predominant logic of the business culture that it seeks to work against.[1]

All of this is to say that the transition from the "university of culture" to the "university of excellence" has rendered the political and economic status of certain concepts or practices ambiguous.[2] As the following section will illustrate, this is particularly true of aesthetics, a discourse that Rhetoric and Composition has generally sought to eradicate since it is understood as inseparable from the suspect notion of literature found in the upper class. I hope to show that aesthetics can not only be separated from the concept of literature that Rhetoric and Composition rightly finds so problematic, but that it may in fact serve as a linchpin for the discipline of English in the coming years.

Aesthetics and the Public Turn

Susan Miller's critique of literature and literary studies in *Textual Carnivals* includes a common condemnation of aesthetic experience as a concept perpetuated by bourgeois elites to obfuscate their privileged status. In the final chapter of *Cultural Capital*, Guillory attempts to construct an understanding of aesthetics that differs from this standard view. From his perspective, recent debates about the literary canon foreground the tendency of critics to regard the aesthetic and the political as "discursive antitheses" (273). Although the Marxist tradition has long been sympathetic toward aesthetics, prevailing opinion sees it as a universalist discourse that unjustly champions certain cultural objects over others, ascribing to them a natural value that is actually quite arbitrary. While he agrees with the critique of universalism that these critics advance, Guillory aims to dismantle the notion that aesthetic experience is inextricably linked to an elite culture. His main target is Barbara Herrnstein Smith, who in *Contingencies of Value* strikes down universalist values by revealing their fundamentally relative nature. For Guillory, her "critique of value has been conducted as the most arid exercise in philosophical debate, as the choice between the two positions of relativism and absolutism" (324). While her analysis has rightly "exposed the groundlessness of 'absolute' values," it has done so "without raising its own discourse of commensuration to the level of historical self-reflection" (324). Guillory bristles against Smith's recourse to the "contingent" and "relative," since these concepts all too quickly overstep the concrete historical processes that make some things more valuable than others. Guillory enlists Pierre Bourdieu to help him resuscitate a notion of aesthetics that moves past the shortsightedness of Smith and others (like Miller), who find literature and aesthetics as interchangeable terms that should both be rejected.

Guillory readily acknowledges that, given the way it has been configured historically, aesthetics deserves the bad reputation it has received. Aesthetics has been defined in two distinct but inseparable ways that divide cleanly according to the broad social markers of "dominating" and "dominated" classes. If aesthetic experience can be understood in terms of the relationship between form and content, where aesthetics is understood as an attention to the formal characteristics that produce content, then neither class has had much of an investment in studying these formal properties. Indeed, the dominated class would appear to have an entirely negative relationship to aesthetics, since its responses to cultural objects are instantaneous and thoughtless, a form of immediate consumption that necessarily privileges the content over the form. If the dominant class appears to offer an escape from this content-oriented immediate consumption, it actually just reifies formal relations as new versions of content, which "effectively suppresses their specificity as relations of contents" (335). More specifically, the only pleasure that the dominant class seems to derive from cultural objects is the pleasure of being able to distinguish itself from the dominated class; the cultural artifacts assigned universal values are merely the tools used to reinforce that distinction. Aesthetic experience is not needed to enter this game of distinction—the art collector doesn't need to know anything about art to feel superior to people who do not own or have access to this art, yet the act of possessing this material is far from engaging with it in any aesthetic sense. In other words, the dominating class defines aesthetics in terms of rejecting immediate pleasure—the sensuous object, instant gratification—in favor of a "deferred pleasure," but this deferred pleasure proves to be nothing more than distaste for immediate pleasure. Thus, although initially it might appear that the dominant class cares about form while the dominated class cares only about the content, Guillory demonstrates, through Bourdieu, that a notion of sheer content prevails in both camps, thereby foreclosing the possibility of actual aesthetic engagement.

At some level, then, aesthetics seems to not exist at all, being canceled out from both directions: "at the level of the dominant aesthetic, the 'pleasure' in aesthetic pleasure is ideally reduced to a zero-degree, to the experience of 'distaste,' while at the level of the popular aesthetic, the pleasure produced by cultural products fails to be aesthetic at all. At neither level is 'aesthetic pleasure' actually experienced by anyone" (333). While Guillory is not disappointed to see the elitist pretensions of bourgeois aesthetics disappear, he does not want to endorse the dominated class's definition of the term either. In fact, the dominated class's rejection of aesthetics conforms to the same content-oriented logic of the upper crust "by the more direct route of rejecting the fetishized forms of the dominant aesthetic just because they are the recognizable signs of working-class cultural dispossession" (335). What both parties overlook, Guillory asserts, is a conception of aesthetics that is not reducible to serving as a mere tool for reaffirming class distinctions. Even if aesthetic experience will always be affected by class antagonisms (as well as any number of other social forces), it should not be seen as simply derivative of them. As Guillory argues, Bourdieu may be right that aesthetic experience cannot be separated from the class system or commodity production. However, "the *specificity* of aesthetic experience is not contingent upon its 'purity.' Is this 'mixed' condition not, after all, the condition of every social practice and experience?" (336). In rejecting the dominant culture's notion of aesthetics as a purification ritual that separates the upper and lower classes, the dominated class actually perpetuates this logic by regarding the very concept of aesthetics as irredeemably impure, a discourse it must reject and excommunicate at all costs. It demands immunity from the immunization that the concept of literature promises to the dominant class.

Instead of following this path, Guillory pursues a course wherein the notion of aesthetics and aesthetic judgment is not completely tethered to class antagonisms. He maintains that aesthetic experience is always already everywhere in society, an essential element in every cultural work, since "the relation of form and content" is "something other than a binary opposition" (335). Indeed, it would be a mistake to see form and content as ever being separable. Content can't exist outside of the formal relations that constitute to it, and formal relations necessarily produce content. As a result, "there is no cultural product, then, which does not possess form, and therefore no way to experience cultural objects without having aesthetic experience" (336). The discourse of canonicity, the broader concept of literature that underwrites it, and the dominating culture's understanding of aesthetics all prove so deeply problematic because they perpetuate "the illusion that aesthetic experience is really *restricted* to the experience of High Cultural works" (336).

Like Guillory, I worry that we may throw out the baby of aesthetics with the bathwater of literature, and that doing so has enormous disadvantages for the future of English studies. Dispensing with the elitism of the dominant class's notion of aesthetics can occur without much of a problem, in many ways because this definition is inseparable from an elite bourgeoisie that is quickly disappearing today and to which the vast majority of those working in literary studies do not subscribe. In fact, as the previous chapter illustrated, the critique of literature as a simple marker of class privilege not only occurred outside of the discourse in something like the criticism of James Berlin, but it also occurred within the confines of literary studies as well, most evident in New Historicism. The more threatening concern comes from the complete rejection of aesthetics that is found within the dominated class. The wholesale rejection of aesthetics that Guillory laments has been smuggled into the discourse of contemporary composition studies through a deep suspicion of the nonimmediate. Composition studies is often accused of anti-intellectualism, and whatever the merits of such criticisms, the more important thing for my purposes is the response that compositionists provide to such charges. Beyond a certain point, compositionists regard intellectual work as not only practically useless but also politically suspicious. The abstract speculation that is inseparable from theoretical intellectual work is typically understood as a diversion from important concrete political and economic matters.

Rhetoric and Composition's suspicion toward theoretical speculation can't be separated from its long-standing critique of the school itself, which dates back at least to Janet Emig's *The Composing Processes of Twelfth Graders*. In that work, Emig lamented how public school teachers promoted arbitrary standards of good writing and thinking; enforcing such standards did little more than reinforce the authority of the school itself. George Kennedy, meanwhile, has criticized the "secondary rhetoric" of the school for divorcing itself from the "primary rhetoric" of the public sphere. Following Kennedy, other scholars have argued that simply incorporating "real world" content into academic essays does not effectively prepare students to write for the concrete audiences they will ultimately encounter. What must be done, many have claimed, is to transcend the limitations of academic discourse by orienting composition instruction toward "real world" writing situations, a movement that has become known as "the public turn" in Rhetoric and Composition.[3]

Miller's *Textual Carnivals* could be seen as a precursor to this "public turn," and the popularity of her book may in fact stem at least partially from its frustration with the lack of instruction in writing courses on composing for concrete "real world" situations. She is critical of the daily themes assigned in composition classrooms where students write about what they find to be "interesting" and about which they "know something," since these exercises separate writing from the important social functions it possesses beyond the schoolroom walls. She writes that a "new purpose for beginning courses must have had something to do with the disappearance of practice in writing generic documents that a student might have to produce outside a classroom" (61). While I would be one of the last people to defend the value of this "daily theme" writing, I am nevertheless skeptical about Miller's push for writing instruction to have immediate real-world applications and focus largely on producing various "generic documents." Her argument makes a number of claims about the connections among writing, economic productivity, and political engagement that warrant close examination. One is the correlation between practical applicability and political progressivism. As her argument makes clear, the emergence of composition served politically conservative agendas insofar as it informed the notion that writing was divorced from socially effective action. New writing assignments "divorce writing from the mundane—or active—reasons that students will write" and provide "a diversion from the actual task of learning to write consequential discourse" (61). Vague, ill-defined theme writing fails to equip students to productively engage in society after graduating, and therefore in danger of becoming politically suspect.

It is no surprise, then, that Miller laments the fact that "the 'social usefulness' of a composition program . . . depends in large measure on a director's ability to leave the uses of writing undefined or tied only to generic processes, forms, and formats that are not openly implicated in social or political conflicts" (167). From Miller's perspective, composition program directors' decision to steer away from the concrete scenes of writing simply rehearses problematic banalities from literary studies about literature as a vehicle for producing a generally sensitive subjectivity. The vague quality of the subject produced in the composition course is a damning sign for Miller, since it betrays this subject's privileged distance from oppressive social arrangements from which it benefits. In other words, the composition student is trained in a manner similar to members of the old bourgeoisie, who certainly know of grimy, industrial labor and the uncouth cultural practices that accompany this labor, but cannot speak about them directly. Miller writes that "composition studies is again implicated in the position that has traditionally preserved literary humanism from details in the 'real' world it claims to know best, but to be free from" (151). Although the word is never explicitly articulated, aesthetics is the key term underwriting Miller's analysis. Her demand for immediacy and concrete writing situations is inseparable from a rejection of the abstract and airier practices associated with a bourgeois notion of aesthetics that she believes troublingly papers over class antagonism.

While we shouldn't discredit the degree to which composition adopts this hazily defined subjectivity from literary studies, we might consider these remarks a bit more charitably. What if a program director's characterization of writing in vague terms was not an evasion of social and political realities but instead the sharpest assessment of them? To provide instruction that simply prepares students for already existing writing practices and genres indulges in a shortsighted understanding of the "real world" that undersells the degree to which this world functions according to perpetual innovation and creation. The most banal practical consequence of this reality is that most of our students will not hold a single job for their entire careers—or even stay in the same company, for that matter—rendering an attachment to narrow concrete objects and skills a recipe for imminent obsolescence (both for workers with those skills and the educational programs that train them). Miller's attachment to the immediate actually renders her proposed pedagogy increasingly less useful than she envisions.[4]

Put another way, an individual's long-term prospects in the labor market revolve around his or her capacity to perform labor that has not become automated by machinery and other technology. In his 1991 *The Work of Nations*, Robert Reich outlined transitions in labor patterns in the second half of the twentieth century, suggesting a tripartite division of industrial work, in-person services, and symbolic-analytic work. Following World War II, industrial workers had a secure and well-paying form of employment in the United States, one made possible with a political-economic arrangement that Reich calls "economic nationalism." Beginning in the 1970s, however, globalization rendered this arrangement obsolete. The mutually beneficial relationship between American workers and corporations was slowly severed. A gap grew between a group of well-paid symbolic analysts (which Reich refers to as the "fortunate fifth" because they constitute roughly 20 percent of the population) and a much larger class of low-paid service work meant to facilitate the consumer goods produced by cheap overseas labor.

Since the publication of *The Work of Nations*, Reich's schema requires the most revision and updating concerning the status of symbolic analysts. While Reich assumes that this group's job security and higher wages will remain more or less preserved, the increasing sophistication of automation has begun to threaten many of these positions (and will continue to do so in the future). To demonstrate to my own students the growing precarious nature of even white-collar work, we briefly survey a website that provides a startling wakeup call for students who believe their college education ensures a secure future. Based on the research of Carl Benedikt Frey and Michael A. Osborne, the site calculates the likelihood that a given profession or occupation will be automated in the next twenty years. For some students, the results upset their belief in the security of pursuing their practically oriented course of study. Accountants and auditors, for example, face a 93.5 percent chance of being automated, computer programmers face a 48.1 percent chance, and market research analysts face a 61.3 percent chance (technical writers, the profession that is often sold as the practical outlet for those students with an interest in language and writing, ironically enough, face an 88.8 percent chance of being automated). Although we can contest the reliability of any given prediction, Frey and Osborne's research highlights how many of today's "good jobs" will soon be transformed into low-wage in-person service work or be eliminated altogether. When students pursue many of today's practical courses of study, part of an elaborate cost-benefit analysis that accompanies the staggering student loans needed to finance higher education, I doubt that they typically factor in the "half-life" of the career itself.

Considering automation's frightening potential, an English degree may actually make more practical sense as a long-term investment than many existing pre-professional majors. If thinking in broad, innovative terms and grappling with the specificities of singular contexts constitutes the most effective bulwark against having one's labor supplanted, then how are we to make sense of the general denigration of the liberal arts—which have proven most adept at producing this flexible thinking—as a useless extravagance that deserves, at best, a marginal and largely ornamental position in the contemporary university? In many respects, the shift toward practically oriented courses of study is an extremely shortsighted endeavor in that it produces workers with soon-to-be-obsolete forms of training and knowledge while simultaneously denying them the opportunity to cultivate the conceptual skills that would allow them to more easily adapt and thrive in new contexts (not to mention the ability to diagnose more effectively the significant problems with this new economic arrangement).

At this point, I would like to translate the language of immediacy and abstraction into the discourse of aesthetics. Rather than consuming the concrete object in all of its immediate sensuousness, aesthetic engagement consists of examining the formal qualities that converged to produce the object. Crucially, it is only when the object is no longer taken for granted as a premade entity that an aesthetic experience can even occur. And perhaps today the slowing down of aesthetic experience to perceive the formal characteristics that constitute an object is more necessary and valuable than ever, if for no other reason than "objects" don't last long today. More specifically, late capitalism operates according to unanchored flows rather than reified objects (or, at least, the perpetual oscillation between the two). As Marx and Engels famously asserted in *The Communist Manifesto*, under capitalism "all fixed, fast-frozen relations, with their train of ancient and venerable prejudices and opinions, are swept away, all new-formed ones become antiquated before they can ossify. All that is solid melts into air" (476). The symbolic-analytic knowledge work of today involves tracing, assembling, and rerouting this complex and often cacophonous swarm of flows rather than territorializing on a specific object and "mastering" it just as it returns to the ether. While there are still "objects" they are continually being modified and transformed by the various intensifications and reversals of the flows that constitute them. Miller's characterization of aesthetic experience and analysis as an escape from reality into abstract speculation ignores the degree to which reality is now abstract and speculative. As Jameson points out in *The Political Unconscious*, "we can think abstractly about the world only to the degree to which the world itself has already become abstract" (51).

If the scenario described earlier accurately captures the contours of contemporary reality, then the most practical education would involve equipping students with the capacities necessary to dealing with ever-fluctuating fluid scenarios. Fortunately, this does not render much of the work done in English studies completely useless. In fact, it suggests precisely the opposite. The future of English studies does not involve overhauling the entire discipline to accommodate harsh new economic conditions but instead in better articulating the ways in which English studies already positions its students to better succeed in these conditions.[5] Indeed, if education as job training constitutes a veritable *dispositif* in the contemporary university, a bundle of conceptual presuppositions that cannot be escaped, then any resistance to the existing situation must work through this predominant logic rather than trying to transcend it altogether. Attempts like Martha Nussbaum's in *Not for Profit*, which valorizes the uselessness of the humanities, fail to register the degree to which such arguments only accelerate the elimination of the liberal arts from higher education. At the same time, however, there are just as many figures who overcorrect Nussbaum's error, emphasizing the importance of immediate skills in education. By my estimation, these are two primary obstacles that must be overcome in refashioning English's "public image": (1) an impulse to retain old notions of "literature" and (2) an impulse to completely territorialize around the immediately practical. As my discussion in this chapter should make clear, both of these tendencies are closely connected to the problematic notion of aesthetics that Guillory and others want to abandon.

The practice of reading serves as a useful example for thinking through some of these complications. Reading is often conceived as a form of passivity that opposes the more productive practice of writing. Translated into economic vocabulary, reading corresponds to consumption and writing to production. The long-held associations of reading with the leisure time that follows a grueling day of labor—or, more directly, with a "leisure class" that does not labor at all—only reinforces the idea that this practice is somehow outside the circuit of production.[6] For these reasons, literature courses are regarded as an indulgence that cannot be afforded in the contemporary university, while composition courses, which more obviously conform to a production model, are still deemed acceptable.

Of course, the schematic I've just outlined is so reductive as to be laughable. Composition studies doesn't jettison reading and interpretation altogether, and its stress on invention strategies certainly constitute a clear version of these practices. Similarly, literary studies is not completely devoid of imparting practical writing skills (although, admittedly, these are often less well defined). Just as Marx saw the chain of production-distribution-consumption as interconnected moments in a cycle rather than discrete practices, we might reconceptualize reading and writing as inseparable activities in a productive process. Rather than choosing sides in the simple binary reading/writing, we should think about the proportions established between these two interrelated practices on a temporal scale—a matter of speeds and slowness. How much reading is necessary before writing, acknowledging that the amount of reading performed changes the goals of writing? Consider a hypothetical example: A certain amount of reading time is required to write an op-ed piece for the newspaper, but perhaps a certain extra amount of reading might convince one that the very act of writing a piece to the newspaper will not constitute an effective strategy for addressing the issue at hand (and that it may actually worsen the problem).[7]

Let's consider a couple concrete examples. Blog writing is a common assignment in newly refurbished Rhetoric and Composition courses with an eye toward the "real world." For advocates of the "public turn," having students compose blogs where they engage with important social and cultural issues provides them with an opportunity to participate more directly in contemporary public debates. Unlike an essay that will only be seen by the instructor, a blog might actually be read by individuals outside the class (or the university) and therefore contribute to some larger civic conversation. But buried within this rationale are a number of presuppositions that warrant further scrutiny; most important, advocates of blogging presume that forms of networked, online communication constitute a transparent medium that can be used to sponsor civil discourse. As Jodi Dean has insightfully illustrated, however, such presuppositions overlook how online communication contributes to what she calls "communicative capitalism." Under communicative capitalism, "messages" are transformed into "contributions" wherein the particular content of any piece of discourse is secondary to the fact that it is an "addition to the pool" of material circulating on the web (58). After arguing that "emphasis on the fact that one can contribute to a discussion and make one's opinion known misdirects attention from the larger system of communication in which the contribution is embedded," Dean explains that participating in online political discussion can actually produce effects that directly counteract the contributor's intentions (60). Deploying Žižek's notion of "interpassivity," Dean claims that the "frantic contributing" of online activity amounts to a "profound passivity" that actually "works to prevent actual action" (60). Online participants can easily assume that online activity frictionlessly translates into material changes in the world; moreover, participating in online communication only strengthens the telecommunications corporations and their subsidiaries that are responsible for many of the social ills being condemned in this online communication.

Dean's analysis should underscore for us the necessity of establishing a proper balance between theory and action. Although blogging and other forms of online interaction can serve valuable ends, one should first carefully consider the resources and constraints of the medium before participating. The university classroom constitutes a valuable space where students might step back from practical activity and analyze the medium of networked communication. Unfortunately, in their denigration of the school as an isolated space and their concurrent pursuit of immediate outcomes, proponents of the "public turn" fail to seize the opportunity the classroom offers for students to engage in substantial forms of "reading" and "reflection."

A similar tension animates my second example. Proponents of the "public turn" have also encouraged students to "partner" with local organizations and assist them with their "communication needs." The worst iteration of such projects—students find a local business and compose promotional documents and other writing—outpaces the excesses of unpaid internships, wherein a student provides free labor for a company. In this case, the student would, through his or her tuition dollars, actually be paying to provide free labor for a company. While the problems with this model are easy to pinpoint, other iterations of "partnering" that lack such egregious edges nevertheless demand closer attention. Having students work with a local nonprofit organization, for instance, avoids the dilemmas of student exploitation, particularly if the nonprofit is contributing to a worthwhile social cause. Once again, though, advocating that students partner with a nonprofit contains within it a number of assumptions that need to be examined. Can we safely conclude that these nonprofit organizations are not part of the problem they claim to be addressing? As Michael Hardt and Antonio Negri detail in *Empire*, many nongovernmental organizations (NGOs) set the groundwork for more overt forms of oppression. Much like the missionaries who preceded colonial intervention in earlier centuries, these NGOs constitute a form of "moral intervention" that can serve as "the first act that prepares the stage for military intervention" in the era of global capitalism (37). While critics of Hardt and Negri have rightly pointed out a number of problems with their sweeping assessment of NGOs, the pair's analysis is important for our purposes insofar as it problematizes a social practice that is incontrovertibly positive at first glance. The push for immediate action bypasses the moment where an incontrovertibly positive practice is examined for any "hidden costs" associated with it. Thus, while I don't want to suggest that nonprofit organizations are incapable of making positive contributions, it behooves us as educators to challenge students to reconsider their most deeply held ideas concerning social progress. In other words, the university's primary mission should be encouraging the kinds of deep reflection that allow one to consider the potential problems with an ostensibly inarguable social institution like a nonprofit organization.

Indeed, I understand reading not as outside of the practices of writing but an integral stage within this productive practice. I'm using "reading"

in the loosest possible way, more as a broad term to characterize the preparatory stage preceding action than as the solitary act of getting absorbed in
a hardbound book (although this practice obviously counts as an important
form of "reading"). Putting it in the action-oriented vocabulary of the
rhetorical tradition, we might think of "reading" as a form of invention—
the discovery and creation of the tools needed to intervene "successfully"
in a given context. In fact, "reading" may be the most important stage
of this productive process, at least if we take seriously Aristotle's definition of rhetoric, which orients almost all of the work done in Rhetoric
and Composition today: the ability in given situations, "to *see* the available
means of persuasion" (37, my emphasis). Aristotle's entire definition pivots
around the act of seeing or observing, and the rhetor's ultimate actions are
inevitably constrained by the degree to which they adequately diagram and
redirect the various forces that have created the situation in which he or she
is immersed. Thinking is not opposed to action but instead constitutes a
specific mode of it. As Gilles Deleuze says in "Intellectuals and Power," his
well-known conversation with Foucault, "there is only action, the action of
theory, the action of praxis, the relations of relays and networks" (207). If
I'm championing reading practices as a certain form of slowing down the
production process, it's not with the aim of halting the process altogether
but of ultimately producing a different outcome. Returning to the discourse of aesthetics, it's interesting that the appreciation of a text's formal
qualities was understood as a form of "deferred pleasure." But we could instead understand aesthetic experience as a form of "deferred production,"
one that would bracket one's immediate impressions of a situation so as to
diagnose the mobile forces that continually shape it anew.

Thinking about aesthetics in these terms not only serves as a way of
linking literary studies to the work done in rhetoric and writing studies
but also provides a ground (of sorts) for the discipline more generally. The
discipline of English would not orient itself around a stable body of knowledge like a literary canon but instead around the various formal relations
and transversal connections that link together any number of different domains. At some level, doing so would merely highlight the interdisciplinary nature of the work that has been circulating within English for quite
some time, providing a coherent but not constricting identity that foregrounds the discipline's wide range of critical and creative investigations.
Whether the umbrella term for this work would be "rhetoric" or "writing"
or "aesthetics" or some combination of the three would largely be a matter of clarifying the already existing connections among these discourses.
Although this is the kind of work that's undoubtedly already been going

on in both literary studies and Rhetoric and Composition, each side has approached issues of form and aesthetics with its own unique set of assumptions and emphases, ensuring that its practitioners illuminate certain formal processes while remaining ignorant of others. If these respective fields were brought into conversation, each field could help point out the other's necessary blind spots.[8]

Where would literary works fit into this schematic? Recall that Guillory sought to recover a notion of aesthetic experience that was not dependent on the concept of literature, which both he and Miller demonstrated to be a tool to preserve clear distinctions between social classes. But there is no reason why the various imaginative works and other cultural artifacts that have been characterized as literature should no longer be taught, as if these objects magically manifested within them the insidious values of the upper crust (or that noncanonical works inherently manifested the values of the dominated culture). As Guillory writes, "no cultural work of any interest at all is simple enough to be allegorized in this way, because any cultural work will *objectify* in its very form and content the same social conflicts that the canon debate allegorizes by means of a divided curriculum" (52). If this were not the case, then there would be no way to explain "the use of the *same* canonical works to inculcate in different generations of students many different and even incompatible ideologies" (63). For our purposes, Guillory's argument underscores that we need not completely dispense with Shakespeare and other canonical figures but that we will need to conceptualize an alternative frame for how they will be approached and deployed.

Perhaps the most effective way of answering this question is by thinking about the relationship between literature and theory. As my earlier analyses have demonstrated, the introduction of literary theory into the discipline of English acted as a threat to the longevity of literature as a concept. The regime of literature was initially so strong that it actually interpolated the deterritorializing threat of theory to further its own ends, both by enlisting it to proliferate the number of interpretations of canonical works or by turning these theoretical interventions into just another canon of important texts. And while the concept of literature still hasn't completely died—recall my analysis in Chapter 1 of its ambivalent configuration within New Historicism—it cannot be said to make the same claims upon us that it once did. At the very least, it is no longer the cultural dominant within the critical community. But if we now operate within a regime of the "interesting"—that is, critical work today is judged not by how well it illuminates certain privileged texts but simply by how well it commands and rewards the attention of its readers—it would seem that theory has become a more useful term for diagnosing the kind of work that goes on today (even work that appears particularly anti-theoretical in the traditional sense).[9] As our opening examination of Vincent Leitch's "planets and constellation" diagram illuminated, the true triumph of theory is the rise of the various "studies" concerning gender, race, media, animals, and a host of other topics; many of these explorations are not primarily invested in literary works although they might use them to in order explore certain questions within their broad research agenda. In this way, literary works have been transformed into a form of theoretical reflection and engagement.

Conversely, the foundational works of French theory emphasized the aesthetic qualities within philosophical inquiry. "Literary theory" was not so much a theory of literature as it was a form of theory that foregrounded its own aesthetic or literary characteristics, underscoring that these formal properties could not be separated from the "arguments" being advanced. Much of the canon of French theory exhibits a daring range of experimentation that examines the relationship between form and content. This is what led many of theory's critics to dismiss it as "merely literature" and for its proponents to deride those who wanted to reduce Derrida, Foucault, and Deleuze to a series of arguments, as if those could be extracted from the stylistic and formal characteristics engaged with in their prose.[10] If theoretical works foreclosed the possibility of decisively extricating form from content, then it should follow that literary works could be considered a particular form of theorizing, since they too assemble a range of material to pose questions or offer provisional strategies to vexing social dilemmas. Of course, "nonliterary works" (and by this I mean writing that does not fall within the recognizable genres of imaginative writing like poetry, fiction, and drama) also conduct this same theoretical speculation, since they too are an assemblage of various forces, suggesting that the discipline might be better served by organizing itself around specific theoretical or conceptual questions rather than the existing divisions between literary and nonliterary texts (although even those boundaries have become increasingly untenable).

In the preceding pages, I have attempted to sketch out a potential future path of the discipline that avoids the problems associated with retaining the increasingly marginal concept of "literature" or migrating toward shortsighted technical training—pitfalls that I regard as two sides of the same coin. My alternative approach to aesthetics not only seeks to overcome these limitations but also gestures toward fruitful connections between literary studies on the one hand and rhetoric and writing studies on the other that could eliminate the unproductive impasses that currently inhibit intradisciplinary conversations. English studies would be able to shed some of its unhelpful historical baggage and thereby recenter itself as a significant player in the university for the foreseeable future rather than an anachronistic oddity occupying a marginal corner of the campus.

But, of course, if this all seems like a too tidy solution to a much more complicated situation, it is. Indeed, even if the discipline can attend to its own past blindnesses and adjust accordingly, it is nevertheless trapped within the broader networks of the university and American culture more generally that will be resistant to (or merely bewildered by) the proposed changes made within the discipline. An updated marketing strategy may not be able to easily pierce the web of preconceptions about the value and purpose of English. Complicating matters further, even if the discipline is successful in becoming a prominent player once again in the university, that victory does not address the labor patterns within the discipline.[11] As the previous chapter stressed, the conflicts between literary and rhetorical education should not be simply conflated with the economic issues surrounding the growing pool of adjunct labor that teaches English courses. In this respect, in spite of the many missteps in Miller's *Textual Carnivals*, the book nevertheless remains admirable in its effort to address in a substantial way the adjunct problem that has only worsened since its publication. So while Guillory provides a more perceptive diagnosis of English studies, including the startling reversal in fortunes between literary studies and Rhetoric and Composition in the contemporary university, Miller should be credited for emphasizing the economic disparities within the discipline that *Cultural Capital* largely elides.

CHAPTER 5

New Things, Old Things: Reading the Latourian Turn Symptomatically

In this final chapter, we turn to the reception of contemporary French sociologist and theorist Bruno Latour within the American academy as a way of demonstrating how many of the tensions within English studies over the last several decades, tensions best illuminated by examining the intersection between French theory and composition studies, operate in the present moment. The final chapter touches on many of the issues that animated the previous four chapters—the structure of literary and rhetorical criticism as a system with its own rhythms, the tension between the specific and the structural, the inevitable reinterpretation of concepts in new environments, and the dynamic between the university and the larger society. Reading Latour's recent incorporation into English studies acts as an extended conclusion of sorts for *The Two Cultures of English*, illustrating how the concepts and practices that we have analyzed remain in force today.

Latour has enjoyed attention from both major spheres of the discipline, and his work seems to offer the possibility of a new paradigm for the discipline. More specifically, he is a figure that many have claimed sounds the death knell for theory and does so while simultaneously deploying key terms from the discourse of Rhetoric and Composition. As a result, Latour appears positioned to inaugurate a potential reordering of the entire discipline. But how exactly is Latour situated with respect to the constantly shifting fault lines that the previous chapters have diagnosed?

After having long been a mainstay in science studies (and a participant of the "science wars" of the late 1990s), Latour crossed over into English studies more generally in the early 2000s, largely on the strength of his "Why Has Critique Run Out of Steam?" essay, which in many respects constituted a mea culpa for much of his previous work.[1] The piece gained attention for highlighting disciplinary norms that had clearly spun out of control, and Latour soon became a model, or, at the very least, a dutiful citation, for a series of new reading practices that were touted to revitalize the humanities in the new century. These new practices, which went by names like "surface reading," "reparative reading," "postcritical reading," and "the descriptive turn," saw in Latour a figure who could spearhead a movement that would challenge long-standing critical orthodoxies, primarily the hegemony of symptomatic reading practices as well as the unquestioned valorization of suspicion. Against models of interpretation that sought to reveal the true meaning of a text lurking beneath its innocuous surface, a practice they saw best concretized in Frederic Jameson's Marxist hermeneutic, "postcritical" critics sought to rally their scholarly peers to turn back to "things themselves." Description, objectivity, trust, generosity—values and practices long dismissed as naive at best and conservative at worst—should be reclaimed. Critics should allow the text to speak for itself rather than imposing some interpretive schema from the outside. Rather than having the critic diagnose the text, the text would instead inform the critic, who would limit him or herself to patient observation and description. Key texts in this vein included Stephen Best and Sharon Marcus's 2009 special issue of the journal *Representations*, "The Way We Read Now," particularly their introductory essay "Surface Reading: An Introduction," as well as Heather Love's essays "Close but Not Deep" and "Close Reading and Thin Description." Eve Sedgwick's earlier essay, 1997's "Paranoid Reading and Reparative Reading," later republished in her 2003 book *Touching Feeling*, served as another familiar touchstone. Rita Felski offered a book-length meditation on these issues in her 2015 *The Limits of Critique*. The movement has since unleashed a bevy of commentary, both positive and negative, with Latour serving as a touchstone.[2]

Rhetoric and Composition's turn to Latour may not be as intense as within literary and theoretical discourse, but it proves substantial nonetheless and speaks to some of the field's most cherished commitments. Some of the earliest Rhetoric and Composition scholarship to engage with Latour was published in the late 1980s, when Dorothy Winsor used him to explicate the writing practices of engineers (not surprising given that Latour's 1987 book *Science in Action* offered an account of the working practices of engineers). Although a smattering of publications, largely confined to technical writing analyses, appeared in the following two decades, a critical mass was not achieved until the early 2010s, at essentially the same point when literary theorists began engaging with Latour.[3] At that point, Rhetoric and Composition's premier publication venues featured articles that treated Latour as a theorist of consequence to the field. Perhaps the most important of these entries was Paul Lynch's 2012 *College English* article "Composition's New Thing: Bruno Latour and the Apocalyptic Turn," which adopted much of the same argumentative strategies that characterized the treatment of Latour in literary circles. Indeed, Lynch positioned Latour in much the same way that the "postcritique" movement did: as someone who details the limitations of critique, limitations that have deadly consequences in the era of climate change. As Lynch writes, "In the apocalyptic turn, contemplation, connection, and cultivation supersede critique as the discipline's central values" (464). Several years later, in 2015, Lynch paired with Nathaniel Rivers to edit a collection entitled *Thinking with Bruno Latour in Rhetoric and Composition*, which assembled some of the most respected names in the field to offer their assessments of Latour; participants included Thomas Rickert, a leading rhetorical theorist, and Marilyn Cooper, former editor of *College Composition and Communication*.

Latour's work appeals to those in Rhetoric and Composition for more than his problematization of critique. Many of the concepts (or at least signifiers) that feature prominently in his thought have long had a comfortable home in the field. For one thing, Latour is a "high theorist" willing to talk about the practice of writing and its capacity to not merely reflect ideas but generate them. Echoing a familiar refrain within Rhetoric and Composition, Latour recently admitted that "if there is one phenomenon I have never stopped wondering at, it's the countless surprises generated by the very material act of writing" ("Life Among" 464). He makes a case for an increased profile for writing as an area of scholarly pursuit; for instance, take note of the fictional sociology professor who appears in a dialogue in the middle of *Reassembling the Social*, who admits that he simply teaches writing now. Latour's method appears to be writing-centered, a process of endless observation and description. Latour laments that writing has been marginalized in graduate education today: "Is it not strange that professors claim to teach PhD students to 'think' and 'study' without ever directing their attention to the subterranean act of writing—which is not to be confused with obeying a format or looking for a 'good style'?" ("Life Among" 465). In calling attention to and attempting to correct the marginalization of writing and writing pedagogy within academe, Latour appeals to foundational concerns of Rhetoric and Composition.

Beyond taking writing seriously, Latour describes certain ontological conditions through recourse to terms that bestow Rhetoric and Composition with a newfound centrality and respect. He characterizes the world as a complex "composition" of heterogeneous elements, and he describes the interactions among these elements in terms of an "assembly" or "parliament of things." The work of negotiating how these elements are combined is frequently described in the language of "diplomacy."[4] Such language cannot fail to appeal to a field that takes deliberation and debate as a key component of its identity. Latour thus allows the "everything's rhetorical" mantra to assume a new meaning, one that sheds much of the baggage that term carried during the era of postmodernism. Rather than being used to describe our limited and interested perspective on the world, and thereby denying the possibility of objective knowledge, the phrase now comes to describe the very texture of the material world itself. In both cases, rhetoric can protest that it does not occupy a more prominent position in the university.

Latour possesses a number of continuities and discontinuities with the theorists that preceded him. In some respects, Latour's emergence as a significant thinker within American academia betrays an uninterrupted continuity with all that came before. Indeed, the opening of Lynch and Rivers's collection begins by anticipating objections from a sizable portion of their audience who will be suspicious of importing yet another continental thinker into the discourse: "'Wait, don't tell me,' we hear the reader. '*Another* French theorist to rescue rhetoric and composition from its intellectual doldrums'" (1). In their effort to frame Latour as a figure worthy of attention, Lynch and Rivers are forced to acknowledge how the turn to contemporary French thought has become so predictable within the discipline that "acquiring another avant-garde European is about as hip as buying a futon" (1). Indeed, Latour's very name only intensifies the ubiquitous French presence on the American scene, his name invoking a range of French stereotypes. Not only does Latour come from a family of famous vintners located in the Burgundy region, but the first syllable of his name is also a definite article in the French language, one of a handful of words that the average monolingual American has picked up on in sitcoms or beer commercials in order to mark the country's citizens' overbearing pretentiousness. Meanwhile, the second syllable brings to mind both Paris's most famous architectural feat as well as the world's premier cycling race hosted by the French each July. Fancy wine, the Eiffel Tower, the Tour de France, stuffy accents. What could be *more* French? Ironically enough, however, while his name would seem to solidify the decades-long occupation of the American humanities by French theory, the academy has positioned Latour's work as an outright repudiation of that era. Latour is regarded as a bold departure from the tenets that unified the loose coalition of postmodernists and poststructuralists.

Reading Latour's own work both with and against the grain, the following analysis not only rejects the idea that Latour constitutes a momentous new era in criticism but also diagnoses how Latour's work helps facilitate that problematic idea. The first part of the chapter examines the core components of Latour's work and compares them to the key French theorists he is positioned as repudiating. This section illustrates that critical claims positing an enormous gap between Latour and his theoretical peers are exaggerated, if not misleading. There are more continuities with the key French theorists than the postcritique movement typically acknowledges. The second part of the chapter then examines a point of curiosity in Latour's recent work, *An Inquiry into Modes of Existence*, as a way of illuminating a crucial conceptual problem plaguing his broader corpus. More specifically, Latour's work—particularly the work that has most attracted critics in English studies—fails to adequately deal with what I am calling here "emergent structures," distributed networks of relations that, although they differ substantially from top-down or centralized structures of control, exert many of the same constraining effects (think here of the second chapter's examination of the serial situation that animated Jameson's critique of Burke).

With these two key dynamics elaborated, the third part of the chapter then reads Latour's uptake within English studies. Through a reading of Lynch's *College English* article, I argue that the idea that Latour represents a major break in the discipline is itself a failure to think rigorously about "emergent structures." Furthermore, Latour is so appealing because his work allows one to avoid confronting the dilemma that emergent structures pose. In other words, one dimension of Latour's work—namely, his actor-network theory (ANT)—authorizes and reinforces another dimension of it—namely, the idea that his work constitutes a substantial transformation within the critical scene today (which is challenged by the lengthy analysis conducted in the first portion of the chapter).

Latour's own failure to grapple with emergent structures gets reiterated in the scholarship that treats him as a radical break from his predecessors. His notion of localized networks that are not predetermined by overarching contexts does not only appeal to critics in terms of the content of their work. It also animates their thinking about what their scholarship can accomplish more broadly. Latour ultimately serves the same function for both spheres of English: the promise of a complete escape from a certain repetitious practice that seems to doom criticism. In fact, Latour's work underwrites a fantasy that criticism can be more than just criticism within a university setting, that it could influence the broader social world in a way that it never has before. But this very fantasy of escaping from the existing confines of criticism is an attempt to escape from an "emergent structure."

Latour and French Theory

In order to assess Latour's reception within the American academy, we must first outline the key components of his thought and situate them within the milieu in which they emerged. Although Latour's work, conducted over the course of roughly four decades, resists any pat summary, a general set of principles animate his thinking. I will now briefly detail four interconnected and mutually reinforcing intellectual commitments: (1) his embrace of the nonhuman in structuring the social world; (2) his emphasis on action as the fundamental ontological principle; (3) his rejection of "context" as a methodological tool; and (4) his distaste for critique as an investigative disposition.

First, Latour's work argues that it is important to acknowledge the role that nonhuman entities play in human affairs. He seeks to abolish any hierarchy between humans and nonhumans, emphasizing how the material world actively shapes social life. As he writes in his early work *The Pasteurization of France*, "there are not only 'social' relations, relations between man and man. Society is not made up just of men, for everywhere microbes intervene and act" (35). Against traditional Durkheimian sociology, which reads inanimate objects as embodiments of values that human society has projected onto them, Latour maintains that nonhumans possess a volition and momentum of their own. In later work like *We Have Never Been Modern*, he pushes this insight even further, insisting that the very division between human and nonhuman, which he regards as the defining gesture of modernity, needs to be dissolved. Too many problems emerge when we demand that nature and culture constitute two separate spheres that operate according to their own incommensurable procedures. In place of these two regimes, he proposes a series of continually shifting "hybrids" or "networks" that interweave the two sides—or, more appropriately, render any distinction between them moot. In incorporating nonhuman entities like microbes into the "social world," the category of the "human" loses its previous coherence and stability.

Second, Latour's work argues that action constitutes the ground through which we should understand the world, a principle advanced most forcefully in the actor-network theory detailed in 2005's *Reassembling the Social*. As Graham Harman, Latour's most vocal explicator, points out, this theory proposes that "there are no nouns in the world, only verbs" ("Demoderning" 253). The centrality of action to Latour's thinking can be seen in the language of "actors" or "actants," which he claims "compose" the world. He regards the social world as a "trail of *associations* between heterogeneous elements" (5). In other words, we must understand the social primarily through the interactions of its actors. The relation between two actors should constitute our primary focus (rather than the actors themselves). Actors derive their composition through their actions, actions that are necessarily connected to other actors in their network. Indeed, the network simply amounts to the sum total of interactions among its participants, both human and nonhuman. Without these interactions, the network effectively ceases to exist, becoming an altogether different network of associations. As Latour explains, ANT claims that social groupings "need to be constantly kept up by some group-making effort" (*Reassembling* 35). Any stability or coherence that exists within a network is caused by the series of actions composing the network, not something that preceded the actions themselves. Latour writes that "the rule is performance and what has to be explained, the troubling exceptions, are any type of stability over the long term and on a larger scale" (35).

Third, Latour's work rejects the notion that social phenomenon can be explained through recourse to "context." He insists that using contextual frames to understand the actions of heterogeneous elements amounts to little more than "stopping the description when you are too tired or lazy to go on" (*Reassembling* 148). Latour targets sociologists who use "social context" as an explanation when they should be committing themselves to the hard work of determining the composition of the social world. It is not too difficult to see how Latour's rejection of context is inseparable from his commitment to action as a fundamental ontological principle. Beginning with "social context" evades the relentless sea of transformations that characterize actor-networks; beginning with "social context" ascribes stability to a volatile scene. As a result, "sociologists of the social" regard actors simply as bearers of a preexisting truth or meaning that originates in the broader social context. In Latour's terminology, elements within an environment are rendered as "intermediaries" of this larger contextual truth rather than full-blown "mediators," which "transform, translate, distort, and modify the meaning or the elements they are supposed to carry" (*Reassembling* 39). For Latour, any discussion of "context" must come at the end of a careful, patient attention to the individual performances of actors within a network since these actions effectively constitute this context. If one starts with a contextual frame, then it only ensures that one will arrive in the same place where one began—with the idea of the "social" as an all-encompassing term, a term that actually explains nothing.

Fourth, Latour's work has a general aversion to the supposed powers attributed to social critique, most clearly evident in his 2004 *Critical Inquiry* essay "Why Has Critique Run Out of Steam?" Here, Latour diagnoses what he regards as a dangerous knee-jerk reaction in the humanities and social sciences, which regard acts of problematizing and deconstructing as unquestionable goods that always result in politically progressive ends. Suspicion of truth and facts is no longer confined to the left wing of the political spectrum. Latour specifically cites Republican strategist Frank Luntz, who deployed the language of postmodern skepticism to reject the scientific consensus concerning manmade climate change. Latour notes that the most pressing danger may no "longer be coming from an excessive confidence in ideological arguments posturing as matters of fact . . . but from an excessive *distrust* of good matters of fact disguised as bad ideological biases" (227). An unabashed critical disposition, found in its most concentrated form in humanities PhD programs, has spread throughout the general culture, resulting in wild conspiracies ranging from those claiming 9/11 was an "inside job" to those insisting that the Apollo program never landed on the moon. He recommends a turn away from deconstruction toward constructivism and a concomitant turn from "matters of fact" toward "matters of concern." From his perspective, orienting oneself toward "matters of concern" involves engaging in a caring and passionate manner with one's object of analysis rather than resorting to a dismissive antifetishism; it would amount to "a multifarious inquiry launched with the tools of anthropology, philosophy, metaphysics, history, sociology to detect *how many participants* are gathered in a *thing* to make it exist and to maintain its existence" (246). The critic should be one who creatively assembles rather than one who simply debunks.

At this point, we should be able to see how these four commitments—the recognition of nonhuman agents, the emphasis on action, the rejection of context, the distaste with critique—are all inseparable elements of his thought. For instance, in showing that nonhuman entities have agency, Latour is able to illuminate that action and transformation are not simply limited to the sphere of human activity; in other words, nonhuman entities' agency confirms that agency, or action, constitutes a transcendental principle. Simultaneously, Latour's insistence on action as a generalized ontological condition complements his argument concerning the failure of traditional sociology's dependence on "social context," since the discipline's reversion to contextual frames inhibits and overlooks important subterranean transformations within networks. Meanwhile, any investment in critique is simply the flip side of a reliance on contextual frames. Given its investment in revealing a hidden truth like "power," "capitalism," or "society" lurking behind innocuous surfaces, critique relies upon the notion of a stable context that cannot keep pace with the dynamic, ever-changing reality of actor networks. Critique's investment in antifetishism precludes it from acknowledging the legitimate power that nonhuman objects can exert. And, finally, the caring, nurturing stance involved in a critic's investment in "matters of concern" is inseparable from the interdependency between human and nonhuman entities that links their fates together.

Having briefly outlined some of the core tenets of Latour's philosophy, we can now address how his writing engages with the key figures of the theory era. While the American academy has positioned Latour in largely antagonistic terms with theory, regarding his allergy to critique and highly legible prose as signs of a diametrical opposition to his predecessors, the relationship is a much more complicated one. There may be more convergences with thinkers like Foucault, Deleuze, and Derrida than the current postcritical moment would feel comfortable admitting. In fact, Latour's work might be used productively to illuminate unappreciated dimensions of canonical theory texts. Leveling any clear distinctions that would baptize Latour as a bold new direction, Yves Citton has recently remarked that "Latour clearly belongs to the glorious generation of Barthes, Deleuze, and Derrida, who promoted the practice of 'writing' (*écriture*) as central both to social life and to theoretical-philosophical inquiry" (315).

In the same way that his emphasis on writing mirrors that found in theory, Latour's emphasis on action or relation as the primary ontological pivot places him squarely with the primary thinkers of the theory era. An investment in relation and action can be traced at least as far back as Nietzsche's famous dictum that "there is no 'being' behind doing, effecting, becoming; 'the doer' is merely a fiction added to the deed—the deed is everything" (*Genealogy* 45). The Nietzschean influence on French theory registers most obviously in Deleuze's *Nietzsche & Philosophy*, which mobilizes "force" as its central concept, and Foucault's "Nietzsche, Genealogy, History," which describes history as the ceaseless interweaving of competing forces. But far from being restricted to commentary on Nietzsche, action finds itself to be central in other canonical texts from the period. In the opening pages of Deleuze and Guattari's *Anti-Oedipus*, for instance, "production" serves as the key term for understanding the world.[5] And, in the companion volume *A Thousand Plateaus*, the primacy of force, action, and connection underwrites the pair's concept of the rhizome, which they argue is "a multiplicity that necessarily changes in nature as it expands its connections," clarifying that "there are no points or positions in a rhizome, such as those found in a structure, tree, or root. There are only lines" (8)—that is, there are only relations that effectively produce the participants in the relation. Meanwhile, although ostensibly confined to questions of linguistic interpretation and representation, Derrida is equally invested in language's creative, productive capacities, most evident in his exploration of J. L. Austin's performative speech acts in *Limited, Inc.* but also in his treatment of phenomena like the American Declaration of Independence.[6]

Along similar lines, Latour's rejection of context resonates with much of the theory era that preceded (or accompanied) him. Like Latour, Derrida bristles at the notion of a readymade interpretive approach that could be applied indiscriminately in any situation: "deconstruction is not a method and cannot be transformed into a method" ("Letter" 273). In his essay "Signature Event Context," Derrida rejects the notion that context could ever be stabilized (or "saturated" in his terminology). Indeed, Derrida's conception of language maintains that the meaning of any word depends on context, but that context is itself only constituted by the heterogeneous elements that compose it—that is, all of the other words within a given situation. Rather than being determined a priori, a word's meaning is derived from how it is used in various contexts, thereby making it possible for forms of substantial "semantic drift" to occur over time. Accordingly, Derrida's analyses were always attuned to the singular status of a given text; rather than graft an exterior concept onto a text, Derrida would allow, through a careful, patient eye, for pivotal terms to emerge within that specific network of associations. While terms like pharmakon, trace, or signature would acquire a singular force within Derrida's treatment of a given text, their importance did not transfer effectively into his next reading. In

2016, Latour commented on the compatibility between ANT and semiotics, explaining that he sees the latter as an "empirical method so as to avoid the flight of concepts into anything like 'thought.' Just like exegesis, semiotics grounds thought in figures that can be described and studied step by step. The continuity of agency is no longer obscured by the multiplicity of its figurations" ("Life Among" 468).

The outright dismissal of preexisting contextual frames reaches a more intense register in Deleuze and Guattari; the entirety of *Anti-Oedipus* could be read as an extended mediation on the limitations of Freudian psychology, which finds the same answers everywhere it looks. Speaking of Freud's analysis of the Wolf-Man in *A Thousand Plateaus*, they lament that for Freud, "there will always be a reduction to the One: the little scars, the little holes, becomes subdivisions of the great scar or supreme hole named castration; the wolves become substitutes for a single Father who turns up everywhere, or wherever they put him" (31). Although institutionalized repackaging of Derrida, Deleuze, and others could transform them into easy-to-use applications, they themselves are unequivocal about the problems associated with using context as a determining force.

Although less pronounced, Latour also shares with poststructuralism a relative lack of interest in the power of critique. The primary figures of theory adopted an approach that can be best illuminated by their engagement with those masters of the "hermeneutics of suspicion": Marx, Nietzsche, and Freud. Recent treatments of critique have tended to conflate the theory era and its nineteenth (and early twentieth) century precedents as part of a single continuum. If Marx, Nietzsche, and Freud constitute the original unholy trinity, they are reactivated by Althusser, Foucault, and Lacan beginning in the 1960s. At one level, conflating these two moments makes sense, particularly since the figures of the 1960s described their respective relationships to Marx, Nietzsche, and Freud using the language of return and recovery. Recall not only Lacan's declaration that his work constituted a "return to Freud" but also Althusser and Balibar's remarks early in *Reading Capital* that they were repeating Marx "by *reading* a text by Marx which is itself a *reading* of a text of classical economics" (24). And, of course, Foucault's engagement with Nietzsche bears many of the hallmarks of a faithful return, with one commentator suggesting that *Discipline and Punish* constitutes a rewriting of the second essay of *The Genealogy of Morals*.[7] Yet, as mentioned in Chapter 3, the nature of that return was far from a frictionless reproduction, instead enacting an interplay of repetition and differentiation that complicates the distinction between inside and outside that critique depends upon.

Put slightly differently, it would be a mistake to conflate the "masters of suspicion" of the nineteenth (and early twentieth) century with the post-structuralists who would revisit them in earnest several decades later; La-can, Althusser, and Foucault all produced novel approaches *through* their engagement with these figures rather than abandoning them altogether. The act of repetition produced something radically different, generating more of a transformation than any external critique could imagine. The poststructuralists' proximity to their objects of study amounted to a form of intimacy and care that resonates with Latour's call for a turn toward "matters of concern."[8] While the primary figures of the theory era cer-tainly indulged in scathing indictment—see Derrida's harsh words for Agamben in the first volume of *The Beast and the Sovereign*, or Deleuze's evisceration of the "new philosophers"—any reading of their thought as simply a critical enterprise fails to do justice to their work.[9]

Against those critics who characterize the theory era as one dominated by critique, it would be better to take a cue from Deleuze and Guattari's *What Is Philosophy?*, which identifies philosophy not as a critical enterprise but instead as a creative one invested in producing concepts. A wild, cre-ative energy animates the poststructuralists' writing, both in terms of their willingness to make daring conceptual connections as well as to engage in surprising formal experimentation. For example, to conflate theory with "critique" would be to fail to register the giddy, mischievous quality of Derrida's *Glas*, a book consisting of two columns, one on Hegel and the other on Jean Genet, that effectively sponsors a lengthy dialogue between two unlikely interlocutors. Even the infamous term "deconstruction," a term that many associate with a thorough extermination of all meaning and cherished values, carries within it a more positive, creative potential. In his short piece "Letter to a Japanese Friend," Derrida grapples with the term "deconstruction," voicing uneasiness about the negative connotations it possesses, particularly in American contexts. He explains that although deconstruction involves "the undoing, decomposing, and desedimenting of structures," it should not be considered a "negative operation." From his perspective, "rather than destroying, it was also necessary to understand how an 'ensemble' was constituted and to reconstruct it to this end" ("Let-ter" 272). Notice here how Derrida's recourse to the word "ensemble" shares much with Latour's notion of the "thing" as an assembly of forces that he described in "Why Has Critique Run Out of Steam?" Derrida re-gards deconstruction in more positive terms and rejects the notion that his analyses are fundamentally destructive.

Despite the numerous instances of overlap, Latour does place some distance between himself and many of his theory compatriots, particularly after his early period of work that was deeply influenced by Hobbes's and Nietzsche's conceptions of reality as a ceaseless struggle for domination. Yet we can see that much of the distance Latour wants to inject between himself and other prominent theorists is a product of either a peculiar interpretation or an acknowledged exaggeration to make a point. Take, for instance, what can only be a thinly veiled mockery of Foucault in Latour's 1998 collaboration with Emilie Hernant, *Paris Invisible City*. In this text, the pair juxtaposes their model of social organization, one embodied in Paris's chaotic sprawl, with a sober, highly regimented model reminiscent of that found in *Discipline and Punish*. Asserting "there are no more panopticons than panoramas," they scoff at the notion that power assumes the centralized, omnipotent forms Foucault's analysis suggests (quoted in Harman, *Bruno Latour: Reassembling the Political*, 127).

And yet Latour's sarcastic, dismissive treatment stems from a particular reading of Foucault's work, one that resonates with the readings previously examined in Chapter 3; like the predominant reading of Foucault in North America, Latour's reading appropriates the panopticon as a metaphor that explains all of society. For both the American academy and Latour, the panopticon is read as a "dream building" rather than, as Foucault proposes, a "diagram of a mechanism of power reduced to its ideal form" (*Discipline* 205). Unlike in Chapter 3, however, where Foucault was read in this way by New Historicists and rhetoricians like James Berlin with an approving nod, thereby transforming him into a version of ideology critique— and not a particularly nuanced one at that—Latour disapproves of the "dream building" formulation for failing to attend to society's rhizomatic structure. Latour criticizes Foucault for advancing a rigid, top-down, all-encompassing model of power, but in doing so ascribes to him a definition of power that Foucault deliberately sought to avoid (recall his insistence that power is "not evil" and should instead be understood as "games of strategy" (*Foucault Live* 447)). The allusions to Foucault in *Paris Invisible City* seek to create novelty around Latour's version of social organization, but in doing so, they only highlight that Foucault already resides in the space that Latour has carved out for himself. Indeed, Foucault is rather explicit about a number of methodological commitments that could easily be attributable to Latour if the citations were stripped away. A series of interviews Duccio Trombadori conducted with Foucault in 1978 are startling for how stringently they insist on many of the same values and practices underwriting Latour's actor-network theory.[10] In a number of areas where

Latour has sought to make a unique mark, we can hear echoes of Foucault that Latour may have failed to detect.

Latour's engagement with Derrida during the opening section of *We Have Never Been Modern* amounts to another instance where he falls into a problematic reading in an effort to distance himself from poststructuralism. Oddly enough, here Latour apologizes in advance for the hasty reductiveness of his remarks, striking a different pose from the biting satire in *Paris Invisible City*. He admits that the following analysis will treat Derrida, along with E. O. Wilson and Pierre Bourdieu, "a bit unfairly." After adopting this conciliatory tone, Latour proceeds to place the three together to illustrate the limitations of approaching the world through narrow disciplinary lenses. Wilson's biological discourse fails to grapple with social forces in any meaningful way, while Bourdieu's sociology cannot fail to stumble when dealing with scientific and technological matters. He then writes that when Derrida "speaks of truth effects . . . to believe in the real existence of brain neurons or power plays would betray enormous naiveté" (6). Yet Derrida, seven years earlier, repudiated precisely this type of reading of his work.[11]

The preceding analysis was intended to illuminate some of the resonances between Latour and the theory era that preceded his entrance onto the main critical stage. Of course, my analysis was too brief to do justice to the richness of all the thinkers involved, neglecting a host of significant intersections and divergences. My primary purpose was simply to show the many continuities running through theory into Latour's work. Or, perhaps somewhat differently, so as to avoid the impression that Latour merely siphons insights from these thinkers, I sought to suggest that Latour should be considered a full-fledged member of that era, regardless of what specific points of emphasis in his work might distinguish him from the rest. In other words, while I do not want to suggest that Latour is saying the same thing as the rest of theory (nor that everyone within that assemblage is saying the same thing, either), I do want to highlight for polemical purposes that the predominant image of Latour—namely, a figure who stands at a great distance from those who came before him—demands revision. Indeed, inspection of Latour's texts reveals that he does not typically seek to create that sense of distance, either. Even in the handful of instances where Latour's desire to accentuate the value of his position leads to troubling interpretations of his peers, it would be fair to conclude that Latour's actual targets are certain strands of Foucauldianism or Derridianism rather than Foucault or Derrida directly (and, as we have also seen, both Foucault and Derrida are at constant pains to distance themselves from the popularized versions of their work that have circulated and outpaced their actual writing). The primary question becomes, then, the origin of the impulse to isolate and elevate Latour. What purposes does that elevation serve? And, perhaps, most important of all, what does positing a wide gap between Latour and his predecessors cover over? What subtle shifts in emphasis between Latour and others are sure to be overlooked by casting them as two incommensurable modes, or with Latour being treated as a decisive improvement in a generalized narrative of methodological progression? To answer these questions, we first need to outline Latour's thinking about the durability of actor networks and their capacity for change, since this material provides a way of thinking about historical transformation that underwrites rhythms in scholarly production.

Latour and the Problem of Emergent Structures

If we had to pinpoint the three most important books in Latour's oeuvre, texts that best encapsulate his intellectual itinerary, they would likely be *We Have Never Been Modern* (1991), *Reassembling the Social* (2005), and *An Inquiry into Modes of Existence: An Anthropology of the Moderns* (2012). Although we might assume that a seamless forward momentum will transport us from one landmark to the next as Latour gradually refines his concepts and commitments, closer inspection illuminates a progression complicated by a countervailing recursive force. *We Have Never Been Modern* provides a rich account of the "modern constitution," which separates nature and culture into two incommensurable spheres. Modernity presumes that the border dividing the two cannot be penetrated, but in doing so has ignored a series of hybrid formations that interweave nature and culture such that they become indistinguishable. Within this text, however, neither the contours of these hybrid networks nor their broader significance are fully elaborated upon. *Reassembling the Social* offers a more robust account of how networks are composed and how they transform over time; the book also outlines a series of techniques for sociologists building networks from scratch while conducting fieldwork. The publication of *An Inquiry into Modes of Existence* seven years later marks a bold new departure, introducing a host of new concepts and terms that few could have predicted from reading his actor-network theory. In this work, Latour relegates networks to a single "mode of existence," proposing roughly a dozen others, all with their own unique characteristics. How this conceptual system squares with his previous work is far from simple. Complicating matters, Latour revealed that he had begun working on *An Inquiry* in the late 1980s, keeping the project a secret for many years. In some respects, the "modes of existence" project actually precedes his actor-network theory, even though the publication timeline positions them as discrete events. Even more confusingly, the "modes of existence" project is meant to correct some of the oversights of actor-network theory. In other words, Latour was developing a solution to a problem that had not yet been fully articulated.

Latour's transition from his actor-network theory to his modes of existence project underscores a tension that will become important shortly. For now, we need only point out why Latour found himself dissatisfied with ANT and a complication involved in his proposed solution. Although he admires ANT for being an incredibly flexible method, Latour is eventually forced to admit that certain liabilities correspond to being so flexible. He confesses that with ANT, "everything equally becomes actor-network" such that "as denounced by Hegel, all cows become grey. When I realized that, I thought something was wrong: it was very well to make an actor network, it *unfolds* the associations. But it does not *qualify* them" (*Inquiry* 311). In the early pages of *An Inquiry into Modes of Existence*, Latour introduces a fictional ethnographer who learns about actor-network theory and quickly encounters some difficulties:

> to her great confusion, as she studies segments from Law, Science, The Economy, or Religion she begins to feel that she is saying almost *the same thing* about all of them: namely, that they are "composed in a heterogeneous fashion of unexpected elements revealed by the investigation." Though she moves "from one surprise to another . . . somewhat to her surprise, this stops being surprising . . . as each element becomes surprising *in the same way*." (35)

There are two important things to note from Latour's admission. First, the exhaustion of ANT, a methodology designed to overcome the "all cows become grey" dilemma, announces that the ghost of "context" has arisen in the most unlikely of forms. Latour's admission should also alert us to the fact that any attempt to evacuate all contextual frames from analysis is a fool's errand. Second, Latour's solution to ANT's limitations presents another dilemma, as it appears to revert back to "modern" formulations that his earlier work rejected. The dozen "modes of existence" that Latour outlines in *An Inquiry* all possess an axiomatic quality; as Barbara Herrnstein Smith points out, acknowledging the existence of the modes is simply treated as a "proper [attitude] taken or given in advance" (Latour's preferred term is "pre[-]position") (343). Latour's *Inquiry* posits a "sharp distinction and mutual incommensurability" between science and religion as existential categories, each with their own "modes of verification" (343). In doing so, Latour appears to be following evolutionary biologist Stephen J. Gould, who divides the world into a sphere of facts governed by science and a sphere of values governed by religion. Gould's division between fact and value, though, is perhaps the clearest instantiation of the nature/culture dichotomy that Latour condemned in *We Have Never Been Modern*. With his modes project, Latour has simply multiplied the number of incommensurable categories populating the world rather than challenging the very notion of incommensurable categories. Has Latour decided to become modern after all?

At this point, on the way toward illuminating Latour's significance for contemporary English studies, I want to suggest that these conceptual snaggles that emerge from *An Inquiry into Modes of Existence* can be used to clarify the nebulous status of Latour's political commitments. Outlining Latour's political orientation will allow us to better understand how his work resonates within English studies, specifically attitudes concerning scholarship's potential for growth as well as its potential impact in the broader public arena.

As with any figure who draws substantial scholarly interest, Latour has solicited his fair share of criticism from thinkers across the political spectrum. Leftists have been particularly harsh, denouncing him for refusing to acknowledge the possibility of radical change and, therefore, revolutionary politics.[12] One should not be surprised by such vociferous charges given Latour's general dismissal of Marxism—in *The Pasteurization of France*, he writes that "capitalism is marginal even today" (173)—as well as his emphasis on gradual reformations within networks, all of which would seem to betray his politically conservative (with a small "c") tendencies. Graham Harman bristles at the many "shot-in-the-dark" (*Bruno Latour* 113) assaults on Latour as a neoliberal, decrying these criticisms as lazy and uninformed takes on his thought. Harman, having had a personal relationship with Latour for many years, asserts: "I can safely describe him (*qua* voter, citizen, and reader of the news) as a politically benevolent French centrist with progressive tendencies" (5). Harman is certainly right to be suspicious of judgments of Latour as a political and economic reactionary, particularly in an era when "neoliberal" has become a fuzzy catch-all form of derision, a term made all the more unhelpful by overuse. I wonder, though, what to make of Harman's defense of Latour as a progressive centrist when the center-left in the Western world today is almost invariably of a neoliberal stripe. More important, the outright detractors and impassioned defenders have the potential of obscuring how Latour's thought illuminates important tensions within the political left today.

Latour's assessment of both capitalism and Marxist analyses of it produces mixed results. His rejection of the "sociology of the social," in which "the social" serves as a prepackaged explanation for all phenomena, extends to traditional Marxist analyses as well. Before looking at a discrete network of local actors, the Marxist critic can simply judge the situation with a one-word answer: "capitalism." Given the dynamic nature of capitalism, which constantly innovates and reinvents itself, Latour does level an important criticism of much of the political left insofar as it remains far too committed to old paradigms and vocabularies that can only clunkily diagnose emerging formations. In this way, Latour's work is compatible with Jameson's insistence, which we examined back in Chapter 2, that any truly Marxist analysis must be as nimble and flexible as capitalism itself. For Jameson, Marxists can only be truly faithful to Marx by being willing to depart from his initial formulations and produce new concepts that respond to the present moment. Interestingly enough, both Jameson and Latour approve of the work of Fernand Braudel, but whereas the former counts Braudel as an important figure in Marxist thought, the latter treats Braudel as an alternative to Marx. Latour's attitude regarding Braudel speaks to his failure to grapple fully with capitalism's inherent volatility, a feature that ultimately constitutes a source of strength rather than vulnerability. In short, then, Latour chastises Marxists in the same way that he does "sociologists of the social." From his perspective, both groups treat their key concept, "capitalism" and "society," respectively, in problematic ways—that is, as a standardizing mold that squashes potential transformations in advance.

Unfortunately, Latour's assessment does not only conflate traditional forms of rigid Marxist philosophy with more dialectical iterations; it also fails to acknowledge the strength of decentralized or acephalous forms of power. Decentralized networks' impressive force is precisely what inspired Jameson's fascination with the serial situation that we detailed in Chapter 2. It similarly underwrites Foucault's meditations on power; he, like Latour, wants to "cut the head off the king" when it comes to our conception of society so as to reveal a series of interlocking and shifting assemblages. Where Foucault differs from Latour, however, is his recognition of the force that such dynamic assemblages can exert, constraining change at both a local and global level (or, perhaps alternatively, if Latour recognizes that fact, he seems relatively untroubled by it, which might come across as political indifference). Regardless, Foucault's grim conclusions perhaps lead Latour to misread his notion of power, with Latour erroneously concluding that Foucault believes power "embraces everything" rather than emerging "from everywhere" (*Sexuality* 93). Latour fails to see that the power that comes from everywhere can combine in unpredictable ways, acquiring a strength that makes it feel as though it embraces everything. Networks or assemblages consisting of a series of feedback loops are capable of forming; these loops can withstand, and perhaps even intensify, from both internal and external resistance. Behavior within the network, even when it differs wildly from one actor to another, does little to modify the feedback loops that constrain the range of possible activity. So while Latour rightly rejects placing situations in rigid contextual frames, instead preferring to compare the relative strengths of networks, his repeated emphasis on the fragility of networks (which need to be constantly reproduced through the actants within the network) underestimates how durable networks can become under certain conditions.[13]

Perhaps the problem with Latour's position concerning the fragility of networks can be better diagnosed by looking at an example from a nominal disciple of this mode of thinking. In the 2016 *New Literary History* special issue dedicated to considering Latour's potential value to the humanities today, Nigel Thrift combines Latour's actor-network theory and "modes" project to assess the organization of the contemporary university. Thrift's chief complaint centers on familiar narratives lamenting how market values have infiltrated campuses at an accelerating clip. From his perspective, too many critics have painted neoliberal economics as an unstoppable force transforming the academy. In rejecting this portrait, Thrift's analysis makes some essential interventions. It rightly takes away the unproductive pleasures of nostalgia, reminding us, much like Christopher Newfield does in *Ivy and Industry*, that there was never an idyllic moment in the past when the university was not engaged with American business interests. Along similar lines, his assessment of Wendy Brown's treatment of the neoliberalization of the university is quite apt. In portraying neoliberalism in monolithic, Manichean terms, Brown ends up idealizing the period following World War II when the federal welfare state assisted in educating a greater swath of the American population—but nowhere near as many individuals as Brown's rhetoric would lead one to conclude. Thrift encourages us to consider the university as a tapestry of different modes of existence, all vying to grow and assert themselves but simultaneously becoming more dependent "on the other[s] to survive to a much greater degree than ever before" (404).

While I agree with Thrift's analysis on the whole, the central thesis—that there are many competing forces operating in the contemporary university—can obscure the relative strength of distinct forces. In other words, the article's argument could easily lead someone to downplay the influence that neoliberal imperatives exert in today's university (in much the same way that a false equivalency like "both sides have a point" levels important distinctions that allow one to assess a situation properly). Thrift clarifies in the conclusion that he is aware of these imperatives, noting that "yes, the idea of the university is under threat because economentality has become more prevalent" (414). Nevertheless, the underlying thrust of his argument—look at the wide variety of conflicting values and practices that populate the university!—can have, perhaps only unintentionally, the effect of downplaying the predominance of one particular mode, and in doing so minimize certain forms of concentrated force. Thrift's analysis may provide a vital dose to cure us of idealized histories of the university, but it may also have the dangerous side effect of offering a misleading picture of the balance and distribution of power within the university today.

In all fairness to Latour, his more recent work seems to recognize the limitations of his previous formulations on networks' durability (or, at least, it can charitably be read in that fashion). Along with such a shift, he has become more polemical and political than his earlier work. In the 2013 Gifford Lectures, he initiates "Schmittian warfare" with climate change deniers; in *An Inquiry into Modes of Existence*, he criticizes the mode of "economics" for smothering other potential forms of organization. Moreover, his attack on economics would seem eerily similar to the Marxist critiques of neoliberal hegemony that Latour had previously dismissed. In any case, his *Modes of Existence* project, in offering a series of stable and incommensurable "modes" that operate in the world, moves toward more clearly acknowledging the possible legitimacy of traditional ideas about the force of "context" (what, in Latour's language, might be understood as "mini-transcendences").

While Harman sees Latour's turn to ideas like "quasi-objects" and "quasi-subjects" as an incidental relapse into modernist dualism, echoing Smith's concerns about Latour's treatment of science and religion as incommensurable modes, we might instead be inclined to read Latour's changing thoughts as an indication that he is finally accounting for the emergence of more durable networks, networks produced haphazardly by a serial situation. Latour's late work would thus amount to a synthesis of the "modern constitution" and the "flat ontology" he proposes in its place. We must begin with a "flat ontology" (roughly corresponding to Deleuze and Guattari's notion of the "plane of immanence"), but out of this space emerge formations of varying degrees of stability, formations we might call "emergent structures." The primary question would thus be how various "modes of existence" come into being and acquire enough stability to approximate the transcendent status that nature and culture were ascribed in the modern constitution. Furthermore, what conditions would be necessary to undermine that stability?

Reading Latour's "modes" project in this way may present some difficulties given that Latour himself presents the modes in an eerily Platonic fashion, as if the various modes of existence existed prior to their emergence from a "flat" ontological plane. Advancing a system of a dozen modes does facilitate more robust multiplicity and transformation than the nature/culture binary of the "modern constitution." Nevertheless, Latour nevertheless remains in dangerous territory of repealing the most valuable aspects of his early work. To preserve these insights, shouldn't we press Latour into admitting that he shouldn't settle on the modes outlined in *An Inquiry*? Couldn't we just as easily suggest the possibility that more modes will one day exist? Shouldn't there be *n* modes? What hybrids might be forming among any number of the existent modes? What new modes might not yet have emerged out of the unpredictable interactions on the "flat ontology" that Latour has spent so much time defending?[14]

Regardless of whether we feel like being generous or not to the potential soft spots in Latour's late work, it is important for our purposes to recognize that the challenge posed by "emergent structures" to Latour's project is a key tension point in the thinker's recent uptake within English studies. Indeed, Latour gained popularity in the American academy several years before *An Inquiry into Modes of Existence* was published in English, meaning that the potential correctives offered in that tome were not what generated the initial interest. We will now turn to that American reception.

English Studies and Postcritique

Having spent a fair amount of time detailing Latour's complicated relationship to the theory era, we can now direct our energies to more fully examining the recent uptake of his thought within English studies. Perhaps the best way to go about assessing Latour's appeal would be through a careful treatment of Paul Lynch's 2012 *College English* article "Composition's New Thing: Bruno Latour and the Apocalyptic Turn." While it would seem confined to the field of Rhetoric and Composition, the dilemmas it brings up can also be used to illuminate trends that apply across the entirety of

English studies. In fact, one point I want to argue is that the fields now face the same structural dilemma.

Lynch's article is instructive because it combines into a single composition the two overriding issues that attract Rhetoric and Composition scholars to Latour: (1) the problems associated with critique and (2) the centrality of "composition" as a concept that illuminates the organization of society and the world. Lynch opens his piece by addressing how scholars in Rhetoric and Composition have increasingly turned their attention toward looming global catastrophe, most notably climate change, a shift that he dubs "the apocalyptic turn" (458). He then focuses on the meaning of the term "apocalypse," forging a link between it and critical thinking, one of the field's cherished tenets. As Lynch explains, critique operates according to an "apocalyptic logic," wherein critical thinking seems to promise revelation, with all its attendant religious connotations. Critique amounts to a "throwing down the idols and getting behind the shadows" so that "we will finally see through a glass clearly" (459). Simply put, apocalyptic logic promises to offer us the unvarnished truth hiding behind appearances. Lynch clarifies that, ironically, the "apocalyptic turn" rejects "apocalyptic logic" because it directly confronts the apocalypse—that is, "serious danger to human flourishing"—rather than trying to get "behind" it. He then proposes that Latour's work can be usefully mined for confronting serious threats without resorting to critique (458).

As his analysis unfolds, Lynch elaborates upon what he sees as critique's two primary deficiencies, namely its problematic understanding of a hidden reality and its self-certainty. Ultimately, these two deficiencies are inseparable. Lynch laments that critique overvalues revealing truth behind a facade. Critique fails to recognize that uncovering truths is not the primary challenge facing our world today; Lynch asks if "we really need close and careful readings to convince ourselves that we live in hard times" (463). Students don't need their teachers to show them the looming apocalypse. Critique also assumes that a hard, stable reality exists which can be represented clearly through the critical act of revelation. In doing so, it fails to register the continual interaction and recombination of elements that exist in the world. Lynch emphasizes Latour's conception of the Heideggerian "Thing," which can also refer to an "assembly," a place where disputes are settled. As Lynch explains, Latour's "Thing" helps clarify how matters of dispute and matters of fact are intertwined. In other words, Latour forces us to recognize that a world where facts and concerns are divorced does not exist. We need to have a conception of facts that recognizes that facts emerge out of disputes among human and nonhuman actors. An old-fashioned understanding of facts as stubborn, immovable objects overlooks this important truth.

A corresponding side effect of overvaluing the act of "getting behind" things, Lynch insists, is that it assumes far too much mastery of the situation. In order to "get behind" the facade and reach the truth, you already have to know how to distinguish between facade and truth. We cannot afford to maintain this sense of mastery in the present. Latour's notion of a "composed world," where things are always in flux, is a proper antidote to an overconfident attitude. What is needed is a greater inclination toward ambiguity, uncertainty, and curiosity. As Lynch explains, in Latour's thinking, "doubt and panic signal the moment when the text, or the Thing, is really beginning" (470); doubt and panic are significant affects because they illuminate the rapid and often unanticipated processes involved in the unending structuring of reality. Channeling Latour, Lynch asserts that we need to embrace the cacophonous mess generated by these fundamental processes of disputation that govern the world.

A number of problems emerge with Lynch's piece, even if we agree with the general goals of the "apocalyptic turn." We should first direct our attention in Lynch's analysis to the way he narrowly defines critique as an operation that reveals transcendent truth. The piece doesn't consider that critique can operate in many other forms, too, none the least of which is the demonstration that there is no transcendent truth or that our access to said truth is blocked. Moreover, defining critique as a revelation of final truth troubles the coherence of the oppositions that organize Lynch's analysis. Recall, for instance, that Lynch proposes that we embrace complexity and confusion over clarity and certainty, stating that "what we lose in focus, we will make up for in richness" (465). To highlight complexity and confusion is in keeping with Latour's insistence that reality is in constant "composition," consisting of a potentially overwhelming number of elements interacting in unpredictable ways. So far, so good. But to counterpose complexity, confusion, and doubt with clarity commits Lynch to valorizing complexity or doubt in itself, which works against Latour's insistence in "Why Has Critique Run Out of Steam?" that cultivating doubt, the value that reigned supreme during the heyday of postmodernism, is the fundamental problem with critique. Incredibly, Lynch's attachment to "confusion" as a god-term leads him to treat climate change, the paradigmatic threat for "the apocalyptic turn," in a way that would flabbergast Latour: he uses Latour's notion of "composition" to *diminish* our sense of the severity of the catastrophic threats of today. Qualifying that he does not want "to encourage a Panglossian attitude" about humanity's current predicaments, Lynch writes that "the idea of the Thing seems crucial for a discipline facing a turn in which the apocalypse seems inevitable. To see it as inevitable is to place it beyond dispute . . . if we assume a dire future as a given, we risk reducing issues to facts" (467). At some level, Lynch rightly intends for his statement to spur people into responding urgently to climate change; if we assume humanity is already screwed and do not act, then we most certainly will be. But the statement can also have the effect of mitigating our certainty in a bleak future, suggesting that the future is more open than the current science concludes (for some climate scientists, we have already passed the tipping points where human intervention, assuming it to be politically feasible, could prevent the most cataclysmic environmental changes from occurring).[15] While many of the specifics of the future remain unpredictable—how severe it will be, what areas will absorb the greatest brunt of the changes—the big picture should be "beyond dispute." Whether intentional or not, Lynch's statement can work against that apocalyptic certainty. The general thrust of Lynch's argument muddies the waters to an unsettling degree.

To approach things from a slightly different angle: Lynch rejects "critique" for aspiring to reveal transcendent truth and replaces it with "disputation," which cultivates uncertainty and negotiation. But "disputation" simply constitutes another form of critique, a critical operation that prompts us to take nothing for granted—precisely the danger that Latour seeks to avoid. Lynch's piece suggests that the way forward is by continually recognizing confusion and complexity, treating these things as scarce resources in need of cultivation. But recognizing the world's complexity and volatility is a necessary but not sufficient condition. After all, in much the same way that students don't really need to be taught that the world is falling apart at a rapid clip, they also don't really need to be taught that the world's dissolution is a complicated, multivariable process. Or, if they do, the acquisition of that knowledge constitutes only the first small step in attempting to address the dissolution. Lynch's article has the unfortunate quality of treating the transition from "object" to "thing" as a form of liberation—that is, recognizing complexity amounts to a saving grace—when in fact it may only serve to obscure the dilemma that climate change actually poses. Unfortunately, this is the inevitable result that emerges from an analysis structured in terms of clarity against confusion, mastery against curiosity, or critique against composition. Is there not a certain clarity, or dare we even say mastery, achieved in admitting confusion? Does critique not constitute a form of problematization? Isn't the shift from "object" to "thing" a revelation of sorts? While trying to avoid doing so, Lynch's argument provides a revelation of its own—that things are more confusing and interwoven than we might initially think they are; we need to think in terms of "things" rather than "objects." This is a good and important revelation to have. But it speaks to the need to preserve a sense of truth, even if that truth is only provisional and in need of constant renegotiation. Lynch certainly recognizes this point, but his notion of an "apocalyptic turn"—a turn that breaks sharply with "apocalyptic logic"— undercuts that acknowledgment.

Rather than blaming Lynch, the confusion may originate in his source material. Despite his insistence to get beyond critique, Latour's own writing is drenched in it. The rhetorical and argumentative features of "Why Has Critique Run Out of Steam?" amount to many of the gestures that he laments within the essay. Latour's dismissal of critique constitutes a performative contradiction that is almost impossible to overlook. A number of critics have commented on this unavoidable aspect of his work, seeing in it perhaps the hard kernel of his appeal.[16] Latour's attempt to evade critique only facilitates its reappearance in subtler but no less significant forms. Much like our analysis in Chapter 1, which characterized criticism as an agonistic field where competition and cooperation bleed into one another with dizzying rapidity, the tensions within Latour's prose imply that critique may be unavoidable, perhaps even an ontological feature of the world on even footing with the "compositional" practices Latour champions.[17]

Critique and composition might best be understood as interwoven material practices. Any attempts to isolate one from the other will prove futile. Current compositions of heterogeneous elements must be torn apart to compose new things; the work of tearing things apart is inseparable from reassembling them differently. Critique and composition are not opposed; they are, at most, distinct stages in a single process (much like our Chapter 4 argued for the inseparability of reading and writing). The "critique" movement in English studies constituted a particular composition of forces, just as the transition to a new form called "composition" requires the force of critique in order to bring it into being. Perhaps we should condemn the most egregious tendencies of the "critique era," what Christopher Castiglia dubs "critiquiness," not for being destructive but for being destructive in a way that did not lead to interesting or productive new compositions. The dynamic between critique and composition underwrites Castiglia's notion of "hopefulness." It also points to the dual sense of "restoration" and "demolition" that Derrida hoped the word "deconstruction" would convey.[18] Perhaps nothing captures the dynamic better than the little boy in a Bruno Bettelheim story, recounted in Deleuze and

Guattari's *Anti-Oedipus*, who muses: "Connecticut . . . Connect-I-Cut!" As Deleuze and Guattari go on to explain, every "flow" in a series of connections simultaneously constitutes a "break" in that assemblage as well (37). Illuminating the fact that Latour indulges in critical practices should not be construed as a "gotcha" moment but instead as a reminder about the inextricable link between critique and composition. Thus, when Lynch, examining the work of another composition scholar, states that he is "interested in asking whether Owens's incipient assignment is an act of critique or an act of composition," we should wonder whether the question poses a false choice (468).

It is not enough to demonstrate that Lynch's essay too readily separates critique from composition. Placing critique and composition on an even plane and regarding them as moments or aspects of a single process forces us to consider other questions. Lynch's turn from critique to composition serves to reintroduce complexity and confusion into a field that has become far too complacent about a number of commonplaces. What does the emphasis on uncertainty and complexity really accomplish for Lynch in the end? Rather than taking the field in a new direction, it subtly repeats a familiar gesture. More specifically, Lynch's article illustrates how the promise that Latour's work will disrupt the habits of his field remains unfulfilled because Latour's metaphors of deliberation—which make him so appealing as a theorist to cite for Lynch and others—simply reaffirm many of the central values of Rhetoric and Composition, values that climate change challenges.

Latour has attracted criticism for his supposedly anthropomorphic treatment of the world, one that prompts humans to talk earnestly with speed bumps and seatbelts.[19] But Lynch's analysis falls into a different trap when attempting to follow Latour's directive to attend to the nonhuman agents in a given system. More specifically, in his description of accounting for climate change as part of a new "Thing," Lynch adopts familiar gestures about hospitably welcoming marginalized groups to the main stage of deliberation. For Lynch, the primary task of the apocalyptic turn involves assembling "a Thing that takes all the actors, human and nonhuman, into account" (469). Lynch turns to Burke's parlor metaphor, which we detailed more fully in Chapter 1, to flesh out his proposal. He insists that a primary task of teaching should be, rather than learning how to enter the parlor and participate in debate, learning how to assemble the parlor and facilitate the participation of others. As he explains, "Latour's vision of the critic asks us to worry less about putting our oar into the Burkean parlor and more about making sure the parlor is available to all. . . . Composing the guest list of the parlor, then, is no small task" (471). Lynch wisely notes that we need to go beyond assuming that being a critical thinker or a passive observer are the only "two ways of being in the world" (470). In doing so, he subtly breaks with the tidy distinction between critique and composition that underwrites the bulk of his analysis. Bringing people into a discussion constitutes a critical act in that it destroys the existing constellation of participants in the parlor.

A problem arises when Lynch describes the climate as one of these previously unacknowledged participants that needs to be escorted into the parlor. That ecological conditions have frequently been marginalized in human deliberation and warrant more careful consideration in the future should be beyond dispute. However, the parlor metaphor carries with it certain connotations that shape our attitude toward the climate in unproductive ways. The parlor serves as the primary site in which important matters are debated and decisions are made; to be outside this sphere is to be effectively insignificant and powerless. Only by being invited into the parlor can one acquire a voice and achieve some form of agency. Unfortunately, extending the parlor metaphor to characterize our relationship with the climate retains a model of human centrality, one with all its attendant privileges. The climate isn't a passive participant that would benefit from a kind, generous welcome from humankind. It doesn't need to be invited into the parlor; it entered long ago, tramping its dirty shoes on the parlor's fine carpet with the toxic waste from outside that we have produced and subsequently ignored. Indeed, humanity's inextricable connection with the environment should illuminate how the parlor metaphor necessitates a dynamic between inside and outside that Latour's flat ontology undermines. In this respect, addressing climate change is not a matter of inviting the climate into the parlor; instead, it is a matter of recognizing that a much larger parlor already exists—has, in fact, always existed—where the climate is a rowdy, increasingly belligerent, participant (but whose belligerence is inseparable from human activity). Although Lynch writes that since humanity is "faced with the unspeakable and the unimaginable, there's little point in assuming the usual position of mastery or expertise" (473), his retention of the parlor metaphor, a commonplace of the field, only perpetuates a notion of human mastery that fails to take in the climate's formidable powers.

The same troubles reassert themselves when Lynch details Latour's "New Constitution" that is outlined in *The Politics of Nature*. In this work, Latour envisions our treatment of the Thing in terms of a bicameral legislature, with a "lower house" that solicits the input of new participants and an "upper house" that works to incorporate those new voices into the existing order. Lynch characterizes the dynamic between the two houses in terms of casuistic stretching (another term borrowed from Kenneth Burke), a practice where new principles are introduced while old principles are retained. As Lynch clarifies, "the new does not replace the old. Instead, the new has to answer to the old, and the old has to accommodate the new" (472). Although it is constrained by a duty to accommodate previously ignored participants, the upper house clearly occupies a power position. Under this arrangement, tradition and the weight of history enjoy a certain implicit advantage. Only out of the beneficence of the democratic spirit does the upper house feel obliged to respond to the demands of the newly recognized voices solicited by the lower house. But this is a fundamentally flawed way to think about climate change. To equate the climate with a silenced, marginalized group is dangerous because it reinforces the anthropocentric tendencies that helped produce the climate crisis in the first place. When it comes to climate change, the old may have to accommodate the new, but the new *does not* have to answer to the old. Responding to the climate is not a matter of being hospitable enough to relinquish some of the pleasures and privileges we derive from the current state of things for the sake of the climate. Responding to the climate is a matter of being willing to relinquish some of the pleasures and privileges we derive from the current state of things for *our sake*.[20] We need to listen to the climate because it will kill (some? many? most? all? of) us if we don't. The climate may have long been ignored and marginalized by the existing order, but it is the ultimate form of power from the outside. And while it is an undeniable fact that, as Lynch reiterates, the "movement of composition . . . can never finally rest because the collective will always have an outside, an excess that will always restart the work of composition," it is far less assured that human agents will always participate in this composition process (472).

A particular modality of power—one comprising a powerful center with a silenced margin demanding recognition—is so ingrained in the field that even a limit case like climate change, which challenges the universality of that model, is simply recast into a familiar, comforting frame. A failure to escape this seductive model was already elaborated in Chapter 2, where Burke, being far too enamored with the action-motion distinction, failed to deal with "history," the unintentional forces produced by uncoordinated individual activity that return to human society with a ferocious insistence of their own. Climate change constitutes the ultimate example of "history": It is a serial situation that loudly confirms that the effects of human activity have an agency distinct from their origins. In rejecting

Burke's action-motion distinction, which only perpetuates the nature-culture divide of the modern constitution, Jameson's Marxism thus already anticipates Latour's flat ontology. His notion of "history" is that of a hybrid network of human and nonhuman actants ceaselessly interpenetrating one another in often unpredictable ways.

Lynch's article wants the field to break out of habits that are unsuitable in a radically new environment. But, as we have seen, a bold new project quickly seems to become a series of familiar gestures. While Lynch's piece struggles to grapple fully with the limitations of the paradigms he has inherited from his field, it at least recognizes that the current moment necessitates revising old habits of thought. Read from a certain perspective, Lynch's article constitutes a Latourian "thing," a constellation of competing forces. Unfortunately, the conservative tendencies of that "thing" are only amplified in *Thinking with Bruno Latour in Rhetoric and Composition.* Whereas Lynch's article wants to face climate change directly but resorts to a deliberative paradigm that softens the harshest edges of the crisis, the collection is striking insofar as Latour's emergence on the scene does not disrupt business as usual. The "apocalyptic" crisis that Latour was initially recruited to tackle is nonexistent in this collection. Given the activist commitments of the field and the general alarm-sounding tenor of Lynch's initial piece, Jeff Rice's entry in the collection detailing how actor-network theory illuminates consumers' participation in the distribution and promotion of craft beer would seem to signal the thorough reorientation of Latour's thought for the field. This is not meant as a slight on the quality of the contributions to the collection, as the entries all attempt to engage with Latour in thoughtful ways (for instance, Ehren Helmut Pflugfelder uses Latour to challenge traditional notions of agency, while Jeremy Tirrell deploys Latour to complicate common understandings of memory in terms of storage and retrieval).[21] Nevertheless, the collection becomes just another occasion to trumpet the core values of Rhetoric and Composition. In several essays, Latour becomes a vehicle through which critics can underscore the importance of civic deliberation and public engagement, while in several others he is used to demonstrate how writing does not merely represent existing realities but participates in shaping them. And, perhaps unsurprisingly, the collection regards the acknowledgment of nonhuman actors as Latour's biggest intellectual contribution, with the contributors framing human relationships to nonhuman actants in terms of Burke's parlor metaphor. Nonhuman agents demand our recognition and deserve to be included in our deliberative practices.

But, once again, the limits of the parlor metaphor become strikingly clear. For example, in the essay "Tracing Uncertainties: Methodologies of a Door Closer," W. Michele Simmons, Kristen Moore, and Patricia Sullivan trace the civic deliberations about building additional railroad lines in Springfield, Illinois. The authors point out that initial plans to build a new rail line through the middle of the city were greeted with hostility since the project would exacerbate already strained racial tensions. An alternative plan was posed that suggested the construction of a high-speed rail rerouting the train traffic around the city. This plan was foiled, however, when project engineers and surveyors identified marshland outside the city limits. In this instance, the marshland "became a figuratively vocal participant in the study" (286). Acknowledging the marshland as "a *nonhuman* actant whose concerns rivaled those of the citizens," the project managers thus "allowed the marshland itself to have its way in the deliberations" (286). While the marshland undoubtedly affected the course of events, the parlor metaphor may obscure rather than clarify the series of relations that comprise this network. Although the essay does not clarify, the project managers' decision to refrain from building on the marshland appears to stem from the inability to construct an architecturally sound railroad in such an environment rather than some generous consideration of the ecosystem itself. And even if such ecological considerations were foregrounded, to what degree would those considerations still be a reflection of human interests? To say that the marshland voiced its dissent and became a full-bodied participant in the deliberation is to ascribe it more agency and volition than it possesses. Although this essay's overemphasis on the marshland's agency does not have the same devastating consequences as Lynch's inadequate emphasis on climate change's agency, both pieces nevertheless illustrate the substantial limitations of Burke's parlor as an explanatory model. The "parlor" falls victim to the same troubles that have besieged the popular interpretation of Foucault's panopticon or his more general meditations on "power"; the parlor becomes an all-encompassing metaphor that can be applied to every situation, thereby rendering the specificities of individual situations stained by the residue of universality. The parlor is just one way to characterize a series of relations; the parlor frames relations in the tones of generous deliberation and genteel disagreement, where maintaining decorum and preserving goodwill remain paramount. But the parlor does not exhaust how one might characterize a series of relations, and using it as a transcendent model creates as many problems as it solves.

English's Next Big Thing

The ubiquity of the parlor metaphor for Rhetoric and Composition illuminates an internal rhythm of scholarly activity, a rhythm that Latour's insertion into the field only accentuates. In this way, it shares much with the postcritique movement that has also turned to Latour for revitalization and a sense of renewed purpose. Although literary theory and Rhetoric and Competition emphasize slightly different features of his corpus, Latour serves the same structural function in both cases. Eric Hayot writes that an entire generation of American academics has come to understand intellectual history as "a succession of novelties articulated as progress" (287). Derrida was replaced by Foucault, Foucault was transcended by Bourdieu, and Bourdieu was replaced by Badiou, with each new thinker treated as an overcoming of the deficiencies of the previous model. When considering the prospects of the postcritique movement, Hayot explains,

> it is by narrating the nature of a thirty-year span *as* a single period and thus by seeing a number of smaller movements that we might have thought of previously as opposed elements in the same larger pattern, that the critique of critique acquires much of its rhetorical and hermeneutic force, and seems to break out of a pattern of historical development that had ground to an ineffectual halt. . . . The "end of critique," even as it demarcates and reframes the small-scale succession of schools under a larger historical umbrella, adopts once more the logic of succession and decline that characterized those schools in the first place. In this way what a certain vision of the end of critique seeks is in fact a *return to critique under another name*, a reproduction of the very historical pattern from which it sees itself as having escaped. (287)

Hayot is blunt in his assessment: "We need to do better" (287). Indeed, Latour is simply the next repetition of a predictable cycle, despite the way his adherents have positioned him as an escape from that cycle altogether. Literary studies' turn to Latour perpetuates a model of intellectual engagement that is not particularly useful. It ignores a wealth of valuable material readily available in its existing theoretical resources—my substantial quoting of Derrida, Foucault, and Deleuze in the first portion of this chapter was intended to underscore that their postcritical ideas could not be considered mere subtext—in order to produce a fairly formalized "critical" reading technique. When the predictable limitations of this "critical" approach manifest themselves, the field turns to a new figure who will overcome these deficiencies. But the desire to install a new movement, one that breaks with the past—in this case, separating critique from composition—only strengthens that continuity at the structural level. Postcritical readings will quickly become another form of routinized critical engagement, aping Latour's "critique under another name" or his fascination with the nuances of local assemblages for their own sake, a fascination that itself repeats the familiar gestures and commitments of the "archival turn" that we detailed more fully in Chapter 3.

Critic Steven Connor articulates Latour's limitations in a slightly different way, but one that allows us to come at the organization of English studies from another angle. Connor explains that "Latour thinks, or writes as if he thinks, that we need a drastic change of philosophy," an altogether familiar gesture in the humanities, and one that is all too easily assimilated into the normal cyclical rhythms of scholarly boom and bust that Hayot details. Unfortunately, a change of philosophy will have minimal effects. This is particularly true when it comes to climate change, the signal issue that Latour uses to justify the importance of his postcritical networked approach. When it comes to addressing climate change, Connor insists, "a change of heart or mind need make no difference at all. A difference to our chances of survival will be whatever results in a dramatic decrease in carbon emissions. That's it. Don't follow the objects or the actants, follow the numbers, for they are what will kill or cure us" (284). By maintaining that climate change is foremost a technical problem, Connor makes clear that changing our feelings about our relationship to the environment will only be valuable insofar as it "helps with the job of engineering" (284). Where Latour fails is participating in "the most common of the dream-machines of the humanities," namely "mistaking epistemology for effect" (284). The mistaking of epistemology and effect is interesting precisely because Latour's philosophy is supposed to redirect our attention toward effects—everything in his philosophy is characterized in terms of action, force, and relations—rather than uncovering an already constructed world. So while Latour performs a valuable service by underscoring that humans have always maintained an interdependent relationship with their environment, his thinking ultimately succumbs to many of the same temptations he argues the humanities need to avoid. Effect becomes another epistemology.

Latour's mistaking epistemology with effect cannot be separated from his underlying fantasy that humanities scholarship can have a substantial impact on society at large. We can see this fantasy operating in Latour's work when he suggests that the theory era helped contribute to the widespread tactics of denial used by the political Right. Latour's assertion ignores the fact that the climate change skeptics were guided by the same public policy outfit that denied that tobacco smoking caused cancer or that coal smoke produced acid rain many decades earlier; that group didn't need the input of Jonathan Culler to achieve its goals.[22] Along similar lines, criticizing the era of critique for failing to stop the social arrangements it analyzes again assigns more agency to the critical theorists than they could ever dream of possessing. Might the skepticism and doubt that Latour laments be a more generalized social affect that infuses the humanities rather than, as he posits, the humanities' work infiltrating the culture more generally? To ascribe academics in the humanities the power, albeit indirectly, to have such a detrimental impact on society is a sign of wishing the humanities could do more. If we have produced such problematic effects, then we could, with the proper corrections, also produce better effects. Why would it be surprising, then, that Latour thinks a change in attitude or perspective will be the solution to the current crisis? But a switch from "critique" to "composition," were such a clean division even possible, would not inoculate the latter from being deployed toward nefarious ends. Today, conservative pundits are just as prone to use the line "we need to have more discussion" as "the science is not certain" when attempting to stall action that would curb fossil fuel emissions.

I will now deploy some of the very symptomatic language Latour rejects. I would argue that Latour's belief in the humanities' influence on the broader society is an effect—dare we say a compensatory fantasy?—of a deeper awareness, perhaps only dimly felt, that criticism does not, and cannot, do the kind of work he ascribes to it. The failure of criticism to enact substantial change in the world has always been an issue for criticism, and much of the postcritique scholarship points out critique's massive failure to stop the wide range of practices it derides. But the idea that shifting to postcritical practices will have a larger social impact is almost certain to create just more disappointment in the future. Latour's philosophy, which rejects the idea that some broad context could determine the interactions of a local assemblage, provides hope that an attitude adjustment within the humanities might spiral out to have a positive impact on the broader community. In this way, Latour's work is so appealing to the discipline because it implicitly promises an escape from the vicissitudes of the serial situation and emergent structures in a moment when these phenomena are more pronounced than ever. His emphasis on the primacy of relations between local actors blots out the degree to which emergent structures have developed out of these local relations to condition and limit potential future transformation. Global capitalism and climate change, two distinct but interrelated phenomena, are massive yet constantly fluctuating systems that did not exist prior to the complex set of practices that initially produced and now sustain them, but they possess a momentum that exceeds the grasp of any individual or small group operating within them.[23] Furthermore, effectively tackling these two systems would require massive coordination among many actors, precisely the kind of large scale effort that is almost sure to be frustrated by the very conditions of the situation itself. In other words, the conditions needed to solve the problem are denied by the existence of the problem.

Climate change intensifies the difficulties of the serial situation since it strips away the one comforting idea that the humanities have long resorted to when confronting issues that require collective mobilization to be resolved: the belief that our teaching will allow more progressive ideas to slowly disseminate throughout society and create a critical mass. But climate change is unfolding at a rate that far outpaces the incremental progress the humanities might achieve in even its most charitable instantiation. As Lester Brown noted all the way back in 2001, "we don't have time to train a generation of teachers, who would train a generation of students, who a generation later will become decision-makers. That's not an option any more. The changes have to come within a matter of years among those of us who are already making decisions" (quoted in Owens, *Composition and Sustainability: Teaching for a Threatened Generation*, 13). Although Brown's statement retains a certain idealism concerning education's impact on social transformation, it nevertheless does important work in recognizing that such idealistic thinking no longer enjoys even the slim prospects of being actualized that it once possessed.

The internal transformations of the discipline are not indicative of some larger sea change. The change that the humanities offer has always been confined to the way we conceptualize things (in some small cases, the conceptual reshaping the humanities offer can have material effects outside the university—although not necessarily the ones intended by the authors—but in most cases, these conceptual innovations make little difference).[24] More important, the practice of changing the way we conceptualize the world—the primary function of criticism—possesses a decidedly conservative function when we consider criticism institutionally. Conceptual reconfiguration is an operation that stabilizes criticism as an entire institution, regardless of whatever disruptions it produces *within* critical history itself. The discipline thrives on conceptual innovations to maintain its internal momentum; without the injection of new ideas, the entire operation stagnates and dies. The turn to Latour may exemplify this more clearly than any major theoretical figure in recent years insofar as he has been configured as a radical break from all that preceded him. As the lengthy first portion of this chapter illustrated, however, claiming that Latour instantiates such a break requires reading both Latour and his predecessors in a way that marginalizes the overwhelming continuities between them. Without positing a substantial break, however, the critical operation would lose the momentum that sustains it. Instituting radical, innovative breaks into critical discourse amounts to a necessary fiction that largely helps the network achieve some degree of equilibrium through constant replication. But what looks like forward progress in the short term only registers, at best, as slight fluctuations in equilibrium in the long term.

When the entire critical apparatus faces external threats that could shrink or eliminate the apparatus itself, the practices within that apparatus are modified to respond to that threat. Nevertheless, they remain practices within the apparatus, which means that their effects are largely confined to the apparatus. In his essay, Connor notes that "the humanities are not so much absorbed in their apparent objects as absorbed in the nature of their absorption in them" (280). Studying and writing about literature become a reflexive activity concerned with demonstrating the value of studying and writing about literature. From his perspective, "the real question at issue in the humanities is always 'what are the power and responsibilities of the humanities?'" (280–281). While Connor insists that the humanities must overcome this navel-gazing tendency, it must be reiterated that much of the humanities' absorption with their absorption has long stemmed from external demands to justify their existence. As Chapter 3 illustrated, Rhetoric and Composition's "absorption" in its own history and its concern with legitimizing itself as an area of intellectual inquiry resulted from its tenuous position within the university. Today, increased administrative pressure and budget cuts have made the two halves of English more similar in this regard than ever before. Both must explain their value to the broader university community or risk being eliminated. Critics have agency but that agency is confined within the local network in which their criticism circulates. Critics have much less agency when it comes to sustaining the institutional networks that facilitate and make possible the scholarly practices in which they do exert some measure of control.

Endless self-defense only encourages the kind of wagon-circling reactions that make productive, more thorough transformations more difficult. The understandable, indeed necessary, preoccupation with short-term survival tactics produces disastrous long-term consequences. Connor and several other contributors to the *New Literary History* special issue on

Bruno Latour consider what role the humanities might play in responding to climate change—most notably, designing new ways to persuade skeptical citizens about the issue as well as finding ways of "maintaining the level of interested stress" for already-supportive citizens so that "the problem of climate change remains something with which we can never permit ourselves to be bored" (Connor 283). These are two commendable recommendations for reconfiguring the humanities in the era of climate change. Yet the combination of interlocking elements that would be needed to facilitate this reconfiguration is daunting to say the least. Even under ideal conditions, how many existing bureaucratic protocols and administrative directives would need to be navigated deftly in order to bring them into being in a timely fashion?

Latour's general appeal for the discipline thus stems from the dream that he can not only break us out of this cycle and renew criticism but also extend criticism's reach beyond the university. But his uptake within English studies only highlights the degree to which criticism's innovations serve to stabilize local networks more than transform them in any fundamental way.

Coda: English Studies and the Uncertain Future

Throughout this book, I have documented the constantly shifting conceptual borders that structure English studies today. I now want to consider the recurring calls to create a more unified discipline that were outlined in the introduction. Since Wayne Booth first beseeched the warring factions of English to reconcile back in his 1982 MLA presidential address, a range of critics have sought to establish common ground that would overcome long-standing divisions (Robert Scholes and Peter Elbow were just two of the more prominent examples offered in the introduction). It is worth noting the similarity between Booth's initial suggestions and subsequent proposals. In a 1984 article for *Profession*, Richard A. Lanham echoes Booth, arguing that lower-division general courses (like first-year composition) should be reconceived as the center of a college education. He proposes a "curriculum that will focus on our society's demands for ever greater and more complex kinds of verbal symbolization" and suggests calling this new curriculum "rhetoric" (12). Lanham's new composition course boasts a more sophisticated "theoretical basis," and in the course plans he lays out, it is clear that he is offering a combination of composition and literary studies (a combination where each side of the Lit-Comp divide will learn something significant from the other camp). Twenty years later, Karen Fitts's and William B. Lalicker's 2004 *College English* article "Invisible Hands: A Manifesto to Resolve Institutional Curricular Hierarchy in English Studies" reaches a conclusion similar to Lanham's. In their piece, Fitts and Lalicker argue that the division between beginning and advanced courses and the split between literature and composition can be overcome through the creation of an "Introduction to Critical Literacy" course for all undergraduates taught by tenure-track faculty in English; they explain that the course "would teach students to recognize and use rhetorical conventions" (446). For Lanham as well as for Fitts and Lalicker, the way to unite English ultimately lies in cultivating a common purpose and set of practices that do not differ substantially from the "critical understanding" that Booth initially proposed.

There are certainly good reasons for adopting proposals for revising and uniting the various factions of English, particularly when considering the current climate of the university. In comparing some of the key figures in both theory and Rhetoric and Composition over the last several decades, my book might be useful for those interested in creating new alliances within English studies. It illuminates previously unrecognized points of contact that could be exploited for productive ends. Chapter 4 adopted much of the optimistic and unifying rhetoric found in the work of Booth, Lanham, Fitts and Lalicker, and many others, proposing a version of English studies organized around an "aesthetics without literature."

The triumphant undertone of Chapter 4 was undercut, however, by my analysis in Chapter 5, which worked against the impulse to establish the "next new thing" that would revitalize the discipline. Given that they both indulge in the fantasy of rejuvenation and newly acquired relevance, my own recommendations and the "postcritique" proponents of the current moment share much in common (in all fairness to my proposal, an "aesthetics without literature" merely asks for a recombination of existing elements rather than a bold new paradigm that razes all that came before). In positing this enormous gulf between past and present, the postcritique movement would seem to conform to what de Man, channeling Nietzsche, concludes about the modern world: "in severing itself from the past, it has at the same time severed itself from the present" (149). Nevertheless, de Man also understands that even his own meditations on the relationship between history and modernity—as well as our own meditations about de Man's meditations—are destined to be absorbed within the historical record. For our purposes, the central question does not so much concern devising a workable solution to reconciling the divide within English studies but instead in implementing such proposals in some feasible fashion. After all, the proposals spanning from Booth to Fitts and Lalicker (and beyond) are remarkably similar. If a solution has presented itself for so long, why does it remain in a perpetual larval state?

As a way to begin answering that question, we might remember that any efforts to unify English must reckon with the fact that divisions are created in the very act of connection. I have attempted to show how a productive synthesis of English's competing interests could be created while at the same time outlining the conditions that make that synthesis difficult to achieve. I began by underscoring two insights from Mezzadra and Neilson's *Border as Method*—(1) borders both divide and connect, and (2) increased circulation actually increases the number of borders rather than decreases them. Chapter 5, on the "Latourian turn," concluded with a similar insight: The inextricable connection between "critique" and "composition" mirrors a border's dual capacity for division and connection. Our analysis has illustrated how this simultaneous movement animates many other disciplinary dynamics. As we have seen, intense divisions can quickly give way to unexpected alliances. Similarly, what appears like shared ground between two parties can actually conceal deeper antagonisms. If the discipline has been structured according to a number of familiar binaries—reading/writing, research/teaching, tradition/innovation—we must recognize that we cannot simply substitute one binary with another. In other words, successfully reconciling one opposition will only exacerbate the tensions between terms in other binaries.

To take just a few examples: In Chapter 1, we observed how criticism as a dynamic system can remain stable only through constant movement and transformation; the true function of criticism is not to reach consensus or produce definitive answers but to spur further debate. Chapter 2 examined an exchange between Burke and Jameson, critics who initially appeared diametrically opposed; their debate ultimately revealed a series of subtle overlaps and divergences that made it difficult to distinguish one figure from the other. Chapter 3 illustrated how a conceptual system (in this case, Foucault's theory of power) could be transformed into a series of alternatives that thereby created a false unity across the discipline. If Foucault held hegemony within English studies for a period in its history, it was not because the vast majority of critics subscribed to his notion of power; instead, it was because the reappropriation of his work for different ends most clearly embodied his ideas about power. In other words, English studies demonstrated or performed his concepts rather than simply restating or applying them.

All of these examples point to a common thread that this book has been tracing since the outset: the vexed status of difference, as both a philosophical and political concept, in contemporary criticism. Crucially, the status of difference has played a role in multiple ways—not only within criticism but also as a force that has structured the field of criticism itself. To understand this dual dynamic, I turn to Masao Miyoshi's essay "Ivory Tower in Escrow," in which he generalizes about the interactions among colleagues in humanities departments at the turn of the millennium, noting how common it is "today to observe a mutually icy-distant silence, which allows everyone to escape into her/his womblike cocoon, talking minimally to the fewest contacts possible. Thus, instead of open discussion and argument at a meeting, perfunctory mail ballots—likely by email—decide issues" (47). But behind this cold silence lies a series of intense, unresolvable struggles: "essentialists contest anti-essentialists; assaults on the 'ludic posties' become the career of 'postludic' academics; post-Marxists reject orthodox Marxists; conventional disciplinary scholars hold in contempt cultural studies writers" (46–47). From his perspective, this lamentable situation came into being through a particular articulation of identity politics, which he believes is "bound to create factionalism and fractionalization" since it regards any form of agreement as "ipso facto suspect and unwanted"; instead of "political engagement" there is nothing but "internecine disputation" (46). Translating it in the words of Chapter 1, it would seem as though there is a fierce antagonism without agonism, a play of stark differences without some complementary unifying undercurrent, one that is necessary to preserve the entire operation. The valorization of difference in and of itself produces an unworkable model of political interaction. As Miyoshi writes, "if the strategy of division and fragmentation is not contained and moderated with the idea of a totality . . . it may very well lose its initial purpose and end up paradoxically in universal marginalization" (41–42).

The tension between difference and totality presents problems beyond staredowns in departmental hallways. Our preceding analysis has been guided by a narrative about the reception of French theory into the American academy; Žižek pithily dismisses the reception as a process wherein "notions of 'European' critical theory are imperceptibly translated into the benign universe of cultural studies chic" ("Rewritten" 195). A pharmacological relationship with difference—that is, one that treats difference as both a poison and a cure—is replaced with one that elevates it into an unalloyed good. Such a Manichean treatment leads to unexpected and likely undesirable alliances. Without a clear and patient documentation of how difference and totality interact within specific contexts, the push for diversity can ultimately accelerate any number of dire economic processes. As Miyoshi succinctly points out, "the corporate system stands to gain under certain circumstances by promoting diversity among ethnic and gender groups as it expands its markets, insofar as it can retain class difference and uneven development—the indispensable capitalist condition for cheap labor" (46). In *Empire*, Hardt and Negri reach a similar conclusion, asserting that those "who advocate a politics of difference, fluidity, and hybridity" as a way of undermining "the binaries and essentialism of modern sovereignty" are ultimately only "pushing against an open door" (138). Late capitalism, as we learned during our analysis of Jameson's exchange with Burke, cannot be equated to any number of social systems that function by squashing difference in the name of standardization and conformity. Although Hardt and Negri's comments are intended for a wide range of postmodern and postcolonial theorists, the preceding analysis has shown how it has played an integral role in internecine struggles within English studies.

The limits of an uncomplicated valuation of difference can be most forcefully felt in the recognition model of politics that typically accompanies it. Although an absolutely indispensable paradigm, the recognition model of politics fails to capture adequately the range of relations that constitute society; it cannot be used as a vehicle for characterizing all social relations without producing a number of mischaracterizations. As Nancy Fraser compellingly articulates in her debate with Axel Honneth, the recognition model of politics can only cover a portion of all the potential relations within capitalist society. Fraser notes how capitalism operates according to a

> quasi-objective, anonymous, impersonal market order that follows a logic of its own. This market order is culturally embedded, to be sure. But it is not directly governed by cultural schemas of evaluation. Rather, the economic logic of the market interacts in complex ways with the cultural logic of recognition, sometimes instrumentalizing existing status distinctions, sometimes dissolving or circumventing them, and sometimes creating new ones. As a result, market mechanisms give rise to economic class relations that are not mere reflections of status hierarchies. Neither those relations nor the mechanisms that generate them can be understood by recognition monism. (214)

Fraser's assessment of a "quasi-objective" order that pursues its own agenda should remind us of Jameson's characterization of "history" as those alienated forces of human activity that return to us with the magnitude of a natural law. Without an awareness of these "quasi-objective" forces, the recognition model falls victim to anthropocentric tendencies, failing to grapple with how power circulates in ways other than through centralized state forms. Thus, while we must insist that a recognition model of politics is an indispensable ingredient for diagnosing and responding to the contemporary world (the election of Donald Trump in 2016 should be proof enough), we must simultaneously be careful not to extend that model into domains where it generates more confusion than clarification.

What does all this have to do with the long-standing divide between literature and composition and the future development of English studies? The tension between the recognition model and its discontents, which our analysis characterized as a difference between an archival and cartographic approach, will remain an animating force within the discipline for years to come. In these final pages, I propose sketching out a few emerging borders in the discipline that will be shaped by these two competing approaches.

Rhetoric and Composition's increasing investment in English as a Second Language (ESL) and English Language Learners (ELL) will be one place where the archival and cartographic approaches clash. We can, of course, rely on familiar theories about a homogenizing American culture and the need to recognize other cultures and forms of global English. These narratives are undoubtedly compelling and will retain much explanatory power in the coming years. But the center-periphery model that underwrites this reading of English in the global world will need to be supplemented with other conceptual frames as dramatic changes occur—changes that concern both the position of the United States in contemporary geopolitics and the American university system's status within it. A more robust and capacious map is needed to recognize that the decline of the nation and its heralded university system will not necessarily unfold at the same pace (recall how Chapter 4 warned us, via Guillory's analysis, of the dangers of conflating the school system with the nation writ large), generating any number of bizarre scenarios within the contemporary university.

More specifically, how will the archival approach, organized according to a center-periphery model, function in scenarios where the United States no longer occupies a dominant position? At the moment, the American university system still remains the envy of the world, attracting more and more students from outside the United States. As universities increasingly rely upon alumni and donors to stay afloat, efforts will be redoubled to secure students from wealthy families in the developing world. In the background, there will be the steady decline of America on the world economic stage, as China assumes the leading role in the global economy.[1] As a result, the United States, along perhaps with the English language itself, will no longer retain the dominant position it has long assumed, thereby challenging many of the presuppositions that have long guided work in the discipline. How exactly will we understand the relationship between an international student from a wealthy family enrolled in an English course taught by an adjunct instructor who is paid by the course? How are we to characterize this student's relationship to the broader university? In the coming decades, recourse to an archival center-periphery model may be of limited value.

The conflict between cartographic and archival approaches will also undoubtedly structure future approaches to the question of "remediation" in higher education, a question that is likely to intensify. It has become a familiar truism that a four-year college degree now carries the same weight that a high school diploma once did because of the need for more advanced skills in the "new economy." However true that might be, it is also worth noting that as the public primary and secondary educational system in the United States is hollowed out from within, much of that initial schooling will be shifted, perhaps quietly, to the universities. Such a shift will conform to the now familiar neoliberal theme of transforming a public good into a private investment; students will effectively finance a portion of their education that they had previously received through the state. Additionally, the education that these students will receive in college will be supplied using labor patterns that have yet to affect primary and secondary school educators (note how the adjunct crisis in higher education has revealed how the salaries for a startling percentage of university instructors pales in comparison to those of high school teachers, who still retain some minimum degree of worker protection from the state, however tenuous it might be). Under such dire labor conditions, remediation is likely to become an increasingly slow, unsteady, and frustrating process. Put simply, the issue of incoming student preparedness will only grow, and the first-year composition course, which has long shouldered an unfair burden for student preparedness in general, will be a major battleground in attempting to alleviate the problem. Retaining an individualized focus on the question of remediation, one that examines the issue largely through the lens of shame and stigmatization, will only further muddy the issue by ensuring that significant structural factors stay hidden in the wings.

Finally, the conflict between the archival and cartographic approaches will assume new dimensions as both climate change and global capital reach dramatic tipping points. In the recent coauthored work *Does Capitalism Have a Future?*, five of the most prominent world-systems theorists—Immanuel

Wallerstein, Randall Collins, Michael Mann, Georgi Derluguian, and Craig Calhoun—speculate on the long-term prospects of the reigning global order. Although far from reaching any kind of consensus, their collaborative conclusion nevertheless predicts substantial dilemmas in the coming decades. This quintet largely differs on which of two major catastrophes—a climate crisis or the end of global capitalism—will arrive first. Whereas Mann believes that significant climate issues will begin to emerge between 2030 and 2050, Collins and Wallerstein claim that global capitalism will falter first, undergoing a series of debilitating convulsions some time around 2040 (Collins believes that major ecological catastrophe will not occur until 2100) (178). All five agree that it is impossible to predict how these two systems—the climate and capitalism—will impact the other, although perilous outcomes are more likely than not. Instead of dwelling on the range of possible doomsday scenarios, we should, for our own purposes, simply remember that as humanity confronts a possibly unavoidable extinction event (not to mention global economic collapse), the relationship between broad, long-term social change and small-scale adjustment and triage will acquire new meanings.

Indeed, in his *Learning to Die in the Anthropocene*, Roy Scranton argues that we will be much better off accepting the dire fate of the planet rather than deluding ourselves into thinking that a series of half-measures will allow us to escape the inevitable. Much like a soldier who believes he is dead even before entering the field of battle, thereby freeing himself of the fear of death, we should treat the disaster of global climate change and all it entails as a foregone conclusion. Doing so will require a radical shift in politics, which, as Lee Edelman so usefully argues in *No Future*, has long presumed the existence of a future. It is therefore worth reconsidering how the cartographic and archival approaches will be configured in this emerging reality.

In order to do so, we can adopt a crucial insight from Jennifer Fleissner's entry in the edited collection *Critique and Postcritique*. In the essay, Fleissner offers an important correction to reigning interpretations of Eve Sedgwick's influential work on "reparative reading." As Fleissner points out, Sedgwick juxtaposes suspicious, "paranoid" reading with reparative, "depressive" reading. Since the essay's publication, many critics have tended to overlook Sedgwick's equation between the reparative and the depressive, instead electing to construct an opposition between a pessimistic paranoid pole and an optimistic reparative one (Latour's essay on critique is similarly underwritten by this pessimistic-optimistic dyad). As a result, critics embracing the reparative have tended to adopt an affect that is far from depressive, namely an "untroubled, self-avowedly depthless cheeriness" (116). But for Fleissner, such formulations mischaracterize the crucial distinction between paranoid and depressive modes: "the difference, rather, lies in the fact that the former mode can imagine solace only in an absolute transformation of the given, whereas the latter tries to make do, meaningfully—and even beyond that, to find real satisfaction—in what is there" (117).

Fleissner's distinction helps clarify what I have been working to detail in this project as the political and conceptual split within English studies; the split revolves around two competing conceptions of temporal and spatial scale. I would suggest that the broad appeal of Latour's work for English studies today is that it feeds the reparative impulse to "make do . . . in what is there." In its unwillingness to grapple with emergent structural forces that can impose surprisingly strict horizons on possible action (something it too quickly conflates with unearned recourse to a nonexistent "context"), actor-network theory takes solace in the prospect that substantial, meaningful changes can still occur at a local level. As such, Latour's theory echoes Burke's championing of "perspective by incongruity" detailed in Chapter 2; the "archival politics" detailed in Chapter 3; and the politics of the "public turn" detailed in Chapter 4. But this critique that I have leveled at Latour and archival politics more generally presupposes the possibility of substantial, long-term social change, a possibility that may quickly be coming to an end. Finding ways to meaningfully "make do"—in other words, "learning how to die"—may become the most capacious form of thinking that the humanities can provide. Doing so would essentially collapse the gap between the broad, structural perspective of the cartographic and the narrow, individualized perspective of the archival. Only by constantly keeping in mind the certainty of macro trends will individual behavior be able to maintain a clear eye toward the dwindling future and avoid the innate response to disavow it.

All of this is to say, then, that the borders within English studies are certain to proliferate at a wild, unpredictable pace in the coming years. Alliances will breed new divisions, which, in turn, will foster new alliances. But the very stability of both the discipline and higher education as a whole will soon begin to feel the weight of history in unprecedented ways, generating all sorts of new and unforeseen divisions and alliances. How will English and its various fields respond to a world of dwindling economic prospects and impending ecological collapse? Perhaps more important, how might analyzing the conflicts within English produce conceptual tools for responding to these broader emerging realities?

ACKNOWLEDGMENTS

Although this book has only one author, it would not have been possible without the contributions, both large and small, from a great number of people.

Foremost, Jeff Nealon played an enormous role in shaping my thinking about all of the material here. Without his unflagging commitment and support, this project simply would not have come to fruition. He is for me a model of both intellectual rigor and academic mentorship. Debra Hawhee reliably offered a perspective that pushed my work in new directions. Rich Doyle was a boundless source of optimism and he provided valuable insights at crucial moments. Claire Colebrook posed a number of penetrating questions about my project that made this a much better book. Jonathan Eburne gave a generous reading of the material that informed my revisions of the introduction and first chapter. Many thanks go to Kit Hume and Jack Selzer for their helpful comments on an early version of the second chapter. Conversations with Stuart Selber, Matt Tierney, Ben Schreier, Michael Bérubé, and Christopher Castiglia helped me refine my thinking on a number of crucial points. In Buffalo, I benefitted greatly from conversations with Roy Roussel as I completed a final round of revisions.

I also wish to thank Michael J. Hogan, Debra Hawhee, and Cheryl Glenn for selecting me as a fellow for the Center for Democratic Deliberation at Penn State during the 2012-2013 academic year; I gained valuable feedback on the project from the Center's writing group, including Professor Glenn, Sarah Rudewalker, Jessica Kuperavage, John Belk, Sarah Summers, and Fabrice Picon. My project also benefitted from a summer research fellowship in 2013 thanks to Sean Goudie and the Center for American Literary Studies at Penn State. I also appreciate receiving a Edwin Earle Sparks Fellowship during the Spring 2014 semester, which allowed me to hole up at home during a cold winter and complete a draft of this book—thanks to Garrett Sullivan for thinking of me. Many thanks to the baristas at Saint's Café, my "second office" in State College, for creating such a consistently welcoming environment to think and write.

Tom Lay was a splendid editor whose keen insight and dedication to the project were crucial to its success. The feedback from the Press's two anonymous readers strengthened the book in innumerable ways. I'd also like to thank Eric Newman for his expert handling of the manuscript during the production process; I deeply appreciate Gregory McNamee's care in copyediting the work.

Many others who were not directly involved in the project nevertheless played a significant role in it coming to fruition. My parents, Stuart and Karen Maxwell, have always been tireless in their encouragement. Despite great geographical distances, Eugene Yacobson, Kevin Hilgers, and John David Devirgiliis were a source of emotional support throughout the project. I'll also be forever indebted to the mentorship that Jane Thrailkill and Gregory Flaxman provided during my undergraduate years at Chapel Hill. And, further back in my personal history, I was fortunate to have had two superb high school English teachers—Vinetta Bell and Henry Dickerson—who instilled in me the importance of close reading and the value of big-picture thinking.

I was also fortunate to have a wonderful group of friends and colleagues who supported me during the day-to-day work on this project. Many thanks go to Ting Chang, Erica Stevens, Matt Weber, Michelle Huang, Ryan Marks, Kris Lotier, Sara and Josh DiCaglio, Robert Birdwell, Jacob Hughes, Ethan Mannon, Adam Lupo, Phil Ortmann, Kyle King, Josh Smith, Josh Tendler, Max Larson, Justin Griffin, Aaren Pastor, Justus Berman, and Matt Price for their encouragement and insight over the years. Evan McGarvey—you made the book! John Steen provided a perceptive reading of the first chapter; Nick Gaskill offered much needed encouragement and guidance on an early version of the second chapter. Sarah Salter was an endlessly committed reader of my work; I feel lucky to have shared so many important professional trials and milestones with her over the years. Abe Foley was a reliable source of thoughtful ideas and productive questions about the project as it slowly unfolded; he was a pretty terrific roommate, too. John Schneider's friendship has been invaluable. Our weekly meetings at Champs during my last two years in State College had a significant impact on the final shape of the book. Finally, Susan Weeber kept me sane through it all. Without her unwavering commitment, good humor, and thoughtful insights, I would have produced a much lesser work. This book is dedicated to her.

INTRODUCTION

1. If one also accounts for the "business and technical writing" jobs, which are typically considered under the umbrella of Rhetoric and Composition and listed in the JIL database, the number may be even higher. Since job listings can list more than one category, the MLA's statistics do not provide a clear picture of how many listings listed both categories. See Modern Language Association's "Report on the MLA *Job Information List*, 2012–2013."

2. The popularity of the abbreviated "Rhet/Comp" might lead a sizable portion to call themselves "Rhet/Compers," but only those with a taste for the perverse would utter the mouthful "Compositionist-Rhetorician" in earnest.

3. Given the strong emphasis on teaching within Rhetoric and Composition—the field proudly carries the banner of the "pedagogical imperative"—it is slightly curious that "critical pedagogy" is located in another orbit.

4. See Walker's *Rhetoric and Poetics in Antiquity* for a thorough account of this dynamic in one historical period.

5. For some examples of the tension between "rhetoric" and "composition," see Coleman and Goodman, "Rhetoric/Composition: Intersections/Impasses/Differends"; Gage, "On 'Rhetoric' and 'Composition'"; Horner and Lu, "Rhetoric and(?) Composition"; Kopelson, "Sp(l)itting Images: Or, Back to the Future of (Rhetoric and?) Composition"; Mulderig; Murphy, "Rhetorical History as a Guide to the Salvation of American Reading and Writing: A Plea for Curricular Courage"; and Swearingen, "Rhetoric and Composition as a Coherent Intellectual Discipline: A Meditation."

6. As of 2010, though, the vast majority of Rhetoric and Composition scholars still remained housed within English departments. See Ianetta, "Disciplinarity, Divorce, and the Displacement of Labor Issues: Rereading Histories of Composition and Literature."

7. Of course, Derrida's statement "there is nothing outside the text" is a translation of "*il n'y a pas de hors-texte*," which is simultaneously translated in *Of Grammatology* as "there is no outside-text" (158). As Derrida has clarified elsewhere, the statement should be read as "there is nothing outside context" (*Limited* 136). The interpretation—and misinterpretation—of Derrida and

other theorists will be a topic of concern in the following analysis, particularly in Chapter 3.

8. See Chapter 5 of Sharon Crowley's *Composition in the University*, "Literature and Composition: Not Separate but Certainly Unequal," for more on the emergence of this division and its durability in subsequent years. See Tuman, "From Astor Place to Kenyon Road: The NCTE and the Origins of English Studies," for another informative history of English studies during the late nineteenth and early twentieth centuries.

9. For a example of someone who treats the 1949 founding of the CCCC as a crucial moment in the field, see Bartholomae's "Composition, 1900–2000." For a discussion of the significance of the 1963 CCCC Conference, see Schilb's "A Tale of Two Conferences," which compares the conference to the 1966 Johns Hopkins Conference that ushered French theory into the American academy. For a treatment of the Dartmouth Conference's significance, see Parker, "From Sputnik to Dartmouth: Trends in the Teaching of Composition."

10. For informative surveys of the establishment and growth of graduate programs in Rhetoric and Composition, see Chapman and Tate, "A Survey of Doctoral Programs in Rhetoric and Composition," and Brown, Meyer, and Enos, "Doctoral Programs in Rhetoric and Composition: A Catalog of the Profession." For a thorough examination of the development of journals in Rhetoric and Composition following World War II, see Anson and Miller, "Journals in Composition: An Update," and Goggin, *Authoring a Discipline: Scholarly Journals and the Post–World War II Emergence of Rhetoric and Composition*. For an example of how scholars attempted to justify the incorporation of rhetoric into the teaching of writing during this decade, see Gorrell, "Rhetoric, Dickoric, Doc: Rhetoric as an Academic Discipline."

11. For an overview of the development of histories of Rhetoric and Composition, see Miller and Jones, "Review: Working Out Our History."

12. The following analysis will unfold in the spirit of Ianetta's recent analysis of disciplinary histories. From her perspective, "combining the histories of composition and literature more fully . . . will help us better understand the inadequacy of narrow discipline-based thinking to solve the problems of either field" (56).

13. One example of this shift can be found in the fact that Cleanth Brooks and Robert Penn Warren's seminal 1939 *Understanding Poetry*, a textbook that helped spread New Critical reading practices, was followed in 1949 by another textbook, *Modern Rhetoric with Readings*. Furthermore, Allen Tate and Warren's location certainly reinforced many of their humanist values. William Jennings Bryan referred to Nashville, home of the New Critic Agrarians housed at Vanderbilt University, as "the center of Modernism in

the South" (quoted in Jancovich, *The Cultural Politics of the New Criticism*, 21). The Tennessee city has another sobriquet, one more fitting of the organicist turn taken by Tate and Warren: "Athens of the South." Boasting a full-scale replica of the original Parthenon in Greece (built in 1897), Nashville aspires to the lofty heights reached by the Ancients.

14. For a more extensive treatment of the themes covered in his MLA presidential address, see the fourth entry in Booth's *The Vocation of a Teacher: Rhetorical Occasions 1967–1988*, entitled "To Warring Factions in an Up-to-Date 'English Department.'"

15. For subsequent responses to the Lindemann-Tate debate, see Brady, "Review: Retelling the Composition-Literature Story"; Crowley's *Composition in the University*, Chapter 2, "The Toad in the Garden"; and McCrimmon, "Across the Great Divide: Anxieties of Acculturation in College English."

16. For an instance of an attempt to negotiate and potentially overcome the disciplinary divide, see Fitts and Lalicker, "Invisible Hands: A Manifesto to Resolve Institutional and Curricular Hierarchy in English Studies."

17. For an insightful look at the genre of disciplinary history of English Studies, see Yood, "Writing the Discipline: A Generic History of English Studies."

18. See Hairston's "Diversity, Ideology, and Teaching Writing" for an extensive criticism of theory's influence on the first-year composition course. Hairston's initial rejection of postmodernism within NCTE publications can be found in "Comment and Response."

19. See Culler and Lamb's *Just Being Difficult?* for a treatment of the dense and disorienting writing typically found in theoretical discourse. Addressing the split between theory and Rhetoric and Composition on the issue of undergraduate essays, a professor of mine once quipped that composition classes taught students to write well while theory courses taught them to write badly. See Crowley's "Literature and Composition," in *Composition in the University*, for traditional humanism's role in the composition classroom.

20. See Cusset for an examination of how French theory informed these movements (and how these movements appropriated this material for their own purposes). Complicating matters even further, Phelps notes that many in Rhetoric and Composition tend to regard theory suspiciously because they do not regard their teaching practice as "an applied science" (863). But this resistance to theory overriding practice is precisely what theory as a discourse was attempting to challenge.

21. While the emergence of theory in the contemporary university is one of his primary interests in *The University in Ruins*, Readings also mentions composition in passing; composition also receives a brief mention in John Guillory's *Cultural Capital* and Wlad Godzich's *The Culture of Literacy*.

Godzich most explicitly connects the two in the introduction to *The Culture of Literacy*, opposing theory to a "New Vocationalist literacy"; he sees both discourses emerging out of a crisis in "classical literacy" (12).

22. For evidence of composition's oscillation between product and process, see Hairston's "Winds of Change" (1982), Kent's edited collection *Post-Process Theory* (1999), and Dobrin, Rice, and Vastola's edited collection *Beyond Postprocess* (2011).

23. See Lanham for an early iteration of this link between composition and theory as the foundation of the general education curriculum. Although Lanham does not speak about theory directly, he recommends that an interdisciplinary, reflective discourse become the center of general education, pointing toward a possible role for theory to occupy.

24. For just two examples of composition scholarship in the 1980s that incorporated theory into the teaching of writing, see Snyder, "Analyzing Classifications: Foucault for Advanced Writing," and White, "Post-Structural Literary Criticism and the Response to Student Writing." In his piece, White even goes so far as to state that while theory has created a crisis for literary studies, writing teachers have "responded to post-structural literary theory with a surprising calm, even general acceptance" (186).

25. For just one indication of the increasing professionalization of Rhetoric and Composition, see Mueller, "Grasping Rhetoric and Composition by Its Long Tail: What Graphs Can Tell Us about the Field's Changing Shape," who has demonstrated that the average article in *College Composition and Communication* in 2011 is much longer and cites more material than an average article in the journal twenty-five years earlier.

26. Harris finds teaching so central to his field's identity that his history of Rhetoric and Composition since 1966 bears the title *A Teaching Subject*.

27. The quotation comes from a chapter in Miller's *Textual Carnivals*, which will receive substantial attention in Chapter 4. For other treatments of the crisis in the humanities, see Bérubé, *The Employment of English: Theory, Jobs, and the Future of Literary Studies*; Bousquet's *How the University Works* and "Tenured Bosses and Disposable Teachers"; Donoghue, *The Last Professors: The Corporate University and the Fate of the Humanities*; Gallagher, "Review: Re-modeling English Studies"; Nelson, *Will Teach for Food: Academic Labor in Crisis*; Newfield, *Unmaking the Public University*; Ostergaard, Ludwig, and Nugent, *Transforming English Studies: New Voices in an Emerging Genre*; and Sledd, "Why the Wyoming Resolution Had to Be Emasculated: A History and a Quixotism."

1. ON THE USE AND ABUSE OF RHETORIC IN COMPOSITION AND THEORY

1. For accounts of agonism in ancient Greece, see Hawhee, "Agonism and Arete"; Vernant, *The Origins of Greek Thought*; and Walker, *Rhetoric and*

Poetics in Antiquity. For a consideration of agonism within poststructuralism, see Weber, "Afterword: Literature—Just Making It." For agonism within contemporary academia, see Di Leo, "Agonistic Academe: Dialogue, Paralogy, and the Postmodern University."

2. For some insightful treatments on Nietzsche's engagement with rhetoric, see Heckman, "Nietzsche's Clever Animal: Metaphor in 'Truth and Falsity,'" and Porter, "Nietzsche's Rhetoric: Theory and Strategy."

3. A number of critics have thoughtfully analyzed de Man's wartime writings; see Felman, "Paul de Man's Silence"; Gasché, *The Wild Card of Reading: On Paul de Man*; and Waters, "Professah de Man—he dead."

4. In all fairness, Miller's work elsewhere advances a more complicated relationship between metaphysics and its deconstruction. See, for instance, "Ariachne's Broken Woof."

5. The first prominent uses of the term "rhetoric" in de Man's corpus were 1969's "The Rhetoric of Temporality" and 1971's "The Rhetoric of Blindness: Jacques Derrida's Reading of Rousseau," the latter bearing an epigraph by Nietzsche; both essays can be found in the collection *Blindness and Insight.*

6. See the October 1963 issue of *College Composition and Communication*, where this "revival of rhetoric" in America begins.

7. For more on Nietzsche in the French tradition, see Descombes, "Nietzsche's French Moment," and Schrift, *Nietzsche's French Legacy: A Genealogy of Poststructuralism.*

8. See Deleuze, "Letter to a Harsh Critic," for more on the creation of "monstrous offspring."

9. For an example of a critic who does take Nietzsche's influence on Burke seriously, see Hawhee, "Burke and Nietzsche."

10. For more on Nietzsche's relationship to democracy, see Hatab's earlier *A Nietzschean Defense of Democracy*, as well as Appel's *Nietzsche Contra Democracy.*

11. Composition's impulse to expand its domain can also be seen in the recent turn to "multimodality," which conceptualizes the act of composition in a much more capacious way. For a key text in the turn to the multimodal, see Shipka, *Toward a Composition Made Whole.*

2. BETWEEN STANDARDIZATION AND SERIALIZATION: KENNETH BURKE, FREDRIC JAMESON, AND RADICAL CRITICISM IN THE POST-FORDIST ERA

1. One of the editors of *The Norton Anthology of Theory and Criticism*, John McGowan, himself an ardent supporter of Burke, laments this trend. However, when assigning Burke in his graduate literature seminars, he finds that the results are invariably negative: "My students' inability

to make heads or tails of Burke did not surprise me. But their indifference did. They find him neither intriguing nor charming. . . . My students
haven't the slightest inclination to indulge Burke or, apparently, my taste for
him" (241).

2. Again, in keeping with one of the guiding insights of this book, it
should be said that none of the subdisciplines are airtight. One need not look
too far to find a literary critic who endorses Burke—I have already mentioned one—or a rhetorical theorist who could do without him. But these are
the exceptions to the rule, and it remains to be seen exactly why today articles
on Burke are commonplace in a venue like *Rhetoric Society Quarterly* but not
Diacritics.

3. Since the late 1970s, many critics have positioned Burke as a theorist
predating the "linguistic turn" in the humanities. For book-length studies connecting Burke to continental thought, see Brock, *Kenneth Burke
and Contemporary European Thought: Rhetoric in Transition*; Chesebro,
Extensions of the Burkean System; Crusius, *Kenneth Burke and the Conversation after Philosophy*; and Wess, *Kenneth Burke: Rhetoric, Subjectivity, Postmodernism*.

4. For other analyses of the exchange between Burke and Jameson, see
Blakesley, "So What's Rhetorical about Criticism? A Subjective Dialogue
Featuring Kenneth Burke and Fredric Jameson"; Bygrave, *Kenneth Burke:
Rhetoric and Ideology*; Tell, "Burke and Jameson: Reflections on Language,
Ideology, and Criticism"; and Wetherbee, "Jameson, Burke, and the Virus of
Suggestion: Between Ideology and Rhetoric."

5. Considering that Burke offers eight pages of corrections to Booth's
assessment of his work, this absence cannot be overemphasized.

6. Elsewhere, in a letter to longtime friend Malcolm Cowley, Burke
associated Jameson with 1970s Yale School deconstruction, dismissively re-
ferring to him as a "Yaley Marxist." Burke and Cowley, *The Selected Correspondence, 1915–1981*, 409.

7. By looking past the frustrating core of the debate, one discovers a
range of fascinating insights. In his recent treatment of the debate, "Burke
and Jameson: Reflections on Language, Ideology, and Criticism," Dave Tell
emphasizes its largely underwhelming effect, particularly Burke's response
essay. Calling the essay "simply not very good" (68) and suggesting that it
amounts to little more than a "glorified Burkean index," (71) Tell notes that
even Burke was dissatisfied with the bulk of his response essay and dismissed
it as "a waste of time" (70). As a way of resuscitating an otherwise disappoint-
ing affair, Tell argues that the debate constituted an "archival event" that can
only be properly understood by examining Burke's personal correspondence
during the period.

8. Burke was often characterized as a renegade New Critic. If he was too much of a formalist for Jameson, he was too engaged with the social for the New Critics.

9. In fact, Jameson has recently engaged in the practice of reinterpreting Burke, using the pentad for his own purposes in a 2009 article for *PMLA*. See his "War and Representation." Burke first developed the pentad in *A Grammar of Motives*.

10. For instance, in one interview, he explains that "no real systemic change in this country will be possible without the minimal first step of the achievement of a social democratic movement; and in my opinion even that first step will not be possible without two other preconditions (which are essentially the same thing): namely the creation of a Marxist intelligentsia, and that of a Marxist culture, a Marxist intellectual presence, which is to say, the legitimation of Marxist discourse as that of a 'realistic' social and political alternative" (*Jameson on Jameson* 13).

11. Elsewhere, Jameson defines Marxism precisely in terms of defeat and dissolution, stating that Marxism stresses the *failure* of all social formations: "inevitable is not the triumphant emergence from capitalism of 'socialism' . . . but rather simply the self-destruction of capitalism (as of preceding modes of production) under its own internal contradictions" (*Jameson on Jameson* 26). Thus, in spite of the support he gives to democratic projects, Jameson can also be counted as one of their fiercest critics (if we understand "critic" to mean a skeptic of the promises that these democratic movements claim to be able to deliver).

12. In fact, we might better understand Jameson's positioning between Burke and Derrida if we examine his tripartite mode of analyzing a literary text as a "symbolic act," an "ideologeme," and an "ideology of form." As we move between modes, broadening the historical scale each time, the overall force of the text diminishes. See *The Political Unconscious* 60–88.

13. On the differences between Jameson and Derrida, see *Ghostly Demarcations*, which includes Jameson's "Marx's Purloined Letter" and Derrida's "Marx and Sons." The differences might be summed up as the slight yet substantial interval between Jameson's "messianism" and Derrida's "messianicity," which the latter emphasizes is a "messianicity *without* messianism" rather than a "weak messianic power": "between 'weak' and 'without,' there is a leap—perhaps an infinite leap" (250).

14. Rather than a complete departure from formalist criticism, the "political turn" in literary studies during the 1980s was a complicated grappling with the insights of deconstruction, distributing critics across the spectrum just elaborated. For many, the limitations of deconstruction became so clear that even Derrida himself abandoned his early career meditations on

language and metaphysics for more pressing political questions concerning democracy, justice, cosmopolitanism, and religion. However, as more recent treatments have emphasized, Derrida's thought remained remarkably consistent throughout his career and the late-era political work should be understood as an extension of his previous investigations. There is no turn from the textual to the political in Derrida insofar as the textual is understood as a type of structure—a structure that challenges the notion of ipseity—instead of a simple reference to literature specifically or even language more broadly. In his later writings, Derrida does not forget the vicissitudes of the text but instead offers a more explicit rendering of the textual quality of law, politics, and history. Derrida's trajectory stands in sharp contrast with numerous literary critics who also engaged with broader social issues beginning in the 1980s but did so in direct opposition to Derrida and deconstruction, believing that a simple turn toward history or context would magically void the problems that his work raises.

15. See Laclau and Mouffe, *Hegemony and Socialist Strategy*, and Mouffe, *The Democratic Paradox*. For a comparison between Laclau and Derrida, see Chapter 5 of Hägglund, *Radical Atheism: Derrida and the Time of Life*.

16. Work in the rhetorical theory journal *PRE/TEXT* confirms this point. See, for instance, Bennett, "Pre/Face: Critical Pluralism and Democracy," and Scott, "The Necessary Pluralism of Any Future History of Rhetoric."

17. For an example of the liberal-plural approach to animal studies, see DeKoven, "Guest Column: Why Animals Now?"

3. MAPPING THE ARCHIVAL TURN IN ENGLISH STUDIES

1. Derrida would revisit Foucault's book many years later as part of a conference celebrating the thirtieth anniversary of its publication; see his "'To Do Justice to Freud': The History of Madness in the Age of Psychoanalysis."

2. I also use the language of cartography in order to link together Foucault with Jameson's well-known concept of "cognitive mapping."

3. Indeed, the very concept of *mal d'archive* in Derrida's *Archive Fever* corresponds to the "cartographic" rather than the "archival."

4. For more on Rhetoric and Composition's investment in archival research, see L'Eplattenier and Mastrangelo, "Archival Research in the Field of Rhetoric and Composition"; Ramsey, Sharer, L'Eplattenier, and Mastrangelo, *Working in the Archives: Practical Research Methods for Rhetoric and Composition*; and Wells, "Claiming the Archive for Rhetoric and Composition."

5. For a compelling account of the "politics of recognition" and its problems, see Fraser and Honneth, *Redistribution or Recognition? A Political-Philosophical Exchange*. Although their recognition-redistribution schematic

does not map cleanly onto my archival-cartographic one, there are a number of important points of overlap.

6. For a useful overview of the early years of writing program administration, see Hartzog. For more recent work concerning writing program administration and its relationship to social justice issues inside and outside the university, see Adler-Kassner, *The Activist WPA: Changing Stories About Writing and Writers*, and Ritter, "Extra-institutional Agency and the Public Value of the WPA."

7. For a broader account of how the energy of the 1960s social movements was incorporated into the university, see Ferguson, *The Reorder of Things: The University and Its Pedagogies of Minority Difference*.

8. As Kenneth Bruffee articulated in an early editorial piece for the *WPA Newsletter* in 1978, there is a "fast-growing tendency in colleges and universities throughout the country to involve whole campuses in writing programs. In many institutions today, writing is no longer perceived as the exclusive province, responsibility, and tough luck of the English department. . . . As a result, the director of the writing program at many schools has been catapulted into a new, important, demanding, and highly visible position of leadership" (7–8).

9. For more on the "affair at U.T." see Brodkey, *Writing Permitted in Designated Areas Only*.

4. TOWARD AN AESTHETICS WITHOUT LITERATURE

1. There is also an emerging "slow" movement, which challenges the "culture of speed" in contemporary life. See Berg and Seeber, *The Slow Professor: Challenging the Culture of Speed in the Academy*; Honoré, *In Praise of Slowness: Challenging the Cult of Speed*; and Walker, *Slow Philosophy: Reading against the Institution*.

2. The transition from "culture" to "excellence" manifests itself in the transition from "reading" to "writing" as the dominant cultural practice. If, as the comments of Yancey and others suggest, reading as a practice has long been associated with the state, then writing as a practice is, historically speaking, deeply intertwined with business. Indeed, as Deborah Brandt notes in *The Rise of Writing*, while reading has long been considered "indispensable to liberty and to the workings of democracy," writing has long been "connected not to citizenship but to work, vocation, avocation, and practical living. The writing skills of everyday people were captured largely for private enterprise, trade, and artisanship" (2).

3. See Wells, "Rogue Cops and Health Care," and Petraglia, "Introduction: General Writing Skills Instruction and Its Discontents," for two examples of the problems involved with simply making the content of writing courses more oriented to the "real world." For two key examples of the

"public turn" movement in Rhetoric and Composition, see Mathieu, *Tactics of Hope: The Public Turn in English Composition*, and Weisser, *Moving Beyond Academic Discourse: Composition Studies and the Public Sphere*. For a challenge to Kennedy's notion of "secondary rhetoric," see Woods' essays "Among Men— Not Boys" and "The Teaching of Writing in Medieval Europe." For a piece that echoes much of the following analysis, see Fleming, "Finding a Place for School in Rhetoric's Public Turn."

4. See Anderson, Reder, and Simon, "Situated Learning and Education," and Geisler, *Academic Literacy and the Nature of Expertise: Reading, Writing, and Knowing in Academic Philosophy*, for treatments of education oriented around abstract ideas compared to education geared toward specific contexts.

5. For a number of prominent popular business publications touting the value of the traditional liberal arts degree, see Anders' writing in *Forbes* and *The Wall Street Journal* and Golsby-Smith's writing in *Harvard Business Review*. See Virno, *A Grammar of the Multitude*, for a treatment of the "virtuosic" qualities required in this environment.

6. Yancey's essay for NCTE advances this idea: "Reading—in part because of its central location in family and church—tended to produce feelings of intimacy and warmth, while writing, by way of contrast, was associated with unpleasantness—with unsatisfying work and episodes of despair—and thus evoked a good deal of ambivalence" (2).

7. See Coogan, "Service Learning and Social Change: The Case for Materialist Rhetoric," and Herzberg, "Community Service and Critical Thinking," for more on the limitations of shortsighted forms of activism in Rhetoric and Composition.

8. And if this shift toward questions of form and process seem be lacking a historical dimension, I want to stress that not only are forms themselves historically embedded and have their own histories, but that the process of history itself might thought of as the mutations of various formal arrangements. For more, see Jonathan Culler's *The Literary in Theory*.

9. See Ngai, *Our Aesthetic Categories*, for a compelling account of the "interesting" in contemporary culture.

10. See Bové's foreword to Deleuze's *Foucault* for an insightful treatment of this issue.

11. Furthermore, debates about reforming the curricula to become more socially and ethically just—Miller's championing of composition studies over literary studies is a prime example—have become largely arcane since the 1990s when changes in lending practices for higher education loans transformed the university into a veritable engine for intensifying (rather than mitigating) social stratification and economic inequality. For more on these changes to policy, see Mettler, *Degrees of Inequality: How the Politics of Higher*

Education Sabotaged the American Dream. For more on how education remains inadequate for addressing economic inequality, see Marsh, "The Literature of Poverty, The Poverty of Literature Classes," and Michaels, *The Trouble with Diversity.*

5. NEW THINGS, OLD THINGS: READING
THE LATOURIAN TURN SYMPTOMATICALLY

1. For informative introductions to Latour's thought, see Harman, *Prince of Networks*; Schmidgen, *Bruno Latour in Pieces: An Intellectual Biography*; and McGee, *Bruno Latour: The Normativity of Networks.* For some important responses to Latour's work within science studies, see Bloor, "Anti-Latour"; Cohen, "Science Studies and Language Suppression: A Critique of Bruno Latour's *We Have Never Been Modern*"; Fortun, "From Latour to Late Industrialism"; Martin, "Knot-work Not Networks, or Anti-anti-antifetishism and the ANTipolitics Machine"; and Pickering, *Science as Practice and Culture.* See Latour and Callon, "Don't Throw the Baby Out with the Bath School! A Reply to Collins and Yearley," for a response to some of these criticisms.

2. For more on "postcritique," see Felski, "Latour and Literary Studies," and Love, "Truth and Consequences." For some important responses to the postcritique movement, see Bartolovich, "Humanities of Scale: Marxism, Surface Reading—and Milton"; Hensley, "Curatorial Reading and Endless War"; and Lesjak, "Reading Dialectically." Also see the 2015 special issue of the journal *Mediations* 28.2. It should be pointed out that Latour has also received attention in the burgeoning area of study known as "new materialism"; for some central works, see Bennett, *Vibrant Matter: A Political Ecology of Things*; Bryant, *The Democracy of Objects*; and Coole and Frost, *New Materialisms: Ontology, Agency, and Politics.* Although he differs from them in substantial ways, Latour is often associated as a member of a loose collective interested in "object-oriented ontology"; for a crucial work on Latour's relationship with this group, see Latour, Harman, and Erdélyi, *Prince and the Wolf: Latour and Harman at the LSE.*

3. For some early work in Rhetoric and Composition using Latour, see Beard's review of *Pandora's Hope: Essays on the Reality of Science Studies* as well as Winsor's "Engineering Writing" and "Learning to Do Knowledge Work." For more recent work, see Barnett "Toward an Object-Oriented Rhetoric"; Brooke and Rickert, "Being Delicious: Materialities of Research in a Web 2.0 Application"; Cooper, "Rhetorical Agency as Emergent and Enacted"; Graham, "Agency and the Rhetoric of Medicine: Biomedical Brain Scans and the Ontology of Fibromyalgia"; Hawk, "Reassembling Postprocess: Toward a Theory of Public Rhetoric"; Mara and Hawk, "Posthuman Rhetorics and Technical Communication"; Marback. "Unclenching the Fist: Embodying

Rhetoric and Giving Objects Their Due"; Miller, "What Can Automation Tell Us About Agency?"; Pflugfelder, "Texts of Our Institutional Lives"; Rice, "Networked Assessment"; Rivers, "Rhetorics of (Non)Symbolic Cultivation"; Sánchez, "Outside the Text: Retheorizing Empiricism and Identity"; and Spinuzzi, "Symmetry as a Methodological Move."

4. Some of the key Latour texts that have appealed to those in Rhetoric and Composition in this vein include "An Attempt at a 'Compositionist Manifesto'" and "From Realpolitik to Dingpolitik: How to Make Things Public."

5. They write that nature and society must be understood as "a process of production" (2) where "everything is production," even those spheres ostensibly outside the productive arena: "*production of productions*, of actions and of passions; *productions of recording processes*, of distributions and of co-ordinates that serve as points of reference; *productions of consumptions*, of sensual pleasures, of anxieties, and of pain" (3, 4).

6. For Derrida's treatment of the Declaration of Independence, see *Rogues*. When explaining why he uses "*savoir*" as opposed to "*connaissance*" to discuss "knowledge," Foucault explains that he uses the former because it captures "the process through which the subject *finds himself modified by what he knows*, or rather by the labor performed in order to know," whereas the latter constitutes a form of knowing where "the subject doing the investigation always remains the same" (*Remarks* 69–70, my emphasis).

7. See May, *Between Genealogy and Epistemology: Psychology, Politics, and Knowledge in the Thought of Michel Foucault*, 78.

8. Consider Derrida's treatment of Lévi-Strauss's structural anthropology in his "Structure Sign and Play," an essay that is typically regarded as a decisive break with everything that came before. Close attention to the text, however, should underscore the absence of haughtiness or dismissive one-upmanship on Derrida's part. Such generosity could be considered a holdover from the "masters of suspicion" that inspired poststructuralism (see Rollins, "Inheriting Deconstruction: Rhetoric and Composition's Missed Encounter with Jacques Derrida," for an insightful account of how Derrida's project is less interested in rejecting tradition than in the question of how one "inherits" tradition). To take the most extreme example, we could note that even Marx's attitude toward capitalism, which is typically framed in terms of unsullied disdain, is much more ambivalent than many of his strident adherents would be willing to admit; despite his grim diagnosis of capitalist reproduction, Marx nevertheless remained fascinated by the system's resiliency, its ability to adapt to unforeseen crises. He remained committed to the nearly impossible task of keeping in dialectical tension the fact that, as Jameson explains, "capitalism is good and bad all at once and simultaneously—the most

productive as well as the most destructive force so far encountered in human history" (*Representing* 8).

9. When asked in an interview what he thought about the "new philosophers," who gained prominence in France during the late 1970s, Deleuze responded bluntly: "Nothing. I think that their thought is worthless" ("New Philosophers" 37).

10. I include a number of quotations here to emphasize the similarities, which should not be downplayed. In a manner reminiscent of Latour's criticism of "sociologists of the social," Foucault clarifies: "I have never presumed that 'power' was something that could explain everything. . . . I tried to coordinate and systematize the different analyses and approaches formulated with regard to power, without depriving them of what was empirical, that is, in a certain sense something that remained to be clarified. *For me, power is that which must be explained*" (*Remarks* 148). Elsewhere, he recognizes the problem of inflexibly applying contextual frames to new and unfamiliar environments, a fact that motivates his rejection of French state-sponsored Marxism during the 1950s, which he complains was "taught like the catechism" and thereby constituted "an object of total disgust" for most youth (135). One must learn from local sites of investigation and feel comfortable creating new concepts to diagnose ever-changing social realities. As he explains,

> thinking back to the period [of the 1960s], I would say that what was about to happen definitely did not have its *own* proper theory, its *own* vocabulary. The changes afoot also occurred in relation to an entire set of philosophical and theoretical systematizations and to an entire kind of culture that had marked approximately the first half of our century. "Things" were about to fall apart, and the right vocabulary didn't exist to express this process. (109)

He also casts a suspicion on the all-knowing critic and insists on the value of learning from participants operating within local settings: "I'm not convinced that intellectuals . . . can point to the essential problems of the society in which they live. On the contrary, one of the main opportunities for collaboration with 'non-intellectuals' is in listening to their problems, and in working with them to formulate these problems: what do the mentally ill say? What is life like in a psychiatric hospital? What is the job of a nurse? How do the sick react?" (151). And look at Foucault's problems with ideology critique, which, while they differ from Latour's, are nonetheless substantial: "I understand how pleasing it can be for some intellectuals to try to be taken seriously by a party or a society by acting out a 'war' against an ideological adversary: but that is disturbing above all because of what it could provoke. Wouldn't it be much better instead to think that those with whom you disagree are perhaps mistaken; or perhaps you haven't understood what they intended to say?" (181).

11. The following statement of Derrida's is worth quoting at length for being both unequivocal and clear:

> I never cease to be surprised by critics who see my work as a declaration that there is nothing beyond language, that we are imprisoned in language; it is, in fact saying the opposite. The critique of logocentrism is above all else the search for the "other" and the "other of language." Every week I receive critical commentaries and studies on deconstruction which operate on the assumption that what they call "post-structuralism" amounts to saying that there is nothing beyond language, that we are submerged in words—and other stupidities of that sort. Certainly, deconstruction tries to show that the question of reference is much more complex and problematic than traditional theories supposed. It even asks whether our term "reference" is entirely adequate for designating the "other." . . . But to challenge or complicate our common assumptions about it, does not amount to saying that there is nothing beyond language. ("Deconstruction and the Other" 123–124)

A thinker criticized throughout his career for writing dense and obfuscating prose, he cannot be accused here of lacking clarity.

12. Some of the most striking criticisms of Latour's political orientation include Brassier, "Concepts and Objects"; Elam, "Living Dangerously with Bruno Latour in a Hybrid World"; Hekman, "We Have Never Been Postmodern: Latour, Foucault and the Material of Knowledge"; Mirowski, "What Is Science Critique?"; and Noys, *The Persistence of the Negative: A Critique of Contemporary Continental Theory*.

13. My analysis here has much in common with Ian Hodder's critique of Latour. For Hodder, Latour's emphasis on "relationality" and "entanglement" tends to downplay the significance of "entrapment." He asserts, "rather than talk of things and humans in meshworks or networks of interconnections, it seems more accurate to talk of a dialectical tension of dependence and dependency that is historically contingent. We seem caught; humans and things are stuck to each other. Rather than focusing on the web as a network, we can see it as a sticky entrapment" (25).

14. A cluster of articles by Latour, Ian Hodder, and Graham Harman in the Winter 2014 issue of *New Literary History* approaches this issue from a slightly different perspective. See Latour, "Agency at the Time of the Anthropocene"; Hodder, "The Entanglements of Humans and Things: A Long-Term View"; and Harman, "Entanglement and Relation: A Response to Bruno Latour and Ian Hodder."

15. Latour in fact cites some of this work in his "Agency at the Time of the Anthropocene" essay. For a more general meditation on human civilization's inevitable demise, see Scranton, *Learning to Die in the Anthropocene*.

16. Steven Connor writes that "Latour is as much driven by the libido of critique as anyone else. Time and again his work lays out the egregious errors of our condition or our understanding of it that must be rinsed away by clear-eyed reflection," (277) his polemics wrapped in a "stylish comedy" that is never "far away from cruelty" (278). Elsewhere, Jennifer Fleissner doubles down on this inescapable feature of Latour's work. From her vantage, Latour's "proposed positive engagement always depends on a great deal of the debunking he supposedly wants to eschew; it's just that what is getting debunked are, again, supposedly those other kinds of critics who want to debunk. There is something, dare one say, *affectively* curious about the result of this: the relentlessly chipper tone combined with the breezy razing of entire fields of intellectual pursuit, as if this were not really what was taking place. And yet I would actually venture to say that . . . it in fact possesses no small role in producing that work's energy and enjoyability for the reader" (116).

17. The 2017 essay collection *Critique and Postcritique*, edited by Rita Felski and Elizabeth S. Anker, boasts a number of analyses repudiating some of the central tenets anchoring the "postcritical" impulse. Toril Moi rejects any dichotomy between "depth" and "surface" reading or between "suspicious" and "gullible" interpretation, insisting that there are simply readers and readings with different points of emphasis and interest. Readers "may of course be more or less subtle and sophisticated, more or less knowing or naive, but it has nothing to do with 'method.'" (34). C. Namwali Serpell, after performing a delightful reading of how clichés function in Jim Thompson's 1952 noir thriller *The Killer Inside Me*, similarly concludes that when it comes to reading critically or passively, "perhaps we read both ways simultaneously, perhaps one way, then the other; in any case, reading is shown to be a layered and variable process irreducible to dichotomies" (175). Meanwhile, other critics challenge the reigning consensus, mobilized by Latour, that critique is a destructive operation diametrically opposed to the more affirmative projects that our contemporary world needs. Christopher Castiglia, for instance, challenges the common conflation of critique with the negative affects— "mistrust, indignation, ungenerosity, and self-congratulation"—typically associated with it, arguing that the critical spirit should be combined with an "imaginative idealism" he calls "hopefulness" (216). Along similar lines, Russ Castronovo admits that while critique is far from synonymous with politics, the former can nevertheless help "produce the conditions for politics to be imagined differently" (239). Even Heather Love, who offers the collection an insightful essay on Donna Haraway, appears to walk back some of the more

programmatic inflections of her previous essays that helped propel the post-critical movement into the spotlight.

18. Derrida laments that "the negative appearance [of the word deconstruction] was and remains much more difficult to efface than is suggested by the grammar of the word (de-), even though it can designate a genealogical restoration [*remonter*] rather than a demolition. That is why the word, at least on its own, has never appeared satisfactory to me" ("Letter" 75).

19. For a good rebuttal of this criticism, see Spinuzzi, "Symmetry as a Methodological Move."

20. Of course, who is counted as part of that "we" is an open question, testifying to the fact that climate change will likely exacerbate existing social divisions rather than alleviate them.

21. Thomas Rickert's insightful analysis of Latour's problematic understanding of "context" shares much with my analysis of Latour's struggles to come to terms with "emergent structure."

22. See Oreskes and Conway, *Merchants of Doubt*, for more on the link between climate denial and the tobacco lobby. See the final chapter of Mirowski, *Never Let a Serious Crisis Go to Waste* for more on conservative tactics concerning climate change.

23. For a recent and compelling account of the interrelation between capitalism and ecology, see Moore, *Capitalism in the Web of Life: Ecology and the Accumulation of Capital*.

24. For other analyses of progressive movements within academic scholarship and their tenuous connection to movements outside the university, see Pierre Bourdieu's analysis of May 1968 in *Homo Academicus* as well as Robyn Wiegman's critique "The Ends of New Americanism."

CODA: ENGLISH STUDIES AND THE UNCERTAIN FUTURE

1. See the work of Giovanni Arrighi, including *The Long Twentieth Century: Money, Power, and the Origins of Our Times* and *Adam Smith in Beijing: Lineages of the 21st Century*, for more on this topic.

Acampora, Christa Davis. *Contesting Nietzsche*. Chicago: University of Chicago Press, 2013.

Adler-Kassner, Linda. *The Activist WPA: Changing Stories about Writing and Writers*. Logan: Utah State University Press, 2008.

Althusser, Louis, and Étienne Balibar. *Reading Capital*. 1968. Trans. Ben Brewster. New York: Verso, 2009.

Anders, George. "Good News Liberal-Arts Majors: Your Peers Probably Won't Outearn You Forever." *Wall Street Journal*, September 11 (2016).

———. "That 'Useless' Liberal Arts Degree Has Become Tech's Hottest Ticket." *Forbes*, August 16 (2015).

Anderson, John R., Lynne M. Reder, and Herbert A. Simon. "Situated Learning and Education." *Educational Researcher* 25.4 (1996): 5–11.

Anker, Elizabeth S., and Rita Felski, eds. *Critique and Postcritique*. Durham, NC: Duke University Press, 2017.

Anson, Chris M. and Hildy Miller. "Journals in Composition: An Update." *College Composition and Communication* 39.2 (1988): 198–216.

Appel, Fredrick. *Nietzsche Contra Democracy*. Ithaca, NY: Cornell University Press, 1999.

Aristotle. *On Rhetoric*. Trans. George A. Kennedy. New York: Oxford University Press, 2007.

Arrighi, Giovanni. *Adam Smith in Beijing: Lineages of the 21st Century*. London: Verso, 2007.

———. *The Long Twentieth Century: Money, Power, and the Origins of Our Times*. New York: Verso, 1994.

Badiou, Alain. *Manifesto for Philosophy*. Trans. Norman Madarasz. Albany: State University of New York Press, 1999.

Barnett, Scot. "Toward an Object-Oriented Rhetoric." *Enculturation* 7 (2010). Web.

Bartholomae, David. "Composition, 1900–2000." *PMLA* 115.7 (2000): 1950–1954.

Bartolovich, Crystal. "Humanities of Scale: Marxism, Surface Reading—and Milton." *PMLA* 127.1 (2012): 115–121.

Beard, David. Review of *Pandora's Hope: Essays on the Reality of Science Studies*, by Bruno Latour. *Rhetoric Society Quarterly* 30.2 (2000): 104–107.

Bennett, James R. "Pre/Face: Critical Pluralism and Democracy." *PRE/TEXT* 7.1 (1986): 77–89.

Bennett, Jane. *Vibrant Matter: A Political Ecology of Things*. Durham, NC: Duke University Press, 2010.

Berg, Maggie, and Barbara K. Seeber. *The Slow Professor: Challenging the Culture of Speed in the Academy*. Toronto: University of Toronto Press, 2016.

Berlin, James. "Contemporary Criticism: The Major Pedagogical Theories." *College English* 44 (1982): 765–777.

———. "Rhetoric and Ideology in the Writing Class." *College English* 50 (1988): 477–494.

———. *Rhetoric and Reality: Writing Instruction in American Colleges, 1900–1985*. Carbondale: Southern Illinois University Press, 1987.

———. *Rhetorics, Poetics, and Cultures: Refiguring College English Studies*. West Lafayette, IN: Parlor Press, 2003.

Bérubé, Michael. *The Employment of English: Theory, Jobs, and the Future of Literary Studies*. New York: New York University Press, 1998.

Best, Stephen, and Sharon Marcus. "Surface Reading: An Introduction." *Representations* 108.1 (2009): 1–21.

Bizzell, Patricia. "We Want to Know Who Are Students Are." *PMLA* 129.3 (2014): 442–447.

Blakesley, David. "So What's Rhetorical about Criticism? A Subjective Dialogue Featuring Kenneth Burke and Fredric Jameson." In *Textuality and Subjectivity: Essays on Language and Being*, 14–20, ed. Eitel Timm, Kenneth Mendoza, and Dale Gowen. Columbia, SC: Camden House, 1991.

Bloor, David. "Anti-Latour." *Studies in the History and Philosophy of Science* 30.1 (1999): 81–112.

Booth, Wayne. "Kenneth Burke's Way of Knowing." *Critical Inquiry* 1.1 (1974): 1–22.

———. "Presidential Address: Arts and Scandals 1982." *PMLA* 98.3 (1983): 312–322.

———. *The Vocation of a Teacher: Rhetorical Occasions, 1967–1988*. Chicago: University of Chicago Press, 1988.

Bourdieu, Pierre. *Homo Academicus*. Trans. Peter Collier. Stanford: Stanford University Press, 1988.

Bousquet, Marc. "The Figure of Writing and the Future of English Studies." *Pedagogy* 10.1 (2010): 117–29.

———. *How the University Works: Higher Education and the Low-Wage Nation*. New York: New York University Press, 2008.

———. "Tenured Bosses and Disposable Teachers." *Minnesota Review* 58–60 (2003): 231–239.

Bové, Paul. "The Foucault Phenomenon: The Problematics of Style." Foreword to *Foucault* by Gilles Deleuze. Trans. Seán Hand. Minneapolis: University of Minnesota Press, 1988.

Brady, Laura. "Review: Retelling the Composition-Literature Story." *College English* 71.1 (2008): 70–81.

Brandt, Deborah. *The Rise of Writing: Redefining Mass Literacy*. Cambridge: Cambridge University Press, 2015.

Brassier, Ray. "Concepts and Objects." In *The Speculative Turn*, 47–65. ed. Levi R. Bryant, Nick Srnicek, and Graham Harman. Melbourne: re.press, 2011.

Brereton, John C. *The Origins of Composition Studies in the American College, 1875–1925*. Pittsburgh: University of Pittsburgh Press, 1995.

Brock, Bernard. *Kenneth Burke and Contemporary European Thought: Rhetoric in Transition*. Tuscaloosa: University of Alabama Press, 1995.

Brodkey, Linda. *Writing Permitted in Designated Areas Only*. Minneapolis: University of Minnesota Press, 1996.

Brooke, Collin, and Thomas Rickert. "Being Delicious: Materialities of Research in a Web 2.0 Application." In Dobrin, Rice, and Vastola, *Beyond Postprocess*, 163–179.

Brown, Stuart C., Paul R. Meyer, and Theresa Enos. "Doctoral Programs in Rhetoric and Composition: A Catalog of the Profession." *Rhetoric Review* 12.2 (1994): 240–251, 253–389.

Brown, Wendy. *Politics Out of History*. Princeton: Princeton University Press, 2001.

Bruffee, Kenneth. "Editorial." *WPA: Writing Program Administration* 1.3 (1978): 6–12.

Bryant, Levi. *The Democracy of Objects*. Ann Arbor, MI: Open Humanities, 2011.

Burke, Kenneth. *Attitudes Toward History*. Berkeley: University of California Press, 1959.

———. *Counter-Statement*. Berkeley: University of California Press, 1968.

———. "Dancing with Tears in My Eyes." *Critical Inquiry* 1.1 (1974): 23–31.

———. *A Grammar of Motives*. Berkeley: University of California Press, 1969.

———. *Language As Symbolic Action: Essays on Life, Literature, and Method*. Berkeley: University of California Press, 1966.

———. "Methodological Repression and/or Strategies of Containment." *Critical Inquiry* 5.2 (1978): 401–416.

———. "(Nonsymbolic) Motion / (Symbolic) Action." *Critical Inquiry* 4.4 (1978): 809–838.

———. *Permanence and Change*. Berkeley: University of California Press, 1954.

———. *The Philosophy of Literary Form*. Berkeley: University of California Press, 1973.

———. *A Rhetoric of Motives*. Berkeley: University of California Press, 1969.

———. "Rhetoric—Old and New." *The Journal of General Education* 5.3 (1951): 202–209.

Burke, Kenneth, and Malcolm Cowley. *The Selected Correspondence, 1915–1981*. Ed. Paul Jay. Berkeley: University of California Press, 1988.

Bygrave, Stephen. *Kenneth Burke: Rhetoric and Ideology*. London: Routledge, 1993.

Castiglia, Christopher. "Hope for Critique?" In Anker and Felski, *Critique and Postcritique*, 211–229.

Castronovo, Russ. "What Are the Politics of Critique? The Function of Criticism at a Different Time." In Anker and Felski, *Critique and Postcritique*, 230–251.

Chapman, David W., and Gary Tate. "A Survey of Doctoral Programs in Rhetoric and Composition." *Rhetoric Review* 5.2 (1987): 124–186.

Chesebro, James W. *Extensions of the Burkean System*. Tuscaloosa: University of Alabama Press, 1993.

Citton, Yves. "Fictional Attachments and Literary Weavings in the Anthropocene." *New Literary History* 47.2 (2016): 309–329.

Clark, Gregory. *Rhetorical Landscapes in America: Variations on a Theme from Kenneth Burke*. Columbia: University of South Carolina Press, 2004.

Cohen, Sande. "Science Studies and Language Suppression: A Critique of Bruno Latour's *We Have Never Been Modern*." *Studies in the History and Philosophy of Science* 28.2 (1997): 339–361.

Cohen, Tom, Claire Colebrook, and J. Hillis Miller. *Theory and the Disappearing Future: On de Man, On Benjamin*. New York: Routledge, 2012.

Coleman, Lisa Hill, and Lorien Goodman, eds. "Rhetoric/Composition: Intersections/Impasses/Differends." *Enculturation* 5.1 (2003), 5.2 (2004). Web.

Connor, Steven. "Decomposing the Humanities." *New Literary History* 47.2 (2016): 275–288.

Connors, Robert J. *The Selected Essays of Robert J. Connors*. Ed. Lisa Ede and Andrea A. Lunsford. New York: Bedford/St. Martin's, 2003.

Coogan, David. "Service Learning and Social Change: The Case for Materialist Rhetoric." *College Composition and Communication* 57 (2006): 667–693.

Coole, Diane, and Samantha Frost, eds. *New Materialisms: Ontology, Agency, and Politics*. Durham, NC: Duke University Press, 2010.

Cooper, Marilyn. "Rhetorical Agency as Emergent and Enacted." *College Composition and Communication* 62.3 (2011): 420–449.

Crable, Bryan. *Ralph Ellison and Kenneth Burke: At the Roots of the Racial Divide*. Charlottesville: University of Virginia Press, 2011.

Crowley, Sharon. *Composition in the University: Historical and Polemical Essays*. Pittsburgh: Pittsburgh University Press, 1998.

———. "Composition Is Not Rhetoric." *Enculturation* 5.1 (2003): http://enculturation.net/5_1/crowley.html. Web.

Crusius, Timothy W. *Kenneth Burke and the Conversation after Philosophy*. Carbondale: Southern Illinois University Press, 1999.

Culler, Jonathan. *The Literary in Theory*. Stanford: Stanford University Press, 2007.

Culler, Jonathan, and Kevin Lamb, eds. *Just Being Difficult? Academic Writing in the Public Sphere*. Stanford: Stanford University Press, 2003.

Cusset, François. *French Theory*. Trans. Jeff Fort. Minneapolis: University of Minnesota Press, 2008.

De Man, Paul. *Allegories of Reading*. New Haven: Yale University Press, 1979.

———. *Blindness and Insight*. Minneapolis: University of Minnesota Press, 1983.

———. Interview by Robert Moynihan. In *A Recent Imagining*, 133–159. Hamden, CT: Archon Books, 1986.

———. "Nietzsche I: Rhetoric + Metaphysics." In *The Political Archive of Paul de Man*, 179–192. Ed. Martin McQuillan. Edinburgh: Edinburgh University Press, 2012.

———. "Nietzsche's Theory of Rhetoric." *Symposium* 28.1 (Spring 1974): 33–51.

———. *The Resistance to Theory*. Minneapolis: University of Minnesota Press, 1986.

Dean, Jodi. "Communicative Capitalism: Circulation and the Foreclosure of Politics." *Cultural Politics* 1.1 (2005): 51–73.

DeKoven, Marianne. "Guest Column: Why Animals Now?" *PMLA* 124.2 (2009): 361–369.

Deleuze, Gilles. *Foucault*. Trans. Sean Hand. Minneapolis: University of Minnesota Press, 1988.

———. "Intellectuals and Power." In *Desert Islands and Other Texts, 1953–1974*, 206–213. New York: Semiotext(e), 2004.

———. "Letter to a Harsh Critic." *Negotiations: 1972–1990*. Trans. Martin Joughin. New York: Columbia University Press, 1997.

———. "On the New Philosophers and a More General Problem." Interview. *Discourse* 20.3 (1998): 37–43.

Deleuze, Gilles, and Félix Guattari. *Anti-Oedipus*. Minneapolis: University of Minnesota Press, 1984.

———. *A Thousand Plateaus*. Trans. Brian Massumi. Minneapolis: University of Minnesota Press, 1987.

———. *What Is Philosophy?* New York: Columbia University Press, 1994.

Derrida, Jacques. *The Animal That Therefore I Am*. New York: Fordham University Press, 2008.

———. *Archive Fever*. Chicago: University of Chicago Press, 1995.

———. *The Beast and the Sovereign*. Vol. 1. Chicago: University of Chicago Press, 2010.

———. "Cogito and the History of Madness." In *Writing and Difference*, 31–63. Trans. Alan Bass. Chicago: University of Chicago Press, 1978.

———. "Deconstruction and the Other." Interview with Richard Kearney. *Dialogues with Contemporary Continental Thinkers*. Ed. Richard Kearney. Manchester: Manchester University Press, 1984.

———. *Glas*. Trans. John P. Leavy Jr. and Richard Rand. Lincoln: University of Nebraska Press, 1986.

———. "Letter to a Japanese Friend." In *A Derrida Reader: Between the Blinds*, 269–276. Ed. Peggy Kamuf. New York: Columbia University Press, 1991.

———. *Limited Inc.* Evanston, IL: Northwestern University Press, 1988.

———. "Marx and Sons." In *Ghostly Demarcations*, 213–269. Ed. Michael Sprinker. London: Verso, 2008.

———. *Of Grammatology*. Trans. Gayatri Spivak. Baltimore, MD: Johns Hopkins University Press, 1974.

———. *Rogues: Two Essays on Reason*. Trans. Pascale-Anne Brault and Michael Naas. Stanford: Stanford University Press, 2005.

———. "Structure, Sign, and Play in the Discourse of the Human Sciences." In *Writing and Difference*, 278–293. Trans. Alan Bass. Chicago: University of Chicago Press, 1978.

———. "'To Do Justice to Freud': The History of Madness in the Age of Psychoanalysis." In *Foucault and His Interlocutors*, 57–96. Ed. Arnold I. Davidson. Chicago: University of Chicago Press, 1997.

Descombes, Vincent. "Nietzsche's French Moment." In *Why We Are Not Nietzscheans*, 70–91. Ed. Luc Ferry and Alain Renaut. Trans. Robert de Loaiza. Chicago: University of Chicago Press, 1997.

Di Leo, Jeffrey R. "Agonistic Academe: Dialogue, Paralogy, and the Postmodern University." *The Comparatist* 37 (2013): 21–36.

Dobrin, Sidney I. *Post-Composition*. Carbondale: Southern Illinois University Press, 2010.

Dobrin, Sidney I., J. A. Rice, and Michael Vastola, eds. *Beyond Postprocess*. Logan: Utah State University Press, 2012.

Donoghue, Frank J. *The Last Professors: The Corporate University and the Fate of the Humanities*. New York: Fordham University Press, 2008.

Dreyfus, Hubert L., and Paul Rabinow. *Michel Foucault: Beyond Structuralism and Hermeneutics*. Chicago: University of Chicago Press, 1983.

Edelman, Lee. *No Future: Queer Theory and the Death Drive*. Durham, NC: Duke University Press, 2004.

Elam, Mark. "Living Dangerously with Bruno Latour in a Hybrid World." *Theory, Culture and Society* 16.1 (1999): 1–24.

Elbow, Peter. "Opinion: The Cultures of Literature and Composition." *College English* 64.5 (2002): 533–546.

———. *What Is English?* New York: Modern Language Association, 1990.

Emig, Janet. *The Composing Processes of Twelfth Graders*. Urbana, IL: NCTE, 1971.

Enoch, Jessica. *Refiguring Rhetorical Education: Women Teaching African American, Native American, and Chicano/a Students, 1865-1911*. Carbondale: Southern Illinois University Press, 2008.

Felman, Shoshana. "Paul de Man's Silence." *Critical Inquiry* 15.4 (1989): 704–744.

Felski, Rita. "Latour and Literary Studies." *PMLA* 130.3 (2015): 737–742.

———. *The Limits of Critique*. Chicago: University of Chicago Press, 2015.

Ferguson, Roderick A. *The Reorder of Things: The University and Its Pedagogies of Minority Difference*. Minneapolis: University of Minnesota Press, 2012.

Fitts, Karen, and William B. Lalicker. "Invisible Hands: A Manifesto to Resolve Institutional and Curricular Hierarchy in English Studies." *College English* 66.4 (2004): 427–451.

Fleissner, Jennifer. "Romancing the Real: Bruno Latour, Ian McEwan, and Postcritical Monism." In Anker and Felski, *Critique and Postcritique*, 99–126.

Fleming, David. "Finding a Place for School in Rhetoric's Public Turn." *The Public Work of Rhetoric: Citizen-Scholars and Civic Engagement*, 211–228. Ed. John M. Ackerman and David J. Coogan. Columbia: University of South Carolina Press, 2010.

Fontaine, Sheryl I., and Susan Hunter. Eds. *Writing Ourselves into the Story: Unheard Voices from Composition Studies*. Carbondale: Southern Illinois University Press, 1993.

Fortun, Kim. "From Latour to Late Industrialism." *HAU: Journal of Ethnographic Theory* 4.1 (2014): 309–29.

Foucault, Michel. *The Archaeology of Knowledge*. Trans. A. M. Sheridan Smith. New York: Pantheon, 1972.

———. *The Birth of the Clinic*. Trans. A. M. Sheridan Smith. New York: Vintage, 1973.

———. *Discipline and Punish*. Trans. Alan Sheridan. New York: Vintage, 1977.

———. *Foucault Live: Collected Interviews, 1961–1984*. New York: Semiotext(e), 1996.

———. *The History of Sexuality, Volume 1: An Introduction*. Trans. Robert Hurley. New York: Vintage, 1978.

———. "The Lives of Infamous Men." In *The Essential Foucault*, 279–293. Ed. Paul Rabinow and Nikolas Rose. New York: New Press, 2003.

———. "My Body, This Paper, This Fire." In *The History of Madness*, 550–574. New York: Routledge, 2006.

———. "Nietzsche, Genealogy, History." In *The Essential Foucault*, 351–369. Ed. Paul Rabinow and Nikolas Rose. New York: New Press, 2003.

———. "Reply to Derrida." In *The History of Madness*, 575–590. New York: Routledge, 2006.

———. "What Is an Author?" In *The Essential Foucault*, 377–391. Ed. Paul Rabinow and Nikolas Rose. New York: New Press, 2003.

Foucault, Michel, and Duccio Trombadori. *Remarks on Marx: Conversations with Duccio Trombadori*. New York: Semiotext(e), 1991.

Fraser, Nancy, and Axel Honneth. *Redistribution or Recognition? A Political-Philosophical Exchange*. New York: Verso, 2003.

Frey, Carl Benedikt, and Michael A. Osborne. "The Future of Employment: How Susceptible Are Jobs to Computerisation?" *Technological Forecasting and Social Change* 114 (2017): 254–280.

Gage, John T. "On 'Rhetoric' and 'Composition.'" In *An Introduction to Composition Studies*, 15–32. Ed. Erika Lindemann and Gary Tate. New York: Oxford University Press, 1991.

Gallagher, Catherine, and Stephen Greenblatt. *Practicing New Historicism*. Chicago: University of Chicago Press, 2001.

Gallagher, Chris W. "Review: Re-modeling English Studies." *College English* 63.6 (2001): 780–789.

Gasché, Rodolph. *The Wild Card of Reading: On Paul de Man*. Cambridge, MA: Harvard University Press, 1998.

Geisler, Cheryl. *Academic Literacy and the Nature of Expertise: Reading, Writing, and Knowing in Academic Philosophy*. Hillsdale, NJ: Lawrence Erlbaum, 1994.

George, Ann, and Jack Selzer. *Kenneth Burke in the 1930s*. Columbia: University of South Carolina Press, 2007.

Ginsberg, Benjamin. *The Fall of the Faculty: The Rise of the All-Administrative University and Why It Matters*. Oxford: Oxford University Press, 2011.

Godzich, Wlad. *The Culture of Literacy*. Cambridge, MA: Harvard University Press, 1994.

Goggin, Maureen Daly. *Authoring a Discipline: Scholarly Journals and the Post-World War II Emergence of Rhetoric and Composition*. Mahwah, NJ: Lawrence Erlbaum, 2000.

Gold, David. *Rhetoric at the Margins: Revising the History of Writing Instruction in American Colleges, 1873–1947*. Carbondale: Southern Illinois University Press, 2008.

Golsby-Smith, Tony. "Want Innovative Thinking? Hire from the Humanities." Harvard Business Review Blog. March 31. blogs.hbr.org/2011/03/want-innovative-thinking-hire. Web.

Gorrell, Robert M. "Rhetoric, Dickoric, Doc: Rhetoric as an Academic Discipline." *College Composition and Communication* 26.1 (1975): 14–19.

Graff, Gerald. "Co-optation." In Veeser, *The New Historicism*, 168–181.

———. *Professing Literature*. Chicago: University of Chicago Press, 1987.

Graham, S. Scott. "Agency and the Rhetoric of Medicine: Biomedical Brain Scans and the Ontology of Fibromyalgia." *Technical Communication Quarterly* 18.4 (2009): 376–404.

Greenblatt, Stephen. *Shakespearean Negotiations: The Circulation of Social Energy in Renaissance England*. Berkeley: University of California Press, 1988.

———. "Towards a Poetics of Culture." In Veeser, *The New Historicism*, 1–14.

Guillory, John. *Cultural Capital: The Problem of Literary Canon Formation*. Chicago: University of Chicago Press, 1993.

———. "The System of Graduate Education." *PMLA* 115.5 (2000): 1154–1163.

Hägglund, Martin. *Radical Atheism: Derrida and the Time of Life*. Stanford: Stanford University Press, 2008.

Hairston, Maxine. "Comment and Response." *College English* 52.6 (1990): 694–696.

———. "Diversity, Ideology, and Teaching Writing." *College Composition and Communication* 43.2 (1992): 179–193.

———. "The Winds of Change: Thomas Kuhn and the Revolution in the Teaching of Writing." *College Composition and Communication* 33.1 (1982): 76–88.

Harari, José. *Textual Strategies*. Ithaca, NY: Cornell University Press, 1979.

Hardt, Michael, and Antonio Negri. *Empire*. Cambridge: Harvard University Press, 2000.

Harman, Graham. *Bruno Latour: Reassembling the Political*. London: Pluto Press, 2014.

———. "Demodernizing the Humanities with Latour." *New Literary History* 47.2 (2016): 249–274.

———. "Entanglement and Relation: A Response to Bruno Latour and Ian Hodder." *New Literary History* 45.1 (2014): 37–49.

———. *Prince of Networks: Bruno Latour and Metaphysics*. Melbourne: re.press, 2009.

Harpham, Geoffrey Galt. *The Humanities and the Dream of the America*. Chicago: University of Chicago Press, 2011.

Harris, Joseph. "Meet the New Boss, Same as the Old Boss: Class Consciousness in Composition." *College Composition and Communication* 52.1 (2000):
43-68.

———. *A Teaching Subject: Composition since 1966.* Logan: Utah State University Press, 2012.

Hartzog, Carol P. *Composition and the Academy: A Study of Writing Program Administration.* New York: Modern Language Association of America, 1986.

Hatab, Lawrence J. *A Nietzschean Defense of Democracy: An Experiment in Postmodern Politics.* Chicago: Open Court, 1995.

———. "Prospects for a Democratic Agon: Why We Can Still Be Nietzscheans." *Journal of Nietzsche Studies* 24 (Fall 2002): 132–47.

Hawhee, Debra. "Agonism and Arete." *Philosophy and Rhetoric.* 35.3 (2002):
185–207.

———. "Burke and Nietzsche." *Quarterly Journal of Speech.* 85 (1999):
129–145.

———. *Moving Bodies: Kenneth Burke at the Edges of Language.* Columbia:
University of South Carolina Press, 2009.

Hawk, Byron. "Reassembling Postprocess: Toward a Theory of Public
Rhetoric." In Dobrin, Rice, and Vastola, *Beyond Postprocess,* 75–93.

Hayot, Eric. "Then and Now." In Anker and Felski, *Critique and Postcritique,*
279–295.

Heckman, Peter. "Nietzsche's Clever Animal: Metaphor in 'Truth and Falsity.'" *Philosophy and Rhetoric* 24.4 (1991): 301–321.

Hekman, Susan. "We Have Never Been Postmodern: Latour, Foucault and
the Material of Knowledge." *Contemporary Political Theory* 8.4 (2009):
435–54.

Hensley, Nathan K. "Curatorial Reading and Endless War." *Victorian Studies*
56.1 (2013): 59–83.

Herzberg, Bruce. "Community Service and Critical Thinking." *College Composition and Communication* 45 (1994): 307–19.

Hodder, Ian. "The Entanglements of Humans and Things: A Long-Term
View." *New Literary History* 45.1 (2014): 19–36.

Honoré, Carl. *In Praise of Slowness: Challenging the Cult of Speed.* New York:
Harper Collins, 2004.

Horner, Bruce, and Min-Zhan Lu. In "Rhetoric and(?) Composition." *The
Sage Handbook of Rhetorical Studies,* 293–315. Ed. Andrea A. Lunsford,
Kirt H. Wilson, and Rosa E. Eberly. Los Angeles: Sage, 2009.

Horner, Winifred Bryan, ed. *Bridging the Gap: Literature and Composition.*
Chicago: University of Chicago Press, 1983.

Ianetta, Melissa. "Disciplinarity, Divorce, and the Displacement of Labor Issues: Rereading Histories of Composition and Literature." *College Composition and Communication* 62.1 (2010): 53–72.

Isaac, Emily. "The Emergence of Centers for Writing Excellence." In *Before and After the Tutorial: Writing Centers and Institutional Relationships*, 131–150. Ed. Nicholas Mauriello, William J. Macauley, Jr., and Robert T. Koch, Jr. New York: Hampton Press, 2011.

Jameson, Fredric. "Cognitive Mapping." In *Marxism and the Interpretation of Culture*, 347–357. Ed. Cary Nelson and Lawrence Grossberg. Urbana-Champaign: University of Illinois Press, 1988.

———. *The Ideologies of Theory*. New York: Verso, 2008.

———. "Ideology and Symbolic Action." *Critical Inquiry* 5.2 (1978): 417–22.

———. *Jameson on Jameson: Conversations on Cultural Marxism*. Durham, NC: Duke University Press, 2007.

———. *Marxism and Form*. Princeton: Princeton University Press, 1971.

———. "Marx's Purloined Letter." In *Ghostly Demarcations*, 26–67. Ed Michael Sprinker. London: Verso, 2008.

———. *The Political Unconscious: Narrative as a Socially Symbolic Act*. Ithaca, NY: Cornell University Press, 1981.

———. *Postmodernism; Or, the Cultural Logic of Late Capitalism*. Durham, NC: Duke University Press, 1991.

———. *Representing Capital: A Reading of Volume One*. New York: Verso, 2014.

———. "The Symbolic Inference: or, Kenneth Burke and Ideological Analysis." *Critical Inquiry* 4.3 (1978): 507–23.

———. "War and Representation." *PMLA* 124.5 (2009): 1532–1547.

Jancovich, Mark. *The Cultural Politics of the New Criticism*. New York: Cambridge University Press, 1993.

Johnson, Barbara. *A World of Difference*. Baltimore, MD: Johns Hopkins University Press, 1988.

Kennedy, George A. *Classical Rhetoric and Its Christian and Secular Traditions*. 2nd ed. Chapel Hill: University of North Carolina Press, 1999.

Kent, Thomas, ed. *Post-Process Theory: Beyond the Writing-Process Paradigm*. Carbondale: Southern Illinois University Press, 1999.

Kindley, Evan. "Big Criticism." *Critical Inquiry* 38.1 (2011): 71–95.

Kitzhaber, Albert R. *Rhetoric in American Colleges, 1850–1900*. Dallas, TX: Southern Methodist University Press, 1990.

Kopelson, Karen. "Sp(l)itting Images: Or, Back to the Future of (Rhetoric and?) Composition." *College Composition and Communication* 59.4 (2008): 750–780.

Laclau, Ernesto, and Chantal Mouffe. *Hegemony and Socialist Strategy: Toward a Radical Democratic Politics*. London: Verso, 1985.

Lanham, Richard A. "Composition, Literature, and the Lower-Division Gyroscope." *Profession* (1984): 10–15.

Latour, Bruno. "Agency at the Time of the Anthropocene." *New Literary History* 45.1 (2014): 1–18.

———. "An Attempt at a 'Compositionist Manifesto.'" *New Literary History* 41.3 (2010): 471–490.

———. *An Inquiry into Modes of Existence: An Anthropology of the Moderns.* Trans. Catherine Porter. Cambridge, MA: Harvard University Press, 2012.

———. "From Realpolitik to Dingpolitik, or How to Make Things Public." In *Making Things Public: Atmospheres of Democracy*, 4–31. Ed. Latour and Peter Weibel. Cambridge, MA: MIT Press, 2005.

———. "Life Among Conceptual Characters." *New Literary History* 47.2 (2016): 463–476.

———. "On Some of the Affects of Capitalism." *Copenhagen: Danish Royal Academy* (2014).

———. *The Pasteurization of France.* Cambridge, MA: Harvard University Press, 1988.

———. *The Politics of Nature: How to Bring the Sciences into Democracy.* Trans. Catherine Porter. Cambridge, MA: Harvard University Press, 2004.

———. *Reassembling the Social: An Introduction to Actor-Network Theory.* New York: Oxford University Press, 2005.

———. *We Have Never Been Modern.* Trans. Catherine Porter. Cambridge, MA: Harvard University Press, 1993.

———. "Why Has Critique Run Out of Steam? From Matters of Fact to Matters of Concern." *Critical Inquiry* 30 (2004): 225–248.

Latour, Bruno, and Michael Callon. "Don't Throw the Baby Out with the Bath School! A Reply to Collins and Yearley." In *Science as Practice and Culture*, 343–368. Ed. Andrew Pickering. Chicago: University of Chicago Press, 1992.

Latour, Bruno, Graham Harman, and Peter Erdélyi. *Prince and the Wolf: Latour and Harman at the LSE.* Washington, DC: Zero, 2011.

Leitch, Vincent. *Literary Criticism in the 21st Century.* New York: Bloomsbury, 2014.

Leitch, Vincent, et al. *The Norton Anthology of Theory and Criticism.* 2nd ed. New York: Norton, 2010.

Lentricchia, Frank. *Criticism and Social Change.* Chicago: University of Chicago Press, 1983.

———. "Foucault's Legacy: A New Historicism?" In Veeser, *The New Historicism*, 231–242.

L'Eplattenier, Barbara, and Lisa S. Mastrangelo. "Archival Research in the Field of Rhetoric and Composition." In *Exploring Composition Studies: Sites, Issues, and Perspectives*, 211–222. Ed. Kelly Ritter and Paul Kei Matsuda. Logan: Utah State University Press, 2012.

Lesjak, Carolyn. "Reading Dialectically." *Criticism* 55.2 (2013): 233–277.

Lindemann, Erika. "Freshman Composition: No Place for Literature." *College English* 55.3 (1993): 311–316.

Love, Heather. "Close but Not Deep: Literary Ethics and the Descriptive Turn." *New Literary History* 41.2 (2010): 371–391.

———. "Close Reading and Thin Description." *Public Culture* 25.3 (2013): 401–434.

———. "The Temptations: Donna Haraway, Feminist Objectivity, and the Problem of Critique." In Anker and Felski, *Critique and Postcritique*, 50–72.

———. "Truth and Consequences: On Paranoid Reading and Reparative Reading." *Criticism* 52.2 (2010): 235–241.

Lynch, Paul. "Composition's New Thing: Bruno Latour and the Apocalyptic Turn." *College English* 74.5 (2012): 458–476.

Lynch, Paul, and Nathaniel Rivers, eds. *Thinking with Bruno Latour in Rhetoric and Composition*. Carbondale: Southern Illinois University Press, 2015.

Mara, Andrew, and Byron Hawk. "Posthuman Rhetorics and Technical Communication." *Technical Communication Quarterly* 19.1 (2010): 1–10.

Marback, Richard. "Unclenching the Fist: Embodying Rhetoric and Giving Objects Their Due." *Rhetoric Society Quarterly* 38.1 (2008): 46–65.

Marsh, John. "The Literature of Poverty, The Poverty of Literature Classes." *College English* 73.6 (2011): 604–627.

Martin, Keir. "Knot-work Not Networks, or Anti-anti-antifetishism and the ANTipolitics Machine." *HAU: Journal of Ethnographic Theory* 4.3 (2014): 99–115.

Marx, Karl. *The Marx-Engels Reader*. Ed. Robert C. Tucker. New York: Norton, 1978.

Mathieu, Paula. *Tactics of Hope: The Public Turn in English Composition*. Portsmouth, NH: Boynton/Cook, 2005.

May, Todd. *Between Genealogy and Epistemology: Psychology, Politics, and Knowledge in the Thought of Michel Foucault*. University Park: Pennsylvania State University Press, 1993.

McCrimmon, Miles. "Across the Great Divide: Anxieties of Acculturation in College English." *College English* 69.2 (2006): 117–126.

McGee, Kyle. *Bruno Latour: The Normativity of Networks*. New York: Routledge, 2014.

McGowan, John. "Kenneth Burke." *Minnesota Review* 58–60 (2002–2003): 241–249.

McQuillan, Martin. Ed. *The Political Archive of Paul de Man: Property, Sovereignty, and the Theotropic*. Edinburgh: Edinburgh University Press, 2012.

Mettler, Suzanne. *Degrees of Inequality: How the Politics of Higher Education Sabotaged the American Dream*. New York: Basic Books, 2014.

Mezzadra, Sandro and Brett Neilson. *Border as Method, or, the Multiplication of Labor.* Durham, NC: Duke University Press, 2013.

Michaels, Walter Benn. *The Trouble with Diversity.* New York: Metropolitan Books, 2006.

Miller, Carolyn R. "What Can Automation Tell Us About Agency?" *Rhetoric Society Quarterly* 37.2 (2007): 137–157.

Miller, J. Hillis. "Ariachne's Broken Woof." *Georgia Review* 31 (1977): 44–60.

———. "Nietzsche in Basel: Writing Reading." *Journal of Advanced Composition* 13.2 (Fall 1993): 311–328.

———. "Presidential Address 1986. The Triumph of Theory, the Resistance to Reading, and the Question of the Material Base." *PMLA* 102.3 (1987): 281–291.

Miller, Susan. *Textual Carnivals: The Politics of Composition.* Carbondale: Southern Illinois University Press, 1991.

Miller, Thomas P., and Joseph G. Jones. "Review: Working Out Our History." *College English* 67.4 (2005): 421–439.

Mirowski, Philip. *Never Let a Serious Crisis Go to Waste.* New York: Verso, 2013.

———. "What Is Science Critique?" Academia.edu. Web.

Miyoshi, Masao. "Ivory Tower in Escrow." *boundary 2* 27.1 (2000): 7–50.

Modern Language Association. "Report on the MLA *Job Information List*, 2012–13." MLA Office of Research, October 2013. Web.

Monaghen, E. Jennifer, and E. Wendy Saul. "The Reader, the Scribe, the Thinker: A Critical Look at the History of American Reading and Writing Instruction." In *The Formation of School Subjects: The Struggle for Creating an American Institution*, 85–122. Ed. Thomas S. Popkewitz. New York: Palmer, 1987.

Moore, Jason W. *Capitalism in the Web of Life: Ecology and the Accumulation of Capital.* New York: Verso, 2015.

Mouffe, Chantal. *The Democratic Paradox.* London: Verso, 2005.

Mueller, Derek. "Grasping Rhetoric and Composition by Its Long Tail: What Graphs Can Tell Us about the Field's Changing Shape." *College Composition and Communication* 64.1 (2012): 195–223.

Mulderig, Gerald. "Is There Still a Place for Rhetorical History in Composition Studies?" In *History, Reflection, and Narrative: The Professionalization of Composition, 1963–1983*, 163–176. Ed. Mary Rosner, Beth Boehm, and Debra Journet. Stamford, CT: Ablex, 1999.

Murphy, James. "Rhetorical History as a Guide to the Salvation of American Reading and Writing: A Plea for Curricular Courage." In *The Rhetorical Tradition and Modern Writing*, 3–12. Ed. James Murphy. New York: MLA, 1982.

Nelson, Cary. *Will Teach for Food: Academic Labor in Crisis.* Minneapolis: University of Minnesota Press, 1997.

Newfield, Christopher. *Ivy and Industry: Business and the Making of the American University, 1880–1980*. Durham, NC: Duke University Press, 2003.

———. *Unmaking the Public University: The Forty-Year Assault on the Middle Class*. Cambridge, MA: Harvard University Press, 2008.

Ngai, Sianne. *Our Aesthetic Categories*. Cambridge, MA: Harvard University Press, 2012.

Nietzsche, Friedrich. *Beyond Good and Evil*. In *Basic Writings of Nietzsche*, 179–435. New York: Modern Library, 2000.

———. *Daybreak*. Cambridge: Cambridge University Press, 1997.

———. *Friedrich Nietzsche on Rhetoric and Language*. Ed. Sander L. Gilman, Carole Blair, and David J. Parent. New York: Oxford University Press, 1989.

———. "Homer's Contest." In *Early Greek Philosophy and Other Essays*, 49–62. Trans. Maximillian A. Mügge. New York: Gordon Press, 1974.

———. *On the Genealogy of Morals and Ecce Homo*. Trans. Walter Kaufmann. New York: Vintage, 1967.

———. "We Philologists." Trans. J. M. Kennedy. In *The Complete Works of Friedrich Nietzsche*, 8:103–190. New York: Macmillan, 1911.

North, Joseph. *Literary Criticism: A Concise Political History*. Cambridge, MA: Harvard University Press, 2017.

Noys, Benjamin. *The Persistence of the Negative: A Critique of Contemporary Continental Theory*. Edinburgh: Edinburgh University Press, 2012.

Nussbaum, Martha. *Not for Profit: Why Democracy Needs the Humanities*. Princeton: Princeton University Press, 2010.

Olson, Gary A., ed. *Rhetoric and Composition as Intellectual Work*. Carbondale: Southern Illinois University Press, 2002.

Oreskes, Naomi, and Erik M. Conway. *Merchants of Doubt: How a Handful of Scientists Obscured the Truth on Issues from Tobacco Smoke to Global Warming*. New York: Bloomsbury, 2010.

Ostergaard, Lori, Jeff Ludwig, and Jim Nugent. *Transforming English Studies: New Voices in an Emerging Genre*. West Lafayette, IN: Parlor Press, 2009.

Owens, Derek. *Composition and Sustainability: Teaching for a Threatened Generation*. Urbana, IL: NCTE, 2001.

Parker, Robert P., Jr. "From Sputnik to Dartmouth: Trends in the Teaching of Composition." *English Journal* 68.6 (1979): 32–37.

Petraglia, Joseph. "Introduction: General Writing Skills Instruction and Its Discontents." In *Reconceiving Writing, Rethinking Writing Instruction*, xi–xvii. Ed. Joseph Petraglia. Mahwah, NJ: Lawrence Erlbaum, 1995.

Pflugfelder, Ehren Helmut. "Is No One at the Wheel? Nonhuman Agency and Agentive Movement." In Lynch and Rivers, *Thinking with Bruno Latour in Rhetoric and Composition*, 115–131.

———. "Texts of Our Institutional Lives: Translucency, Coursepacks, and the Post-historical University: An Investigation into Pedagogical Things." *College English* 74.3 (2012): 247–267.

Phelps, Louise Wetherbee. "Practical Wisdom and the Geography of Knowledge in Composition." *College English* 53.8 (1991): 863–885.

Pickering, Andrew, ed. *Science as Practice and Culture*. Chicago: University of Chicago Press, 1992.

Porter, James I. "Nietzsche's Rhetoric: Theory and Strategy." *Philosophy and Rhetoric* 27.3 (1994): 218–244.

Ramsey, Alexis E., Wendy B. Sharer, Barbara L'Eplattenier, and Lisa S. Mastrangelo, eds. *Working in the Archives: Practical Research Methods for Rhetoric and Composition*. Carbondale: Southern Illinois University Press, 2010.

Readings, Bill. *The University in Ruins*. Cambridge, MA: Harvard University Press, 1996.

Reich, Robert. *The Work of Nations*. New York: Vintage, 1991.

Rice, Jeff. "Craft Networks." In Lynch and Rivers, *Thinking with Bruno Latour in Rhetoric and Composition*, 237–255.

———. "Networked Assessment." *Computers and Composition* 28.1 (2011): 28–39.

Richards, I. A. *The Philosophy of Rhetoric*. New York: Oxford University Press, 1964.

Rickert, Thomas. "The Whole of the Moon: Latour, Context, and the Problem of Holism." In Lynch and Rivers, *Thinking with Bruno Latour in Rhetoric and Composition*, 135–150.

Ritter, Kelly. "Extra-institutional Agency and the Public Value of the WPA." *WPA* 29.3: 45–64.

Rivers, Nathaniel A. "Rhetorics of (Non)Symbolic Cultivation." *Ecology, Writing Theory, and New Media: Writing Ecology*, 34–50. Ed. Sid Dobrin. New York: Routledge, 2012.

Rollins, Brooke. "Inheriting Deconstruction: Rhetoric and Composition's Missed Encounter with Jacques Derrida." *College English* 69.1 (2006): 11–29.

Rood, Craig. "'Understanding' Again: Listening with Kenneth Burke and Wayne Booth." *Rhetoric Society Quarterly* 44.5 (2014): 449–469.

Rose, Shirley K. "Review: The WPA Within: WPA Identities and Implications for Graduate Education in Rhetoric and Composition." *College English* 75.2 (2012): 218–230.

Rose, Shirley K., and Irwin Weiser, eds. *The Writing Program Administrator as Researcher*. Portsmouth, NH: Boynton/Cook, 1999.

———.*The Writing Program Administrator as Theorist*. Portsmouth, NH: Boynton/Cook, 2002.

Ross, Andrew. *No Respect: Intellectuals and Popular Culture*. New York: Routledge, 1989.

Said, Edward. *The World, the Text, and the Critic*. Cambridge, MA: Harvard University Press, 1983.

Sánchez, Raúl. "Outside the Text: Retheorizing Empiricism and Identity." *College English* 74.3 (2012): 234–246.

Schilb, John. *Between the Lines: Relating Composition Theory and Literary Theory*. Portsmouth, NH: Boynton/Cook, 1996.

———. "Composition and Poststructuralism: A Tale of Two Conferences." *College Composition and Communication* 40.4 (1989): 422–443.

Schmidgen, Henning. *Bruno Latour in Pieces: An Intellectual Biography*. Trans. Gloria Custance. New York: Fordham University Press, 2015.

Scholes, Robert. *The Rise and Fall of English*. New Haven: Yale University Press, 1998.

Schrift, Alan. *Nietzsche's French Legacy: A Genealogy of Poststructuralism*. New York: Routledge, 1995.

Schrift, Alan, ed. *Why Nietzsche Still? Reflections on Drama, Culture, and Politics*. Berkeley: University of California Press, 2000.

Scott, Robert L. "The Necessary Pluralism of Any Future History of Rhetoric." *PRE/TEXT* 12.3 (1991): 195–209.

Scranton, Roy. *Learning to Die in the Anthropocene*. San Francisco: City Lights, 2015.

Sedgwick, Eve Kosofsky. *Touching Feeling: Affect, Pedagogy, Performativity*. Durham, NC: Duke University Press, 2003.

Serpell, C. Namwali. "A Heap of Cliché." In Anker and Felski, *Critique and Postcritique*, 153–182.

Shaughnessy, Mina P. *Errors and Expectations: A Guide for the Teacher of Basic Writing*. New York: Oxford University Press, 1977.

Shipka, Jody. *Toward a Composition Made Whole*. Pittsburgh: University of Pittsburgh Press, 2011.

Simmons, W. Michele, Kristen Moore, and Patricia Sullivan. "Tracing Uncertainties: Methodologies of a Door Closer." In Lynch and Rivers, *Thinking with Bruno Latour in Rhetoric and Composition*, 275–293.

Sledd, James. "Why the Wyoming Resolution Had to Be Emasculated: A History and a Quixotism." *Journal of Advanced Composition* 11 (1991): 269–281.

Smith, Barbara Herrnstein. "Anthropotheology: Latour Speaking Religiously." *New Literary History* 47.2 (2016): 331–351.

Snyder, Carol. "Analyzing Classifications: Foucault for Advanced Writing." *College Composition and Communication* 35.2 (1984): 209–216.

Spellmeyer, Kurt. "After Theory: From Textuality to Attunement with the World." *College English* 58.8 (1996): 893–913.

Spinuzzi, Clay. *Network: Theorizing Knowledge Work in Telecommunications.* New York: Cambridge University Press, 2008.

———. "Symmetry as a Methodological Move." In Lynch and Rivers, *Thinking with Bruno Latour in Rhetoric and Composition,* 23–39.

Stallybrass, Peter, and Allon White. *The Politics and Poetics of Transgression.* Ithaca, NY: Cornell University Press, 1986.

Stewart, Donald C. "The Status of Composition and Rhetoric in American Colleges, 1880–1902: An MLA Perspective." *College English* 47.7 (1985).

Stiegler, Bernard. *For a New Critique of Political Economy.* Trans. Daniel Ross. Cambridge: Polity, 2010.

Strickland, Donna. *The Managerial Unconscious in the History of Composition Studies.* Carbondale: Southern Illinois University Press, 2011.

Swearingen, C. J. "Rhetoric and Composition as a Coherent Intellectual Discipline: A Meditation." In *Rhetoric and Composition as Intellectual Work,* 12–22. Ed. Gary Olson. Carbondale: Southern Illinois University Press, 2002.

Tate, Allen. *Essays of Four Decades.* London: Oxford University Press, 1970.

Tate, Gary. "A Place for Literature in Freshman Composition." *College English* 55.3 (1993): 317–321.

Tell, Dave. "Burke and Jameson: Reflections on Language, Ideology, and Criticism." In *Burke in the Archives: Using the Past to Transform the Future of Burkean Studies,* 66–83. Ed. Dana Anderson and Jessica Enoch. Columbia: University of South Carolina Press, 2013.

Therborn, Göran. *The Ideology of Power and the Power of Ideology.* London: New Left Books, 1980.

Thrift, Nigel. "The University of Life." *New Literary History* 47.2 (2016): 399–417.

Tirrell, Jeremy. "Latourian *Memoria.*" In Lynch and Rivers, *Thinking with Bruno Latour in Rhetoric and Composition,* 165–181.

Tuman, Myron. "From Astor Place to Kenyon Road: The NCTE and the Origins of English Studies." *College English* 48.4 (1986): 339–349.

Veeser, H. Aram, ed. *The New Historicism.* New York: Routledge, 1989.

Vernant, Jean Pierre. *The Origins of Greek Thought.* Ithaca, NY: Cornell University Press, 1982.

Virno, Paolo. *A Grammar of the Multitude.* New York: Semiotext(e), 2004.

W.E.B. Du Bois Research Institute at the Hutchins Center. "About." hutchinscenter.fas.harvard.edu/about. Web.

Walker, Jeffrey. *Rhetoric and Poetics in Antiquity.* New York: Oxford University Press, 2000.

Walker, Michelle Boulous. *Slow Philosophy: Reading against the Institution.* London: Bloomsbury, 2017.

Wallerstein, Immanuel, et al. *Does Capitalism Have a Future?* New York: Oxford University Press, 2013.

Warren, Robert Penn. "Knowledge and the Image of Man." In *Robert Penn Warren: A Collection of Critical Essays*, 237–246. Ed. John L. Longley. New York: New York University Press, 1965.

Waters, Lindsay. "Professah de Man—he dead." *American Literary History* 7.2 (1995): 284–303.

Weber, Samuel. "Afterword: Literature—Just Making It." In *Just Gaming* by François Lyotard and Jean-Loup Thébaud. Trans. Wlad Godzich. Minneapolis: University of Minnesota Press, 1985.

Weisser, Christian. *Moving Beyond Academic Discourse: Composition Studies and the Public Sphere*. Carbondale: Southern Illinois University Press, 2002.

Wells, Susan. "Claiming the Archive for Rhetoric and Composition." In *Rhetoric and Composition as Intellectual Work*, 55–64. Ed. Gary A. Olson. Carbondale: Southern Illinois University Press, 2002.

———. "Rogue Cops and Health Care: What Do We Want from Public Writing?" *College Composition and Communication* 47 (1996): 325–341.

Wess, Robert. *Kenneth Burke: Rhetoric, Subjectivity, Postmodernism*. Cambridge: Cambridge University Press, 1996.

Wetherbee, Ben. "Jameson, Burke, and the Virus of Suggestion: Between Ideology and Rhetoric." *The Henry James Review* 36.3 (2015): 280–287.

White, Edward M. "Post-Structural Literary Criticism and the Response to Student Writing." *College Composition and Communication* 35.2 (1984): 186–195.

Wiegman, Robyn. "The Ends of New Americanism." *New Literary History* 42.3 (2011): 385–407.

Williams, Jeffrey J. "The Little Magazine and the Theory Journal: A Response to Evan Kindley's 'Big Criticism.'" *Critical Inquiry* 39.2 (2013): 402–411.

Winsor, Dorothy A. "Engineering Writing/Writing Engineering." *College Composition and Communication*. 41.1 (1990): 58–70.

———. "Learning to Do Knowledge Work in Systems of Distributed Cognition." *Journal of Business and Technical Communication*. 15.1 (2001): 5–28.

Woods, Marjorie C. "Among Men—Not Boys: Histories of Rhetoric and the Exclusion of Pedagogy." *Rhetoric Society Quarterly* 22 (1992): 18–26.

———. "The Teaching of Writing in Medieval Europe." In *A Short History of Writing Instruction: From Ancient Greece to Twentieth-Century America*, 77–94. Ed. James J. Murphy. New York: Routledge, 2012.

Yancey, Kathleen Blake. "Writing in the 21st Century." *National Council Teachers of English* (2009): 1–9.

Yood, Jessica. "Writing the Discipline: A Generic History of English Studies." *College English* 65.5 (2003): 526–540.

Žižek, Slavoj. *First as Tragedy, Then as Farce*. New York: Verso, 2009.

———. "Have Michael Hardt and Antonio Negri Rewritten the Communist
Manifesto for the Twenty-First Century?" *Rethinking Marxism* 13.3/4
(2001): 190–198.

INDEX

1960s social movements 14, 94, 102, 109,
    119, 121, 213n7

Acampora, Christa Davis 29
Adams, Kate 109
Adler-Kassner, Linda 213n6
Adorno, Theodor 73
aesthetics 131–132, 141–148, 152–154,
Agamben, Giorgio 167
agon 26, 28–29, 33–35, 44, 89, 196
Agrarian movement 8
Althusser, Louis 107, 166, 167
American Comparative Literature As-
    sociation 132
Anders, George 214n5
Anderson, John R. 214n4
anecdote/anecdotalism 101
animal studies 22, 91
Anker, Elizabeth S. 219n17
Anson, Chris M. 206n10
Appel, Fredrick 209n10
Aristotle 3, 25, 27, 30, 35, 39, 47–48, 57,
    152
Arnold, Matthew 55
Arrighi, Giovanni 220n1
Auerbach, Eric 102
Austin, J. L. 165

Badiou, Alain 117–118, 186
Balibar, Étienne 166
Barnett, Scott 215n3
Barthes, Roland 52, 63, 92–93, 164
Bartholomae, David 206n9
Bartolovich, Crystal 215n2
Bate, Walter Jackson 38
Beard, David 215 n. 3
Benjamin, Walter 95
Bennett, James R. 212n16
Bennett, Jane 215n2

Berg, Maggie 213n1
Bergson, Henri 68
Berlin, James 15, 17, 105–109, 111,
    113–114, 129, 138–139, 144, 168
Bérubé, Michael 208n27
Best, Stephen 157
Bettelheim, Bruno 180
Bibliothèque Nationale 98
Bizzell, Patricia 5–6, 11
Blair, Carole 27
Blakesley, David 210n4
Blass, Friedrich 27
Bloor, David 215n1
Booth, Wayne 9, 10–12, 63, 90,
    193–195, 207n14, 210n5
Bourdieu, Pierre 142, 143, 169, 186,
    220n24
Bousquet, Marc 15, 113, 208n27
Bové, Paul 214 n. 10
Brady, Laura 207n15
Brandt, Deborah 213n2
Brassier, Ray 218n12
Braudel, Fernand 173
Brereton, John C. 7
Brock, Bernard 210n3
Brodkey, Linda 213n9
Brooke, Collin 215n3
Brooks, Cleanth 206n13
Brower, Reuben 38
Brown, Lester 189
Brown, Stuart C. 206n10
Brown, Wendy 48, 174
Bruffee, Kenneth 213n8
Bryan, William Jennings 206n13
Bryant, Levi 215n2
Burke, Kenneth 8, 9, 17–19, 22, 25–26,
    44, 56, 60–92, 94, 106, 129, 160,
    181–184, 195, 197, 201, 209n1,
    210nn1–7; *Attitudes Toward History*

241

Lightning Source UK Ltd.
Milton Keynes UK
UKHW041206021118
331638UK00019B/106/P